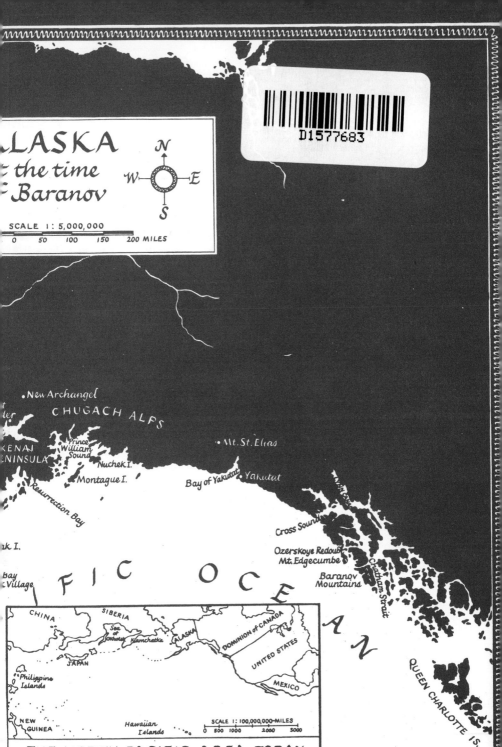

Lord of Alaska

BARANOV AND THE RUSSIAN ADVENTURE

Irene Stephens
Box 398
Soldotna, Ak.
99669

Lord of Alaska

BARANOV AND THE RUSSIAN ADVENTURE

Hector Chevigny

BINFORDS & MORT, Publishers
PORTLAND, OREGON
1971

Lord of Alaska

LIBRARY OF CONGRESS CATALOG CARD No. 51-4156
ISBN: 0-8323-0055-1
EIGHTH PRINTING

Printed in the United States of America
by
Metropolitan Press, Portland, Oregon

FOR
Claire, Toni, and Paul

Author's Note

Stating dates in any work drawn largely from eighteenth century Russian sources must be often guesswork. Where the record is confused and contradictory, I arbitrarily chose the time sequence that seemed to me most probable considering the facts of time and geography. Where dates seem established, I state them, with few exceptions, in modern terms, changing them from the old Julian calendar notation which even standard histories still give.

For the same reason, where the old Russians used one place name and modern maps another, I chose the latter.

I trust that all who helped me gain access to the materials for this book will forgive my singling out for special thanks: Clarence Andrews, the distinguished Alaskan historian; Dimitri Krenov, University of Washington, for his loan of translations of Baranov letters; Kenneth Wiggins Porter, the biographer of Astor; the Moscow office of the USSR Society for Cultural Relations with Foreign Countries; Dr. Herbert Priestley and C. Gregory Crampton, Bancroft Library, Berkeley; Dr. Avrahm Yarmolinski, New York Public Library; Laura C. Cooley, Los Angeles Public Library; Robert Schad, Huntington Library, San Marino; Dr. Nicholas Rodionov, Library of Congress, and officials of the National Archives, Washington, D.C. For much data I recall with gratitude the Rev. Andrei Kashevarov, late pastor of St. Michael's Cathedral, Sitka, and the late Prof. Edmond Meany, great authority on Pacific Rim history. My thanks for help in translations go to the Comte Georges de Kervily and Nikolai Levienne; for technical advice on Russia to Dr. Simon Mitchneck; for clerical assistance to Rita Mohr. For his patience and skill spent editing the manuscript, I must express my gratitude to Robert O. Ballou.

H. C.

Contents

CONTENTS

Lord of Alaska

BARANOV AND THE RUSSIAN ADVENTURE

Foreword

THE Yankee and British shipmasters who sought along its bewildering array of inlets, bays, islands, and fiords for furs to sell at Canton called the region, simply, the Northwest Coast. A curving strand almost three thousand miles in length, it comprises the present coasts of British Columbia and Alaska and follows the reach of the Aleutian Islands almost to the tip of Asia.

Old maps, however, call it Russian America, giving proper credit to the people who settled and, in a measure, civilized it. Russia claimed it for a century and a quarter and her occupation of it is still evinced by the generous proportion of Russian blood in native veins, by the existing Russian speech in many sections, by the bulb-domed churches of Russian Orthodoxy whose priests still minister to the natives from Sitka to Unalaska, and by the surrounding geographic names—Shelekhov Straits, Voskressenski harbor, Pribylov Islands, Pavlovski village, the Baranov mountains and many more.

As you sail eastward from the shallow, often ice-locked, reef-enclosed Sea of Okhotsk on the Siberian coast and first sight the Aleutian Islands you are struck at once by the fantastic desolation of the seascape. The westernmost Aleutians rise from the restless, repellent, slate-gray seas like crags in Doré etchings, twisted and tortured beyond belief in testimony of their violent volcanic origin, and warning the mariner to keep his distance from their concealed sawlike teeth, white with the droppings of the millions of seabirds that forever wheel and cry in the surrounding mists like lost children. You realize, then, that this is of a pattern with the Asiatic coast; Japan has its earthquakes and Kamchatka its smoking peaks, but here the process of formation seems to go on still.

Then, in spite of the fact that the drift ice from the Arctic lies but a few miles to the north, you notice the warmth. On one side of the Aleutians lies the Bering Sea, on the other the Pacific—or rather *Kuro Siwa*, the Japan Current. The Aleutians are a gigantic boom that keeps them apart. The Current sweeps up from near the Equator on a slow, cosmic swirl past the Japanese Empire, turns along these Aleutians and warms them, turns again along the mainland to California, where it makes its last turn to gather warmth to carry north.

The Bering seems unhappy at being thus barred from mingling with warmer waters. In winter its resentment is savage. Its vast northern surf charges the Aleutians again and again until it seems they surely must give way before the onslaught. The wind howls and bellows in sympathy, the seabirds protest the warfare with desperate cries, and the poor little ship unfortunate enough not to have found anchorage in some rocky cove is often sent scudding helplessly under bare poles far out into the Pacific.

In summer, however, the Bering has sullenly to retire, the receding drift ice gnashing its teeth with futility, and it contents itself with a sort of guerrilla warfare. To keep watch over the Aleutians day and night, it sends clouds that cover the region with rain for hours, days, weeks on end. Rare and charming indeed is the day when the close-hanging mists and dark clouds part to let the sunshine grudgingly through. Then the Aleutians can be startlingly beautiful.

With rain, wind, and surge apparently creating nothing but gloom and these very islands at best seeming insecure perches liable to disappear, it seems impossible that human beings can live on them and call them their native soil. "We live like our brother, the sea otter," the Aleut natives told the first white men, and it was almost literally true. The sea is their proper medium. The prospect of an hour's walk on land fills them with unease, but they will fasten their little walrus-hide *bidarkas*—brother to the Eskimo's *kayak*—to their bodies and, armed with bows and arrows and double-bladed paddles, will face journeys of hundreds of miles through roaring seas with laughs and squeals of joy.

They are heavy-bodied, sparse of hair, and colored lightly like the northern Japanese they somewhat resemble. Their clothing against the sea and everything for dealing with that medium are artfully contrived, but of the science of living aland they were, until the Russians came, virtually in the Stone Age. They were surprised to hear that food should be stored against winter; they looked on starvation and scurvy as the inevitable concomitants of the "dark months." Their homes were simple holes in the ground roofed with sod. They had no warlike tendencies but were simple, trusting, and friendly. But they can be roused to wrath, by extremes of cruelty or treachery, and engage in insane, shocking reprisals.

As you continue to sail eastward, the impression of terrible newness passes somewhat as larger and larger islands appear with green and russet lichens covering the highlands, which soon assume the aspect of mountains. Then, the forefront of Alaska Peninsula, the beginning of the mainland, comes slowly into view. Here are some of the most awesome heights of the world, mountains and glaciers fronting the sea and giving way to gigantic bays and inlets, fringed by incredible forests and filled with the thunder of cataracts that forever drain the snow fields in the distance. However, the familiar fogs and mists remain, and the rain continues to fall.

Indeed moisture pervades everything. Its abundance gives virile life to the forests of hemlock and fir and to the dense undergrowths of huckleberry and fern, and keeps their old enemy, fire, from destroying them. Everything seems strong, enormous, and filled with sap that never recedes, even in winter. The soil underneath, wet and covered with centuries of mold, is deep, rich, and friendly to seed. Past a barren glacier region on the mainland, from the Bay of Yakutat south to the Columbia River, it is a northern jungle.

The mainland natives seem invested with the strength, grandeur, and richness of their land, just as the Aleut islanders are touched with the poverty of theirs. The Tlingits—or Kolosh, as the Russians called them—were the strongest in heart and body, the most intelligent, the most formidable when aroused, and the most cruelly ferocious of all the natives of the American coast. Strong, too, of temperament, the Kolosh numbered all the tribes and septs of their race from Yakutat to Juan de Fuca Straits in one masonic alliance. Above their clusters of long communal houses built of logs three and four feet thick in which ten to sixty families might live, rose those strange totem poles which are neither gods nor gods' representations but complex expressions of interfamily relations, tribal histories, and kinships with the living things of land, sea, and air. Their civilization was definite, their arts developed to the point of formalism; they practiced democratic government yet upheld grades of aristocracy, attested to by the flattening of the heads of the well-born in childhood. Like piratical vikings they put to sea in long, perfectly fashioned canoes, seating thirty warriors armed with helmets, breastplates, and shields. They wandered hundreds of miles from their bases, to Puget's Sound and the Columbia River, up to the Aleutians and even along the Bering coast, in search of booty and slaves to labor in their villages or to offer as human sacrifices.

It seems strange historical irony that it remained for the least maritime nation in Europe, and as late as 1745, to start taking all this region. Surely it was a prize for a seafaring people. The timber was there in abundance for ships, the broken coast offered unlimited sanctuary, and trade routes were near. Across the ocean at Canton lay a market willing to pay much for furs, and the world has never known a fur country like this. On the Aleutians, red, arctic blue, and silver foxes bred unmolested but for occasional killings by the natives. In the surf from Attu Island to California the little sea otter, bearer of what was even then the world's costliest and loveliest fur, played by the millions unhunted. In the Bering Sea lie two small islands, the Pribylovs, which are still the seal's world breeding grounds. To this day a man can kill a thousand with a club in a few hours; from a distance on a June day their barking sounds like far-off artillery thunder. In those days the whale swam by unsought. Fish abounded by the ton for the taking. In the interior lay hidden metals enough to pay national debts. But the maritime nations of Europe by 1745 were too exhausted by their terrific colonial expansions to be curious. For two hundred years Spain had not ventured beyond Mexico. In England a prize of twenty thousand pounds sterling, which parliament put up to revive interest in finding the Northwest Passage, went by default. Only an occasional Dutch trader putting in at Nagasaki came anywhere near.

The first people to suspect that something interesting lay across those waters were the *promyshleniki* of the Siberian backwoods. The term means frontiersman, advance guard, the fur hunters of the lonely Siberian *taigá*. They were a peculiar breed, numbering only a few thousands, but daring and reckless out of all proportion to their numbers. Their principal ancestry was Cossack from the Caspian region and they preserved Cossack customs, though their blood had long since been heavily diluted with the native strains of Asia. For a hundred years they gazed across the fog-draped bosom of the Pacific from the shores of Kamchatka and itched to investigate what lay across; for rumors persisted among the natives of the Anadyr to the far north that indeed another *bolshaya zemlya*, another great land, was across those waters and rich in furs. The ancient records preserved at some of their old outposts hint that bolder spirits once or twice built *lodki* of loose boards and crude sails in which to sail eastward; but of course they never returned.

The promyshleniki were born of the days when Tsar Ivan the Terrible in the sixteenth century set out to restore order in the infant Russian Empire, and sent an army to clean out the nest of Cossack robbers along the Caspian who ignored his orders to cease robbing English merchants trying to ascend the Volga. Eight hundred and fifty of them, resenting this enforcement of the peace, crossed the Urals into Siberia under the *hetman* Yermak Timofiev in search of a land where they could enjoy their brand of freedom.

They found a sick and effete oriental empire, a sorry inheritance of the days of Genghiz Khan and his Mongol hordes, with the strongholds of which they proceeded to make short work. Yermak then sent messages back to the Kremlin offering to conquer the rest of the broad plain before him if the tsar would extend both blessing and forgiveness for former crimes. Tsar Ivan gave both and added the jewel of Siberia to his crown.

Yermak died in 1584 but his men kept his promise in a conquest march unparalleled in the history of the white race for speed and completeness. In fifty years they cut and slashed their way across Asia and in 1636 stood at last on Pacific shores, where they founded an outpost and named it Okhotsk. In one lifetime a continent had become Russian. In forty years more, all of what is now Siberia had passed under the dominance of the promyshleniki, as the conquerors came to be called.

As more of their freedom-loving people joined them, fleeing from the rule of Tsar Boris Godunov, they attacked China and captured the Amur River and valley down its length toward a second foothold on the sea. Possessed, by this time, of a habit of conquest, and an insatiable restlessness, they showed every sign of overrunning the land whence their remote ancestors had come. China, in fury, cut off the ancient trade in tea and medicines with Russia. The most curious thing about the promyshleniki is their continued obedience to the Kremlin. They fell back from the Amur at once upon the tsar's angry reaction to the loss of his tea. The Chinese emperor sent his Jesuit advisers to the Mongol border to negotiate a new trade treaty with the tsar's envoys and there, in 1669, it was agreed that, in return for stopping further promyshlenik penetration, China would grant the privilege of so many caravans of furs annually across the Gobi desert, and of a trade station in Peking. Further, it was agreed that no Russian could enter the Chinese Empire except at two points, one of these to be Fortress Mai-mai-cheng, some two hundred English miles below the then village of Irkutsk. Most of this was confirmed by a second treaty in 1728.

Swiftly, then, the promyshleniki turned to hunt furs. Now people in whom Tartar, Mongol, Yakut, and Tungus blood had all but obliterated their original Cossack strain, they still traveled in small bands, each with its traditional Cossack "nine bags of provisions," electing their leader or deposing him by popular vote as had been done for centuries, and owning all things in common. They deployed on their shaggy Mongol ponies over the steppes, through the taigá, into the frozen Anadyr on the hunt for fox and bear but mostly for sable. And with every band went the gatherer of *yassack*, or tribute in furs, forcibly extracted from native tribes in the name of the tsar.

Only the Pacific and the Arctic stopped them. And longingly they gazed across the Pacific, for stories of the bolshaya zemlia across it sounded as if they might be truthful.

When Peter the Great became tsar at Moscow he wished Russia to shake off her ancient preoccupation with her own affairs and take interest in the world at large. In 1725 he sent the Danish sailor Vitus Bering to Okhotsk to build two ships in which to chase Europe's favorite will-o'-the-wisp, the search for the Northwest Passage, and to ascertain whether Asia joined America.

Bering sighted the mainland of the Northwest Coast, but died following shipwreck on the island that still bears his name. His men, however, in 1742 found their way home, toothless with scurvy and gaunt with starvation but wearing around their bodies as clothing and using as sleeping blankets furs of the sea otter, seal, and arctic blue fox to the value of a fortune.

Peter the Great was dead and the old Asiatic apathy had redescended on Muscovy when Bering's men returned, else their discoveries might have created the sensation they deserved. But the promyshleniki were fully alive to the values of Bering's discoveries. They wasted not a minute. With characteristic improvidence they had killed off most of the Siberian sable, implausible as that sounds, and Irkutsk, now the clearing house for trade in furs with China, had to send to England for Hudson's Bay Company skins with which to keep up the trade balance in tea—to which import had been added of recent years silks, nankeens, and copper goods. With whoops of joy the promyshleniki abandoned their shaggy ponies in order to begin the construction of a *shitika*, a sort of galley of green timbers lashed together with leather thongs, in which they put forth under the Cossack sergeant Emilian Bassov to find Bering's Island. In 1745 they returned with another fortune in furs to confirm the richness of the region.

In 1746 the *Yevdoika*, commanded by the peasant Mikhail Novodchikov who had been with Bering, discovered the Aleutians.

Thereafter between two and six vessels put out early almost every summer—the old records show only the numbers of those which returned. Forty to seventy men were on each—hunters and sailors. We read of cargoes brought back worth sixty, eighty, a hundred thousand rubles in the fur markets of Irkutsk, whose trade balance was thereby saved. The Chinese paid enormous prices for sea otter—in the earliest days of the trade as much as three hundred gold rubles' worth of trade per skin. The crews put forth *na paik*, on shares with the commander and builder of the boat. As usual the gatherer of yassack went along to claim the tribute in furs from the Aleuts. Each vessel would locate an island, winter on it, kill off all the animals, and return in spring. As for what they did to the people on the islands, "God was high in His heaven and the tsar far away."

Each year the ships had to go a little further along the Aleutian chain in search of fur grounds undestroyed the previous year, and that meant that each year the ships had to be a little bigger and stronger. The old shitika of green timbers and leather thongs would no longer do. In twenty years, Russian vessels of respectable size, financed by wealthy Siberian merchants, were sailing the length of the Aleutians to the mainland itself.

Suddenly Europe heard of it. Like dogs, England, France, and Spain jumped out of a sound sleep, pointed to the north, and growled. What was Russia up to? What secret imperial policy was back of all this? Quickly the three countries roused themselves to almost simultaneous though independent action. Madrid sent orders to colonize California without delay; and the mission chain was thrown northward to Sonoma. In 1774, the viceroy of Mexico ordered an exploratory expedition northward, and sent a second the following year. The fortification of San Francisco

Bay was ordered. A decade later another Spanish expedition set
out, to return with news so disturbing that Spaniards were sent
to establish a colony at Nootka Sound, in latitude 49 degrees, just
beyond the claims of Bering. In England, parliament renewed the
prize of twenty thousand pounds sterling for discovering the
Northwest Passage, and this time a claimant stepped forth—Captain James Cook.

Cook discovered the Sandwich Islands and cruised up the
Northwest Coast. Despite the prior claims of Bering and the un-
disputed presence of Russian traders all around him, he calmly
proceeded to give bays, inlets, and mountains English names that
they still bear and that in many cases the Russians themselves
adopted. Even France, amid her revolutionary troubles, found
time to send La Pérouse on his fruitless exploration in the same
general region.

The merchants of Irkutsk in Siberia were deeply disturbed by
all this foreign prowling. The old Chinese treaty limiting trade
to that one section of the border still operated, and they enjoyed
a monopoly of handling the furs. Their worst fears were realized
when European traders came quickly on the heels of the explorers.
Captain James Hanna came up the Northwest Coast, off the beaten
track to Canton, in a sixty-ton brig and bought from the Kolosh
560 otterskins, which the Chinese bought for five thousand pounds
sterling—a startling profit over what he would have obtained for
his cargo ordinarily by taking it to Canton. The Chinese were
willing to pay high for sea otter, no matter who brought them,
Russians or English, and it was easier to buy them right at Canton
than to have to send expeditions across The Gobi to Fortress Mai-
mai-cheng on the Russian border. Other British merchants followed
at once. The Yankees, hungry for business under the squeeze
of the British East India Company, also smelled the kill from
afar; in 1788, Captains Kendrick and Gray, engaged by Boston
merchants to investigate, appeared off the coast and returned to
report favorably. The very next year the Yankees came in quick,
fast little vessels to buy otter from the Kolosh too. Upon the

discovery of rich growths of sandalwood on the Sandwich Islands, for which the Chinese also paid high, the balance of commerce within a year or two passed from the old trade routes.

Prices for furs fell sharply in Siberia. The merchants begged St. Petersburg to acknowledge the Northwest Coast as Russian by right of discovery and conquest, which had never been officially done.

The merchants of Irkutsk were strong and aggressive. Their unifying influence was the Merchants' Guild, to which by law they had to belong, and their boldness came from the laws affecting trade issued by Empress Catherine the Great on her accession to the throne in 1762. Not Russian at all but German by birth and breeding, Catherine was nevertheless deeply enamored of the French; she made French speech, manners, and the new liberal ideas stemming from France virtually mandatory on her entourage and created in her capital that strange state of mind known as Petersburg Russianism. The merchants she freed under the doctrine of *laissez faire*, then being born as a current economic faith.

To the merchants, long inhibited by confiscatory taxes and restrictions regarding foreign trade, this was like new wine. Irkutsk plunged heavily into financing ships going to America and the Guild blossomed with partnerships, insurance pools, and corporations. The two largest firms were the Golikov-Shelekhov Company and the firm owned by Pavel Lebedev-Lastotchkin. When foreign competition threatened their investments, true to their pattern the world over, they screamed to the government for protection.

But Catherine was, on the face of it, consistent. If the merchants sought dangers under their new freedom, they had to face them. She was willing to free trade but not to protect it. Moreover Catherine's mind never encompassed all of Siberia; she never grasped the fact that so simple a thing as persuading China to abrogate the old treaty limiting trade to one point on the border and which allowed no Russian ships to enter a Chinese port would have solved the whole problem. She was far too interested in her quar-

rels with Sweden and Poland and with her efforts to open the
Dardanelles to turn her attention to such legendary places as Fortress Mai-mai-cheng, Canton, Okhotsk, and Northwest America.

She dismissed the matter in 1769 when she wrote, ". . . it is for
traders to traffic where they please. I will furnish neither men,
ships, nor money. I renounce forever all possessions in . . . America." Later, when there was talk of colonies, she tartly observed,
"England's experience with American colonies should be a warning to other nations to abstain from such efforts."

About 1780 the Irkutsk merchant Grigor Shelekhov took matters into his own hands. If the government would not move to
hold the American coast or issue patents affirming Russian claims,
he would, at his own expense, plant a colony there himself which
would stand as a visible sign of occupancy and, in the event of
trouble, possibly force the Crown to his help.

Shelekhov was truly a self-made capitalist. Born at Rylsk in the
Ukraine about 1730, he came to Siberia when young, probably in
search of his fortune. He does not seem to have come as an exile
but of his own volition. For a time an employee of the custom-
house on the Chinese border, he later became an itinerant trader
in the taigá around the Gulf of Okhotsk, exchanging powder,
shot, sugar, and tea for sableskins. About the time the merchants
were freed for foreign commerce, he built a few sloops to trade
among the northern Japanese islands. But he itched to get into
the tremendously lucrative, but dangerous, sea-otter trade, and in
1776 built his first large vessel, in partnership with another. After
three successful voyages he was an important merchant of Irkutsk
and formed the Guild's largest corporation in partnership with
Ivan Golikov, an elderly, shrewd, and very wealthy man exiled
for life from the Ukraine because of certain manipulations with
government accounts.

Characteristically, the business alliance was cemented by Shelekhov's marriage to a kinswoman of Golikov's. His first wife had
died shortly before, leaving at least one son and a daughter aged
fifteen. Natalya Alexyevna, the new Gospozha Shelekhova, was a

clever and astute person with great capacity for intrigue. In a day when Siberian women had hardly emerged from *terem* she engaged boldly in her husband's affairs. Later she became the first white woman to set foot on America's Northwest Coast, though that is ahead of the story.

It seems to have been she who shrewdly perceived, when news was brought of Cook's ruthless assumption that the Russians did not exist in the Pacific, that it was useless for merchants to appeal further to the St. Petersburg which, though it had freed them, failed to understand them, and that it was time to use that freedom to its utmost.

It was a tremendous thing for a private Russian firm to decide to found a permanent colony on the American mainland. Hitherto, traders had established only temporary camps. A permanent colony would cost a veritable fortune and would take many men and supplies. Larger ships than had ever been built would be needed. That meant much iron, and iron was an expensive luxury on the Siberian coast. A glance at the map shows the reason: it had to be imported from Europe to Irkutsk, and then travel two thousand more miles to Okhotsk, eight hundred of which were by pack horse over the Stanovoi mountains separating the steppe from the coast. There had to be cattle, too, and sheep, dogs, seeds, and farming implements. A different breed of men had to be found— less brave, perhaps, but more reliable.

By the summer of 1783, however, three vessels were built and named the *Three Saints*, the *St. Michael Archangel* and the *God's Friend Simeon and Anna His Prophetess*. The *God's Friend* was a sloop but the first two were galiots—large of hold, broad of beam, with square gaff mainsails and rudders two fathoms long, and equipped with sweeps for tacking and bucking winds—the best they knew how to build at Okhotsk.

Shelekhov himself took charge and, with his wife Natalya, sailed on August 16, 1783, with 192 men, the largest group to leave Siberia in this manner. The Shelekhovs were on the *Three Saints*, which was under Captain Stepan Izmailov. On leaving Okhotsk

Gulf a squall separated the *St. Michael* from them and, after a time-consuming search, Shelekhov gave up and agreed to winter on Bering Island. After a season of the best discipline ever seen in those parts, the two remaining vessels again set sail in June of 1784.

They lost the *God's Friend* in the fogs as they neared the Aleutians. Shelekhov, having learned how futile searching for lost ships could be, kept on. Fortunately, the missing sloop reappeared off Unalaska Island and on August 3, a year out of Okhotsk, the two vessels entered a fine little harbor along a pleasing stretch of grassy coast. This was picked as the settlement and named Three Saints Bay.

If Izmailov thought he had guided Shelekhov to the mainland, he was mistaken. This proved to be Kodiak Island, a hundred miles long and fifty broad. Fortunately it lies close to the mainland. The natives seemed to know and distrust Russian occupation and Shelekhov had a battle on his hands, but his luck held; the sun went into eclipse. The Kodiak islanders promptly made peace on his promise to restore the sun. The story is told in a curious little book that Shelekhov himself wrote, *The Travels of Grigor Shelekhov, Russian Merchant*, apparently to impress St. Petersburg. It is the work of a firm, determined but dishonest mind, and claims many things he did not do.

To have told the truth would have been marvel enough. He undoubtedly was an excellent organizer. A neat settlement was built comprising some four or five log houses decorated in Russian style, a ropewalk, a blacksmith shop, barns for the animals, a commissary, and countinghouse. The two navigators were kept busy exploring, and on Cook's Inlet, one of the vast estuaries indenting the mainland, an outpost was established and named Fort Alexander in honor of the empress's grandson.

In the spring of 1786, Shelekhov's belief in his personal star was strengthened by the reappearance of the *St. Michael*, three years after she had left port. In March he prepared to return home and transferred command to Konstantin Samoilov, an old-time promyshlenik. His orders for the future were models of their kind;

they included directions for sanitation, prevention of scurvy, teaching the Aleuts, establishing new posts along the mainland, the pushing of explorations as far south as latitude 40 degrees and, finally, the exclusion of rival traders from the occupied territory "by peaceful means, if possible."

Shelekhov and his wife returned to Irkutsk after four years, determined to make capital of their work without delay. They found changes. Golikov had been pardoned in a general amnesty after his years in Siberia and allowed to return home to the Ukraine. Shelekhov gave Governor General Jacobi copies of his maps and records and petitioned for the attention of Petersburg. His ambition now was boundless. He intended to ask for a monopoly of all the fur trade in the Pacific.

This naturally turned the Guild against him. The merchant Pavel Lebedev-Lastotchkin, the next largest firm, threatened to put up a rival colony and take the bloom off Shelekhov's accomplishments if he persisted in such demands, even though Shelekhov held stock in the Lebedev Company.

Suddenly Shelekhov, to his surprise and pleasure, was summoned to St. Petersburg with the hint that he could expect good news. He went with his wife and youngest daughter, Anna. Old Golikov, by an almost miraculous circumstance, had talked with Empress Catherine and seized the chance to speak of Shelekhov. The Imperial College of Commerce was ordered to investigate Shelekhov's claims and achievements and decide on the Pacific question once and for all. Governor General Jacobi put in a strong word for Shelekhov, declaring that a portion of the Baltic fleet must immediately be sent into the Pacific, and that the Golikov-Shelekhov Company should be granted the exclusive rights asked for— it was the only way to protect the Aleuts from the excesses of vagrant traders, he said.

Unfortunately, Shelekhov ruined his own case by talking too much. Had he been content to rest on the bare record of his achievements he might have won. Certainly the College of Commerce found in his favor, at first. There was even a recommendation of a subsidy from the treasury to the tune of two hundred thousand rubles, without interest. But he bragged about discovering Kodiak, whereas it was proved that others had landed and traded on it long before him, and his absurd claim to having received every native of Kodiak into the Orthodox Faith was exploded.

He pulled every intrigue he could, among other devices telling high-placed members of the Orthodox clergy that he was willing to pay out of his own pocket for an expedition of missionary priests, so great was his concern over the souls of the Aleuts. Apparently he said this to the Archimandrite Iosaph Bolotov of Valaam Monastery on Lake Ladoga, a sincere but not critical man; he certainly gave the Archimandrite ten shares in his company for the Church as an incentive to speak well of him. Another intrigue was with the empress's current lover, Plato Zoubov, a relative of his wife Natalya Alexyevna, no less. A third lay in the deep interest his daughter Anna had stirred in the heart of Nikolai Rezanov, a promising young courtier of noble blood who was friendly with Catherine's court poet, Gabriel Derzhavine. But it all came to little. The most he got was the concession to consider exclusively as his company's what he now occupied and might colonize later, and a couple of swords and gold medals for himself and Golikov, inscribed, ". . . for their services, rendered Us by their noble deeds."

Late in 1789, Shelekhov had perforce to return home. Reports from his colony showed that things had gone no better there than in Petersburg. Not once had an exploratory vessel stirred from Three Saints Bay since he left; the only outpost was still the one he founded on Cook's Inlet; and Lebedev-Lastotchkin had carried out his threat and planted a rival post, unfortunately also on Cook's Inlet. The number of furs being sent was small and yet the colony screamed for more supplies. By letter he deposed Samoilov from local command and appointed a navigator of Greek blood, Yevstrate Delarov, although he knew that Delarov was no administrator either.

It was imperative he find a man with initiative and energy to keep his colonial enterprise from failure.

The man he did find lived to push the Russian advance until the Russians had footholds even in California and reached out for another on the Hawaiian islands. This book is about him, and the people and country who became his.

Lord of Alaska

". . . a rough, rugged, hard-drinking old Russian; somewhat of a soldier, somewhat of a trader; above all a boon companion of the old roystering school, with a strong cross of the bear . . ."

—WASHINGTON IRVING, *Astoria*

1

···

Aleksandr Baranov, *Mestchannin*

B ARANOV'S origins were humble in the extreme. Kargopol, where he was born to the storekeeper Andrei Baranov in 1747, lies near the old Finnish border in what used to be the government of Olonyetz. In Baranov's time the region was sparsely settled, dotted with innumerable lakes. One village was very like another, built of logs and with the roads between invariably axle-deep in mud. "Deaf villages," they were called, for a tsar could be dead and another crowned for months before the more distant *mirs* heard about the event.

In former times, when Russia's only seaport was on the White Sea and the highway running past was traveled by Dutch and English merchants on their way to the fairs in the interior, Kargopol had been of some importance; but when Peter the Great opened the Baltic and built St. Petersburg, ignorance descended on the land. The people were for the most part Great Russian by blood, but many among them showed strains of Finnish, Swedish, Tchudi, and Tartar blood. They were big, kindly, and strong; skillful with few tools other than the ax. Pious, they did not indulge in such European abominations as shaving the beard or using tobacco.

Aleksandr Andrevich was the oldest of four children; after him came his brother Pyotr and sisters Avdotya and Vassilissa. Aleksandr, far from being typical of his region, was small and delicate of frame, quick of mind, clever with his hands. His hair was flaxen in color and very fine, his expression mobile and alert, and his disposition friendly and gregarious; yet there was a sharp edge to his good-fellowship that manifested itself in his delight at besting others at bargaining. It showed in the faint Tartar look of his eyes.

There used to be an old legend of the days when Vassili the Blind was grand duke at Moscow and the last of the Tartar invasions swept up from the Crimea which told how a certain mirza nicknamed Barán—"the Wild Ram"—abandoned his Tartar chieftainship and remained behind to become a Christian and follower of the blind tsar. He had fallen in love with a fair Lithuanian princess with whom he founded the family name of Baranov. But ten generations back is a long way to seek ancestral influences. Baranov's fair hair could have come from Sweden or Finland more simply than from that long-dead Lithuanian princess, and his eyes from almost anywhere in Russia.

His father's class was that of *mestchannin*, or lowest grade of small trader, ineligible even to membership in a town guild of merchants and but a couple of steps removed from the peasant class itself. In a country like Olonyetz, though, storekeepers became by circumstance dominant figures. The elder Baranov engaged extensively in bartering, especially in skins, and whole families depended on his judgment for their supplies of tea, sugar, salt, gunpowder and, occasionally, their muskets. Andrei Baranov had to read and write a little and keep his accounts, and such knowledge as he gained he transmitted to his son. Probably this was all the early education Aleksandr Andrevich had. The records show no school in the village. Perhaps the priest taught the children, but even that would have meant little, for the village priests of the day were seldom above the villagers themselves and indeed were often held in but scant respect by their neighbors.

Aleksandr loved to roam the woods, with a heavy Moscow musket when powder could be afforded, with a sling when it could not, in search of fur-bearing animals, the skins of which he expertly dried and stretched to send to Moscow, and also to in-

dulge his fondness for examining rocks. He would follow down
the bright veins in rocky hillsides and was always asking questions
about coal and mineral deposits. That kind of interest was rare
among his people. Aleksandr Andrevich was indeed a curious boy.

Soon he awakened to the existence of a world outside these
forests. Gangs of neighbors often went to work out of the district
in winter, to Moscow or down the Volga, and they brought back
stories of what there was to see. The noblemen who owned the
estate of the district was seldom home but lived at St. Petersburg,
where the tsar was. The Old Believers still cursed the name of
Peter the Great for introducing the ways of Europe into Russia
and called him Antichrist. The occasional sable trapped in the
woods was eventually sent, he learned, all the way to China to be
traded for tea and cloth. When he was fifteen he could not curb
the growing force of his curiosity and he ran away to Moscow.

It must have been a profound shock to that slight, fair-haired
boy wearing sacking for shoes to see Moscow for the first time,
to realize there could be so many people in the world, so many
houses not built of logs, such huge markets, so many churches
with their multi-colored domes, so many and such huge bells to
fill the air at all hours. It must have been even more of a shock
to realize that among all these people there were so few to give
him a kopek for the bread he could see in the markets. And, confusion of confusions! it was a German who gave him a job in spite
of the good Orthodox, who persisted in hating Germans more
than any other people.

Shortly after he arrived, the city began to fill with five times
as many people as usual and to take on twice as much color, because it was preparing for the crowning of an empress in the
Kremlin church—it was whispered that she had put away her husband, the Grand Duke Peter, and had seized power for herself by
an intrigue with the army. On the great day, he climbed the fa-
çade of a building and looked out over the ocean of people in Red
Square to see the German woman who was later to be known as
Catherine the Great ride through the crowd in a carriage behind

mounted Cossacks who cleared the way with whips. He knew this was the closest he would ever come to such a person but he was not abashed. He cheered with the rest. Millions more would not get even that close.

Moscow had changed little since the days of Peter the Great. Nobles and merchants were still strictly separated by class barriers, and the merchants themselves, heavy with centuries of tradition, drew differences sharply among their own ranks.

As Baranov grew to manhood, Moscow taught him what it meant to have been born a lowly mestchannin. By nature friendly and convivial, he began to avoid Russian society and seek out the less class-conscious company of foreigners who have always formed so distinctive a feature of Moscow's commercial life. The German firms predominated but there were also many Swiss and Dutch and a few English firms—bankers, manufacturers, importers and exporters trading in Russia, Siberia, with the Baltic states, and down to Azov and Astrakhan. Each nationality lived more or less exclusively in its *gostinnui dvor* but they met freely in the same dram shops and *kafenes*.

It was from members of this same group that Peter the Great, in an earlier day, had received his revolutionary ideas. And now Baranov gained many ideas not consistent with the time-honored customs of old Russia, and at the same time he achieved a rough familiarity with the German language.

He came to realize, too, that illiteracy was shameful, and speedily sought to remedy his lack of knowledge of letters. His handwriting through the years acquired ease, even a sort of boldness, but all his life certain solecisms with the hard and soft signs of the alphabet were to betray his origins. He was astonished to discover the world of books and took naïve delight in exploring the big Moscow markets for cheap editions of Russian classics which he greedily devoured. Whenever he could find one he bought treatises on metallurgy and mineralogy, though he knew he had but a small chance to achieve a career in that field. His destiny was that of a trader. So he studied textiles and became an expert on linens and nankeens. Ciphering came easily to him and he learned the German way of bookkeeping when clerks in Russian houses were still figuring with the old abacus.

He seems to have risen to the status of clerk with one of the German firms, but he eventually broke away from Moscow. The new freedom of movement granted business by the Empress Catherine loosened the hold of the ancient Moscow houses on national trade and Baranov returned to his native Olonyetz as agent for Siberian imports. At Kargopol he married a woman whose name is completely lost and begot a daughter. Baranov seldom spoke of his Russian wife in later years and his actions indicate that his union with her was not a very satisfactory one. In 1780, when thirty-three, he left his wife and emigrated to Siberia with his brother, Pyotr.

He had done a great deal for his brother, paying for his education and training as a trader and taking him as a partner in his ventures. Baranov was generous where friends or relatives were concerned. He conscientiously sent money for the care of his wife and child. His first business venture in Siberia was as an itinerant trader among the villagers of the big government of Irkutsk. As a sideline he took on the task of gathering the tax on liquor imposed by the government but administered by private individuals.

Farming out the gathering of certain taxes to wealthy individuals who bid for the business was one prime abuse that the administration of the Empress Catherine had never corrected, and in the matter of vodka, the curse of the old Russian countryside, it was a dirty business indeed—but very profitable. Wealthy merchant Ivan Golikov had long held the franchise by the simple expedient of bidding higher for it than anyone else. Working for Golikov, Baranov apparently made his stake as quickly as he could, and then embarked on a completely original enterprise.

It was based on his old interest in mineralogy. In partnership with a German and a Russian he opened a small factory for making glass by means of a process of which he had read. The enterprise proved successful, for up to then glass had been an expensive importation. Baranov's achievement created nothing less than a furor. From far-away St. Petersburg the very chancellor of the empire, Count Ostermann, sent him a letter of commendation for contributing to Siberia's pitifully few industries. The local branch of the Imperial Free Economics Society invited him to read a paper on business management. He was a success. He was found to be trustworthy as well as intelligent. He gained friends. But his class still militated against him; membership in the Irkutsk Merchants' Guild was never offered him. He turned, as before, to the foreign merchants, of whom there was a large number in Irkutsk, for his best friendships.

He had been in Irkutsk eight years when he decided to break away. He had been finding the doing of business in the Russian manner, by interminable conferences with partners over every small decision, increasingly distasteful. He decided to go with his brother into the north, to the tundras of the Anadyr, to open a trading business with the Chukchi natives, the isolated villages of Old Believers, and a few exiles. Profits might not be large but in such country there would be distinctions only between the clever and the stupid. He would listen to no offers to go elsewhere on behalf of others and proceeded with his plan to put his share in the glass factory in trust to support his family at Kargopol and start for the Anadyr the following spring, in 1788.

That year Grigor Shelekhov and his clever wife returned from their adventure of founding a colony in America. Shelekhov scoffed at the idea of Baranov wasting his talents in the Anadyr and proposed that he go to Kodiak Island to manage his colony; but Baranov refused, and in a way that deeply offended Shelekhov. He had had enough of partners and intrigues, he said; he wanted to be subject to no more.

When he and his brother started to pole their flatboat loaded with trade goods down the Lena River, twelve hundred miles toward Yakutsk, Baranov was forty-two years old. He was still a small man by comparison with his fellow Russians but hard of body and wiry, and quick of movement. His face had not lost its old mobility and its alert look. The Tartar look of his eyes had become accentuated by life in the open. His flaxen hair was beginning slightly to thin.

At Yakutsk they transferred their goods to reindeer and went on to the north. They established headquarters at Ishiginsk on the Sea of Okhotsk, and outposts in the interior. Since the opening of the American fur grounds, the north had been less frequented by traders, the sables had increased, and by the summer of 1790 the brothers Baranov had a fine pile of furs worth many thousands of rubles to send to Irkutsk. They were on their way to success.

They were deep in debt but these skins would amply repay everything. On the way through the taigá toward Yakutsk with his furs, Baranov learned a lesson he never forgot to the day of his death. The very guns, powder, and shot they had sold the Chukchi natives were turned against them and every sable stolen.

The situation facing Baranov was highly unpleasant. He had neither funds nor credit with which to resume operations. If his shares of property at Irkutsk were seized to pay his debts his family would be destitute. He sent his brother back to Ishiginsk to guard what was left; then he went on himself with a couple of horses across the Stanovoi mountains to see Johann Koch, the district military commander, whom he had known well in Irkutsk.

It was mid-August of 1790 when Baranov, following the Okhota River down from the mountains, came to the forty-odd log houses, the church, the commander's residence, and the barracks for the district Cossack police making up the village of Okhotsk, Russia's only seaport on the Pacific, to tell the story of his catastrophe to Johann Koch.

Tied up at the little wharves jutting out from the beach lay Shelekhov's high-pooped galiot, the *Three Saints.*

At a time when many Germans had come into Russia attracted by the high pay offered for specialized knowledges or administrative ability, Johann Koch had left Hamburg and entered the Russian army as a surgeon. He served throughout the bloody campaign against the Turks to its victorious conclusion in 1777, then assisted in the conquest of the Crimea. For reward he found himself attached to the military entourage of the governor-general of Eastern Siberia, who in 1784 appointed him commander of the District of Okhotsk.

In practice Koch's command extended all the way across the Pacific to America. That is, he had an assumed jurisdiction over the ocean, questionable in theory in view of the fact that the Crown had never claimed Russian America, but necessary because of its factual Russian occupation. Now Koch stood ready to extend actual sway at any time, for the Empress Catherine grew old and the next sovereign would undoubtedly make the territory officially Russian. It must be held together in the meantime. The questions involved required the utmost tact. Koch could not, for instance, send out an official altogether in his name. He must do his work through the co-operation of traders.

He had been doing what he could by requiring the traders setting out in ships to plant copper plates stamped with the imperial coat of arms in the ground of new discoveries and to keep maps of their locations. He required crews setting out to take an oath of allegiance, and held their navigators responsible to him for their behavior. And when the vessels returned the furs had to be counted in his presence before a division of shares was made.

The plan had seemed to work well enough. But suddenly the questions involved became acute. Direct from Petersburg in a weekly dispatch marked with "three feathers" to show urgency came the announcement that Sweden had commissioned an English privateersman of fourteen guns to go into the Pacific and destroy the Russian fur business, the result of a declaration of war between Sweden and Russia.

Simultaneously the merchant Shelekhov, who had just been in St. Petersburg, came with the same disturbing news. A supply ship was about to go to his colony, the first in two years, and he was plainly worried. He admitted that in an emergency he could not trust his chief at Kodiak, the Greek Delarov. Someone of honesty, enterprise, and initiative should be sent, with which opinion Koch agreed, but there seemed no one he could find.

Into this situation walked Aleksandr Baranov in the necessity of an immediate change of fortune, and looking to Koch like the answer to a prayer uttered by a man more pious than himself.

But it took the utmost diplomacy on the part of the commander even to bring the two men together. Shelekhov balked at Baranov. He had once offered the man the post and did not intend to be insulted by a second refusal. And Baranov at first refused even to discuss the matter, saying he knew Shelekhov and Golikov too well to become involved in their enterprises.

But neither man had much choice, really. Shelekhov had to make a change at Kodiak and another vessel could not put out for another year; it was then August and too late in the season. Baranov was certainly a clever, resourceful, intelligent, and responsible man —the only one available. And Baranov knew in his heart that this situation must be, if not the hand of Providence, certainly at least its index finger. So Koch finally got them together, perhaps over an encouraging bowl of punch in his house.

Shelekhov told of founding his colony on Kodiak, his appoint ment first of Samoilov as his chief, then of the Greek Delarov, and his disappointment in both. Since he himself had left America not one exploratory voyage had been taken to claim new lands, not one outpost founded since he planted Fort Alexander on Cook's Inlet. Yet there were two vessels out there—the galiot *St. Michael* and the sloop *God's Friend Simeon*.

Shelekhov also told him that the government had given him the right to occupy exclusively wherever he colonized. That was an opportunity he could not let slip. He had sunk a fortune already in this colonial venture. Baranov must make up his mind without delay. The galiot *Three Saints* would soon be loaded and the fifty new men going for service to the colony to replace the ones who had served out their five-year terms would soon be all picked and ready to leave. As it was, the *Three Saints* was overdue to sail; it was already dangerously late in the season for her to make Kodiak without encountering the autumn gales. And his offer was generous, ten shares in the Golikov-Shelekhov Company during five years of service.

Still Baranov demurred. He acknowledged the generosity of the offer, but said that he must first discuss the matter privately with the commander.

To Koch, Baranov spoke his mind freely. He told of his humble beginnings, his station in life, some of the reasons for his going into the Anadyr. Koch had spoken of government matters, of the need for planting evidences of new discoveries at secret places, of what to say if the English came by with exploring fleets, or the Spanish from Mexico, of what to do if that English privateersman Cox came by under Swedish colors. How could a mestchannin, of no standing whatever, assume any authority? The meanest pen-pusher, providing he held government rank, could come out there and overrule him! What would happen when the Empress Catherine died and the Russian Navy came out to take control? Where would he be then, but at the door, cap in hand, waiting for those officers to invite him in like a *muzhik*, at their pleasure?

Apparently Koch was a most sympathetic listener and a most tactful persuader. Acknowledging the reasonableness of all of Baranov's arguments he assured him that he could fall back on government authority when it was necessary. He, Koch, would back him to the limit in case of trouble with Shelekhov. It was a pity that, due to official governmental policy, his authority would extend only to the Shelekhov interests. But he was to observe other traders and report any misconduct on their part to Koch. Among the Shelekhov men, insubordination, rape, stealing, and knowingly spreading venereal disease was to be punished by measures up to flogging. Murderers and illicit distillers of vodka were to be sent home for trial.

What had Baranov to lose? Five years! And if things went well he should come back after that time wealthy.

The sense of Koch's arguments was inescapable, and in addition there was perhaps the strongest argument of all—Baranov's immediate, pressing need. The compensation Shelekhov offered him would pay all his debts at Irkutsk, secure his property, safeguard his family, refinance his brother in the Anadyr, and indeed if all went well there would be a handsome profit left over. He would be only forty-eight when he returned.

He hesitated no longer.

2

Last Voyage of the *Three Saints*

T HE weather is often bad at Okhotsk. The fogs roll in from the ocean and rain falls often and violently. The great Gulf of Okhotsk, when it is not ice-locked, swirls with flotsam washed in by the Japan Current through the teeth of the Kuriles.

The settlement itself and the adjoining coastal region, as rough a human population and as mixed as that of any country still in the frontier stage, was, for long after Baranov's time, the last stand of many a Russian malcontent, fleeing before the advance of the more sophisticated city populations. Exiles for political crimes were often sent there. The Old Believers moved there for freedom of thought. Bands of Chinese and Mongolian outlaws sought refuge from their own land in the surrounding taigá. The sable hunters, the promyshleniki, made the town their headquarters, as did also the crews who made a profession of sailing for the merchants in the sea-otter trade. Prominent among these latter were the navigators of the ships, who considered themselves a race apart because they possessed some instinct for bringing bottoms through the Aleutian reefs without mishap. They formed a tight little society, one tenet of which seemed to be the determination to keep their secrets a monopoly, another seemingly never to be sober while ashore.

Such a man was Dimitri Botcharov, skipper of the *Three Saints*. That vessel left port August 30, 1790, her square gaff mainsail and auxiliary jib bellying solidly before the wind that would sweep her safely past the Kurile reefs and out to open sea with her cargo of supplies—fifty-two men and Baranov, the new colonial chief—to Shelekhov's colony, eighteen hundred nautical miles away.

Seven years had passed since Shelekhov had built the galiot and sailed in her himself to found his colony. She had not been taken from the water since, except to be pulled up on beaches for the winter. Her timbers, but for the grace of her three heavenly protectors, should long since have fallen apart. Fortunately the strain of tacking the heavy craft could, in emergencies, be eased by long sweeps manned by both passengers and crew.

Down in the hold bawled several cows in concert with the baaing of sheep. Hogsheads of sugar, sacks of salt and rye meal, boxes of tea bricks, bales of tobacco, bolts of Chinese cloth, and hardware of all kinds took up the space not grudgingly permitted to passengers and crew. On deck were several pieces of artillery, mostly falconets on swivels and one-pounders of Chinese brass, removed from the poor Okhotsk stores for the defense of Kodiak Island.

A few of the men going for service with the Company were of the old promyshlenik tradition but Shelekhov had not picked most of them for their independence. Some, of course, had been to the islands before, and were returning now, after drinking up their profits. One was an artilleryman of army experience. As far as possible all were chosen for their skill with their hands, though a few were completely inexperienced. All, including skipper and crew, had signed articles before the Okhotsk commander swearing they were in their right minds and knew what they were getting into, that they had no venereal disease, that they would remain faithful to the imperial government, and binding themselves for not less than five years to the service of Golikov-Shelekhov, providing that at the end of that time they were not in debt. Of the fifty-odd aboard probably the only three literates were the skipper, Baranov, and a young bookkeeper he had selected as his assistant named Ivan Kuskov.

The skipper bore every mark of being a drunkard, but he was an old Shelekhov man, having brought the *God's Friend Simeon* through when Shelekhov journeyed to America. The merchant insisted on employing him. Botcharov and Baranov failed to hit it off from the beginning. Baranov distrusted drunkards and from the start Botcharov resented the fact that a rank landlubber had been appointed to the post of Shelekhov's chief manager.

At sea, however, Botcharov demonstrated his worth. Sobering immediately, he brought the *Three Saints* out of Okhotsk Gulf with a skill that seemed miraculous to all who knew the dangers. He navigated largely by instinct, his instruments being limited to a compass and such crude charts as he and previous skippers going over the route had drawn. On hitting the open sea the galiot wallowed in the troughs like a bewildered cow, her old timbers creaking and groaning alarmingly. The passengers had to be kept constantly at the pumps.

A few days out, somebody prodded Baranov out of his intense seasickness in his foul bunk with the news that the water casks must all be leaking, for the supply was almost gone. Someone, on filling them, had seemingly wished to sabotage Shelekhov's expedition. Ill, bewildered, frightened, Baranov made his way wildly to the poop to order Botcharov to stop at the first island they saw; but Botcharov contemptuously replied they could all go on short rations, he was stopping nowhere until Unalaska, halfway across; it was the only safe thing at the season. At sea Botcharov was commander.

Botcharov's real value now showed itself. Head winds struck them and for four long weeks the galiot bucked them obstinately as the men pulled at the sweeps and labored at the pumps on a gill of water a day apiece—and that soon crawling with living things. All kept eyes strained in the scudding mists for a sight of Unalaska Island's Makushin peak.

On October 7 they sighted it and none too soon, for in addition to the marks of thirst, scurvy had appeared. Men dropped at the sweeps from weakness, breaths were offensive, a few teeth fell out of pain-deadened gums. On October 9, with fervent thanks to God, they dropped anchor in Unalaska's Koshigin harbor. Hurriedly they dropped the water casks in the small-boats and, muskets in hand, pulled for the beach and the flat, treeless, grassy landscape behind it.

Anchorage had to be some distance out, for the beach was very sloping. The grass looked good and the men not skiffing water casks or detailed to kill seal for fresh meat rafted the live stock ashore for pasturage. It was only to be a temporary stop, for a day or two, though from now on greater speed would be made on the journey. They were in the lee of the Aleutian chain and the worst should be over.

Nowhere could a native be seen, although some hundred yards back from the beach were dugouts, *barabaras*, which the old hands said were typical Aleut dwellings. A door opened into the mound of earth serving as the roof, and a short ladder led into the one room, but in each dugout there had been little left but an unbelievably foul reek of rotten fish and aging seal meat.

During their second night ashore, a hoarse shout called everyone's assistance to the *Three Saints*. A breeze had come up and she had dragged her anchor inshore, like a stubborn old cow pulling up stakes for the barn. The breeze sharpened into a squall. Suddenly there was a sharp crack and she seemed to sigh and settle down for the winter; she was on a rock. The men managed to get the skiffs launched despite the high surf beginning to pound the beach, but the sea came in too fast for the pumps. The galiot was simply too old; her bottom was giving in.

The squall beat up into a gale. Botcharov, yelling hoarsely above the scream of the rigging, superintended taking the cargo ashore. All night the men labored like fiends, feeling their way by the fitful light of the moon as the scudding clouds occasionally revealed her, getting the goods on rafts which they maneuvered so that the surf would throw them cleanly onto the beach.

Dawn found a good part of the cargo saved, though the artillery had been mostly lost, and also showed the continuation of the storm and the old galiot bearing it with bad grace. Indeed, by noon she began falling to pieces and the disconsolate men roamed the beach, gathering the wood as it was washed up for fuel and shelter and salvaging all the metal attached to it they could.

There was nothing to be done but prepare for a winter here. The first task, after improving shelter, was to make friends with the inhabitants.

Hesitantly, at first, the Aleuts returned to their dugouts alongside which the Russians had dug their own, then more boldly when they learned the leader of these Russians would not let his men harm them. They brought a few quarts of cranberries preserved in candlefish oil—the delicacy of the region—and some bundles of dried salmon, *yukola;* but not many, for the Aleuts were not themselves provident. What little sugar and flour had not been ruined was soon used up.

"For a long time we had to eat without salt what meat and fish we could get," recorded Baranov, "but later a dry sack was found under the snow and I could issue a small pinch to each man on Monday."

All winter the gales raged with unexampled violence, driving the surf mountain-high. Shooting seals was impossible. The fox in the highlands had disappeared despite the most diligent search of the hunters. Although they had kept the little jar of kvass-yeast, they had no flour or sugar to mix with it for the making of a brew to help prevent scurvy. Almost every man developed some symptom of that disease before the gales abated and fresh seal meat again made its appearance.

As time went on, the Aleuts became more friendly. The women were shyly agreeable to bedding with the Russians for the winter in return for a few articles of iron apiece—iron is the Aleuts' most precious metal; so for some it wasn't bad, but others disliked their odor and found the bone labrets the women affected in their lower lips unforgettably hideous. The women farther west were more attractive, the old hands said.

For iron, too, many of the men bought Aleut clothing, abandoning their canvas jackets and even their traditional sheepskin caps for waterproof seal-gut *kamleikas* sewn with water-expanding gut thread, wooden Aleut rain hats, and boots cleverly sewn of the esophagus of the seal.

Before the start of the worst of the winter's gales Baranov broached to the island elder, the *toyon*, the subject of getting word of his plight to Delarov. Although Kodiak Island was a good seven hundred miles away, the elder immediately agreed to send five bidarkas and nine paddlers, two in each canoe, if one Russian would go. Lots were drawn and Aleksandr Molev drew the short one. Molev carefully dressed in a good Aleut seasuit, stepped into the forward hatch of one of the two-hole bidarkas, pulled the draw strings of the walrus hide taut about his middle, and in a few minutes disappeared with his companions in the mists.

Six months later, nothing had been heard from Molev. If he had succeeded in getting word to Delarov, Baranov felt sure the latter would have sent one of his two available ships, either the galiot *St. Michael* or the sloop *God's Friend Simeon.* Meanwhile, Baranov learned the Aleut tongue—a simple one—practiced the handling of their marvelously mobile little bidarkas and, when the weather cleared, learned how to hunt sea otter. He was determined to master every detail of that occupation. The search for the little animal whose fur is the loveliest and most expensive on earth was his reason for being in this vast desolation. Patiently he sat for hours in a bidarka, one of a circle of twelve similar watchers in six other canoes, waiting for the telltale bubbles to rise and mark the diving place of one of the animals. He saw the arrows drawn back as the little snout pushed for air and heard the twang of the bows as the animal dived in fright, necessitating another long wait, or was impaled to be drawn into the canoe. Guns, he found, frightened it away for good.

Baranov was also taken to the sea otters' feeding grounds where he watched them play in surf like hundreds of dogs, leaping, diving, swimming. He learned that July and August are the best months for otter, for then the surface of the sea is quietest, but that they never migrate and may have young at any time. He saw many females swim by with their single-born pups and he watched them break clams with their teeth and place the food in the pups' mouths. He looked at prime skins dried on frames and blew into their jet-black, glossy surfaces to marvel at the silver sheen beneath. A good pelt measuring five feet in length by two wide would fetch a hundred rubles in trade with the Chinese!

By April it was decided to start building three large *baidars*—open skin boats—big enough to get them to Kodiak under sail. It seemed certain that something had happened to Molev. In the old days the men would have patiently waited for some passing trader to pick them up, but under the sort of contract they now had the stores they were using were charged to their accounts; and unless they got to work soon, they would end their five years' term in debt to the Company instead of with pay. Almost a year of their term had already passed.

Three light frames thirty feet long from the *Three Saints*' timbers were put together and covered with walrus hide sewn with whale-gut thread by the skillful hands of the Aleut women they pressed into service. In May they were ready to sail. Lots were drawn to pick the five who would stay behind to guard the cattle and stores and to determine the places of each man in the boats.

Baranov then gave his final orders to Botcharov, with whom his relationship had been none too good during the difficult winter. One boat only—Baranov's own—would go direct to Kodiak; the other two, under Botcharov's command, would turn at the tip of Alaska Peninsula and go north on the Bering Sea side to explore Bristol Bay. This exploration had been one of the specific orders of Shelekhov, who wanted a portage across the peninsula found in the event of attack and the necessity for withdrawal from Kodiak Island. After looking at Bristol Bay, Botcharov would then portage his boats across the peninsula, using them again to cross Shelikof Straits and go around Kodiak Island to Three Saints Bay.

It was an order that showed haste to get things done rather than an understanding of difficulties in the way of such a feat. The natives of Alaska Peninsula were known to be very unfriendly and the attitude of the Bristol Bay Eskimos was unknown. The Russians' only conceivable advantage would lie in their firearms—a doubtful one inasmuch as they would be wet a good part of the time.

But Baranov was stubborn and the men obeyed, remembering the authority of Koch. Doubtless under the old ways Botcharov would have called for a show of hands to decide the wisdom of the decision, or would have demanded Baranov's deposition, but Baranov represented a new leadership and for the first time the promyshleniki looked to one with authority beyond themselves.

The three baidars parted company at Isanotski Strait on May 21, the two under Botcharov turning north toward Bristol Bay and Baranov's continuing eastward under the propulsion of sails made from the *Three Saints'* canvas.

There was little room for movement for the sixteen men in the boat cluttered with gear. They brought no provisions but depended on shooting a seal when they could, bringing down birds, catching a stray salmon or cod in the little net they kept always trailing in the water from the stern, and digging clams on the beaches when they stopped for the night. They were seldom out of sight of those beaches and were always prepared to start paddling furiously whenever a blow seemed imminent. Fortunately the weather remained uniformly fair. In the distance schools of blackfish often spouted and porpoises were seen at their games. Whenever they beached, gulls and cormorants rose with harsh, startled cries. Every fourth day they remained ashore forty-eight hours to let the hide of their baidar dry out. It was slow going. It was the middle of June before they had traversed half the distance.

Wet all day with spray, sleeping without cover on the damp beaches, often eating their clams and fish raw, Baranov at last succumbed to a fever. When it turned to a light delirium the man chose a protected cove and made camp. One of the old promyshleniki shook his head and said to his companions, "Here is one who won't last long in this climate." At dawn Baranov rose to his feet, ordered the baidar to sea again, but he collapsed and the men decided to stay ashore until his fever subsided. They wrapped him in what few skins they had and placed him close to a roaring fire of driftwood.

Days later, Baranov lay again in the prow of the baidar and watched the landscape change from the desolation of the Aleutians to the approaching mainland through fever-bright eyes. Now the baidars were skirting the mainland, yet the men continued to sleep on the islands offshore for fear of the natives. No fires any more, lest they advertise their presence.

One evening they beached at a rocky inlet and were cautiously reconnoitering for a camp-site, muskets leveled, when they froze on hearing a shout and seeing an emaciated individual in a ragged Aleut kamleika come stumbling toward them over the rocks and babbling Russian. The figure fell to his knees on recognizing them, burst into tears, and made the sign of the cross. It was Aleksandr Molev. Behind him were three Aleuts in a similar state of semi-starvation.

Molev the previous winter had come within a hundred miles of Kodiak but had overridden the advice of his Aleuts and camped on the mainland. They were raided, six Aleuts were killed, and their bidarkas all wantonly destroyed. The four survivors barely reached this island alive, where they had since been living on raw clams and dead seals washed up on the beach.

Taking Molev and the Aleuts into the already crowded baidar the next morning, they sailed on. At length they reached the point from which they had to try crossing Shelekhov Strait to Kodiak, one hundred and thirty miles out of touch with land. They took on what extra water they could and rationed their food. They were hopeful of the attempt; despite their hardships and illnesses no one yet was dead.

3

* *

Baranov Reaches Kodiak Island

IT was July 8, nearly a year after they had left Okhotsk, that
Baranov and his men landed at the village of Three Saints Bay
on Kodiak Island, and, looking like long-haired bewhiskered
ghosts, were met by the Greek Delarov. Baranov himself was in delirium from the fever he had contracted, and it was not until the
middle of August that he was able to walk about and examine his
new domain. Botcharov and his men who had been sent to Bristol
Bay had not yet been heard from.

Three Saints Bay was a charming spot, dreamy and reposeful.
Baranov saw it for the first time at the best season of the year, when
the mists clear away for hours at a time, when the Pacific ocean
before it looks blue and guileless and the verdure gleams a brilliant
green. Successful farming could be done here; soil was good, water
plentiful. The pastureland stretched on a smooth slope for twenty
miles to the mountain range ridging the middle of the huge, hun-
dred-mile-long island. Yet the cattle and sheep brought by Shelekhov had not greatly increased—the bears took them, the men said
—and there were only a few patches of potatoes and turnips under
cultivation, and a little tobacco being grown as an experiment. The
men felt that they were here to hunt furs, not to do agricultural
and domestic chores.

Nor had the settlement greatly changed since Shelekhov left it.
The logs had of course weathered in the sea winds, but there were

still only the five or six cabins built with an attempt at Russian style of roof and gable, a bunkhouse, the blacksmith shop, the commissary for dispensing supplies, the ropewalk, the storehouse for furs. The only accretion was a large community of Aleuts, made up of natives of the place and hostages from villages trading with the Russians.

The village swarmed with children, dozens of whom the Russian hunters had begotten of the Aleut women. Among those waiting Botcharov's safe return, for instance, was his half-caste son Ignatii Dimitryevich.

The hunters took mates because the women were as essential to domestic economy as they were pleasant for creature comforts. No male fingers were capable of doing the intricate sewing necessary to make waterproof *mukluks*, seagoing kamleikas, or the extraordinary feather *parkas*. A few trifling gifts to the girl's father cemented the alliance. The women and men were generally faithful to their chosen mates. There was little trading around.

The trouble was the strong attachment ensuing between the hunters and their offspring. One of the best characteristics of the Russian heart is its warmth for children. Shelekhov had made an absolutely unbreakable rule that no children could be taken to Russia. In the Aleut code the child belongs to its mother, not its father. Forcibly taking one away caused great anger among the natives. Because of this many a hunter eligbile to return home with Delarov in spring doubted if he would ever leave.

Delarov baptized them all, the old navigator Stepan Izmailov generally standing as godfather. They made few attempts, however, to induce the adult Aleuts to accept baptism. They argued that they had always got along without religion; why give them rules which they would only disobey? Besides, it made the Russians uncomfortable to sleep with baptized women; it somehow made a sin of one of the few real pleasures the country afforded.

The situation that Delarov reported was far from comforting. Within the village itself matters were well enough. Delarov had been just, firm, even-tempered but not very enterprising. He kept his village scrupulously clean. The natives obeyed him.

But outside the village there were more distressing prospects. Big as Kodiak was, the supply of furs was beginning to run out. Whoever would continue making profits must begin an intensive drive for other footholds. Unless Botcharov returned with a report that there were good furs to the north, the drive must be to the southern mainland coast inhabited by the powerful and warlike Kolosh. It would take many men to secure a foothold among them. Moreover, summer was the only feasible time for exploration and conquest, and that was also the time of the main drive for sea otter.

But Baranov was not discouraged. He knew that Shelekhov, in two years and with no more men than Delarov had, had not only established this settlement but explored a portion of the mainland and planted the outpost of Fort Alexander on Cook's Inlet. No other post had since been established and now even Fort Alexander had a rival, also on Cook's Inlet, put there by the Lebedev-Lastotchkin Company. How much of all this was Shelekhov's fault and how much Delarov's? Wherever the blame belonged, other companies besides Lebedev-Lastotchkin might also set up permanent bases and in the future there might be strife.

Certainly the fault seemed Shelekhov's, as Delarov demonstrated from the records. The merchant had indeed been stingy with men and supplies to the point of crippling operations. No supply ship had ever brought more than the barest replacements in rigging and canvas for the ships. Even such necessities as powder and shot had always had to be rationed.

The record of comforts sent was naturally much worse. Tea, sugar, and alcohol were luxuries, and tobacco something that every man eked out with willow bark. The loss of the *Three Saints* meant that now everybody would go without for one more year; what little flour and tea was now in the commissary was kept for the most special holidays.

With most of the men under Delarov privileged to go home in

spring, the fifty-odd whom Baranov had brought—providing Botcharov got them back from Bristol Bay—would not round out the force to one hundred and fifty, and twenty of those were at Cook's Inlet. Surely not an imposing list of resources to back an enterprise of such vital interest to the Russian Empire.

Even less attractive were Baranov's resources of transportation. The Company now owned only the *St. Michael* and the *God's Friend Simeon*, neither in any better condition than the *Three Saints* had been at her crack-up. To make matters worse, when Delarov left in spring Baranov would have only the sloop with which to start a program that could not longer be delayed if this enterprise was to pay dividends.

At Okhotsk, Baranov had feared his complete ignorance of navigation but now it came home to him as his most formidable obstacle. Helpful as Delarov was in all else, he was united with his fellow navigators in keeping their secrets a monopoly. This left Baranov at the mercy of Botcharov, if he came through alive from the north, or of old Stepan Izmailov, who was at present the skipper of the *God's Friend*. Baranov could hardly decide which man, Botcharov or Izmailov, he distrusted the more. Izmailov was patriarch of the Okhotsk skippers and long a Shelekhov man; he had piloted the merchant's first Pacific ventures to success. But he was vain, un-coöperative, and crotchety. He ran a private distillery, the only one who dared, making an evil liquor of fermented crab apples and cranberries that nobody but an old-time promyshlenik could have imbibed for long. Despite his age he was still hale and children of his ran all over the place. Baranov shuddered to think what would happen if Botcharov got through alive and these two combined against him; he almost hoped they would stay drunk on that cranberry vodka. That would at least immobilize them partially. Sober they would be full of intrigues against him. From the start Izmailov had made no secret of his contempt for Shelekhov's appointment of a landlubber as chief.

Botcharov came through. On September 25, two large baidars with sails rounded the bay, and the whole settlement helped onto the beach the thirty-two salt-caked, thirsty men sent to explore Bristol Bay. All were alive but Botcharov said their survey had revealed nothing of value, unless it was the negative result that they could cross off the northward as a direction for activities. Bristol Bay was a huge expanse of shoreline with many Eskimo villages, peaceable enough and friendly, but few sea otter were there and only a poor showing of bear, marten, fox, and other furs of inferior value. However, Botcharov had planted the copper shields as ordered and had given the chiefs the imperial coat of arms on copper to show to wandering foreign shipmasters.

Baranov then set out to explore what he could of Kodiak before the winter gales set in. He found it strange that not even that task had ever been adequately done. Asking no favors, he elected to go by canoe, with native guides.

He noted that the timber line bisected the island straight as a ruler; the northern half, instead of grass, bore a good stand of timber, some of it excellent spruce. It would have been far better to put the colony here in the first place—building materials were nearer to hand. He noted one bay, the site of an Aleut village called Chiniak, that would have been ideal, and thought of moving the colony there. But he could imagine the outcry of protests that would follow the suggestion.

He was impressed by the size of the Aleut population of Kodiak and its neighbor, Afognak Island. There must be four or five thousand, he estimated, of whom at least fifteen hundred must be grown males. Some of the larger villages had hundreds of canoes. The elders at each place received him amiably and acknowledged the sovereignty of the Russians. They had often contributed *artels* of canoes to Delarov for otter hunting and, like their Unalaska brethren, were not afraid of long journeys of hundreds of miles in them. Baranov's busy mind began pondering the storming of some new position along the southern coast with a large body of these Aleuts, or at least of turning over all fur hunting to them, in order to free the Russians' hands for other work. He had yet to learn that the Aleut cannot long sustain an enterprise and, like a child sent on an errand, dawdles along the way unless he is under constant supervision.

Nor did Baranov yet realize the truly deadly fear in which an Aleut holds the Kolosh. But he was intelligent enough to realize that his theory would need much testing before it could be tried on anything important. As he turned his canoe back to escape the October storms, it seemed that the test must be made—unless by some miracle Shelekhov sent new ships and at least five hundred men. Training the native population to his uses seemed the best solution to be found.

Returning home, he found visitors. Botcharov's call on the Bristol Bay Eskimos was being returned. They came dressed in skin garments, in contrast to the Aleuts' feather parkas and seal-gut clothing. The stout chief told Baranov, through an interpreter, that he was pleased to meet *Nanuk*, the great white hunting leader; he had come to place himself under Nanuk's hegemony and had brought bales of foxskins and bear to trade for the goods Botcharov had assured him were for sale.

Baranov watched the long process of barter with keen interest. As with the Aleuts, iron was the precious metal of the Eskimos. Iron meant superior tips for their weapons, new strength for canoes and passable ornamentation. The visitors remained several days, feasting and drinking (they loved the vodka but spat out the tea when they thought their hosts were not watching).

As always, Baranov had many questions. Yes, the interior of their country was vast and in winter very cold. No, they had never heard of anything resembling the Northwest Passage and believed that if anything like it existed, it must be so far north as always to be frozen. They confirmed Botcharov's report—they had few sea otter. At length they took their departure, leaving as a parting gift to Nanuk two Eskimo girls aged sixteen or seventeen captured during a raid on a village in the interior.

This present Baranov received with distinct pleasure. The girls seemed more intelligent and less gloomy than the Aleuts and did not disfigure the lower lip with bone labrets. The elder, a comely wench, modest and shy, "I took in to care for me and my house," as he recorded. Like all her kind she was obedient, pleasant, and skillful with the needle.

Having thus readied his domestic economy against the oncoming winter, the first waters of which now drummed down from the leaden skies in daily earnest onto the shakes of his cabin, life must have taken on renewed hope for Baranov. Something could be accomplished despite the poverty of his resources.

"The fulfillment of all my plans," he wrote to Shelekhov, "depends of course on Providence. My first steps into this country were attended with misfortune, but I am determined to change that luck or go down fighting. Want and hardship I can bear when," he added with a touch of obvious diplomacy, "the sacrifice is made for true friendship."

Then, remembering Shelekhov's injunction always to add something for prying official eyes, he wrote: "Send me a priest. Choose one who is intelligent, able to get along with others, not bigoted, and above all, sincere."

4

Warfare at Cook's Inlet

PERHAPS Baranov would have felt less confident had he known what was happening meanwhile on Cook's Inlet.

"Inlet" is too diminutive a word for this great arm of the sea. When Captain Cook entered it with his vessel, its size, rugged grandeur, and boiling tiderace convinced him that he was on a great river and that this must be the Northwest Passage at last. Two hundred miles inland he discovered the truth, and he named the place where he veered his vessel for the last time "Turnagain Arm."

High mountain ranges throw peak after peak to the skies on all sides. On the east stand the guardians of the mysterious Ilyamna country, dominated by Ilyamna volcano, a pillar of brown smoke by day, by night a ruddy glow. The west shore is really a mountainous tongue of land—Kenai Peninsula—on the other side of which lies another huge estuary of the sea, Prince William Sound.

Off Kuchekmak Bay, on this peninsular side, Shelekhov had established his one outpost. Like his main base it had changed little, except for the weathering of the logs of the palisade and the gathering of moss on the carved wooden coat of arms over the gate. Inside were bunkhouses for the men, sheds for curing and storing furs, a community kitchen, the usual bathhouse. Commander of the force of twenty men was Vassili Molokhov, an intelligent and dependable promyshlenik with many years experience in the fur trade. Second in command was the old Cossack Samoilov, once Shelekhov's trusted lieutenant but now relegated to minor rank because of his failure to function satisfactorily as chief at Kodiak.

Life was not bad, here at Fort Alexander. The natives were neither Kolosh nor Eskimos but true Indians known as Kenaitze, handsome in appearance. After a period of aloof suspicion they had been won over to great friendliness, and now traded freely with the Russians and left their daughters as hostages. The Russians in return kept them supplied with trade goods and made their daughters happy with many children. It was a fine life.

About three years before, when Shelekhov had returned to Irkutsk and was agitating his brother merchants with talk of getting a monopoly because he had established permanent bases, his rival Pavel Lebedev-Lastotchkin had also dispatched a ship for the same purpose, under Pyotr Kolomin, with a small force of less than thirty men.

Although Lebedev-Lastotchkin had told Kolomin to occupy some new place on the mainland, although Shelekov had instructed *his* managers to exclude rival traders from occupied places "by force if necessary," Kolomin stopped at Kodiak Island to ask about the best place to settle; and Delarov, with equal amiability, advised him not to put his small force in danger at any unknown place but to go on to Cook's Inlet where his own men had pacified the inhabitants.

Kolomin accepted the invitation, sailed his galiot to the mouth of the Kassilov River some fifteen miles from Fort Alexander, and put up his own stockade, setting over the gates a crude wooden carving of the imperial arms in imitation of the others' and flanking them with his two little brass one-pounders on swivels.

The English explorer, Vancouver, left a description of Fort St. George, as they named the place, that bears repeating. "On our arrival we were saluted by two guns from a kind of balcony . . . repeated on our landing, where we met two Russians who came to welcome us and conduct us to their dwelling by a very indifferent path, which was rendered more disagreeable by a most intolerable stench, the worst, excepting that of the skunk, I have ever had the inconvenience of experiencing, occasioned, I believe, by a deposit made during the winter of filth, offal, etc., that now had become a fluid mass of putrid matter . . . We were, however, constrained to pass some time in this establishment . . . The only refreshments they had to offer were some cold boiled halibut and raw dried salmon, intended to be eaten with it by the way of bread." But Vancouver also confessed that the Russians got along very well with the natives and treated them as brothers.

Delarov's sending of the Kolomin force to this place had been one of the acts that had infuriated Shelekhov, though the Greek had acted in good faith. Shelekhov owned shares in the Lebedev-Lastotchkin Company, and Delarov could not understand why the two should nevertheless be rivals. In time, Lebedev-Lastotchkin became equally annoyed at the actions of his own men. Instead of opposing the Shelekhovski and trying to best them at fur trading, the two sets of hunters fraternized. They divided up the villages between them and frequently visited back and forth to make plans for common expeditions in search of furs, exchange crumbs of tobacco, tell stories, sing, get drunk when they had any liquor, or vary their boiled halibut and dried salmon with the delicacy of the region—cranberries preserved in candlefish butter. All men are brothers, says the old proverb. Why fight the merchants' quarrels?

When Shelekhov returned to Irkutsk with the boast that he had succeeded in getting the clever Aleksandr Baranov to go to his colony as chief, Lebedev-Lastotchkin decided to change his management, too, picking out two of the most notorious of the old freebooting promyshleniki he could find and sending them to America. What his exact orders to them were can only be conjectured, but evidently they were to prevent the Shelekhov men from establishing further footholds on the mainland and to drive them from what they had. The two were named Grigor Konovalov and Amos Balushin. How their job was to be done was apparently left to their peculiar brand of discretion.

So, during the month when Baranov lay abed with fever at Kodiak, the galiot *St. George* came sailing up Cook's Inlet. She passed both Fort Alexander and Kolomin's fort and kept on to a river's mouth, sixty miles up, where her men hauled her up on the beach with ropes and proceeded, using her hull as one wall, to build a new redoubt. This was the old method of "holing in" for winter.

Puzzled, because he recognized the vessel when she passed his port, Kolomin sent a messenger offering assistance. The reply came that Grigor Konovalov had been appointed to supreme command in America and that Kolomin must at once deliver up his fort, men, and furs.

Now Kolomin had long been expecting a successor; his term was up and he had had no supply ship since he came. But to deliver up furs to anybody but the commander at Okhotsk was unheard of. On an accurate government count depended his and his men's profits. Kolomin retorted he had to have proof of such strange orders.

Konovalov and Balushin delivered their replies in person. They came in canoes backed by several Cossack promyshleniki, beached before Fort St. George, and sauntered up to the gates manifesting much contemptuous amusement at the brave little fort. Konovalov, a huge man wearing the sheepskin cap of the Cossack leader, had his huge hairy hands thrust with his pistols in his broad leather belt. Amos Balushin was a squat, truculent creature.

Kolomin was no coward and all this show made him angry. He demanded the reason for the hurry in assuming command.

"Lebedev-Lastotchkin has ordered you deposed because you are a weakling and incompetent," answered Konovalov. "You failed to obey orders about ousting the Shelekhovski from this region. To-morrow morning Balushin comes to take command. Have your accounts ready to turn over at that time."

Leaving this peremptory order, Konovalov left.

That night Kolomin held long council with his men. When, at dawn, Balushin appeared with a squad of men and they beached canoes, they found a welcoming committee—the St. George men stood on their palisade with cocked muskets. Balushin's confident smile turned to a scowl of rage. He shook his fist at the closed gates, shouted that their refusal to obey orders would be reported to Konovalov, and curtly told his men to re-embark.

Unfortunately at that moment, several long native canoes with the gaily painted prows of the Kenai people came bearing down on the fort. The paddles were being dipped slowly and there was much laughter, for these were relatives of the hostages at the fort and had come to visit for a few days and trade for furs. At a shouted order from Balushin, his men rushed the astonished Indians and drove their canoes quickly to the beach. The men were forced out at musket's point, the girls seized, their screams stopped by gags and their hands tied, and they were thrown into the Russians' canoes. Then the bundles of furs were taken from the Indians, and as Balushin's men paddled quickly away the interpreter shouted at them that this was the first warning to keep away from Fort St. George.

By nightfall all of Cook's Inlet was in a tremendous hubbub over this outrage. The girls had been taken to Fort St. Nicholas, as Konovalov called his redoubt, plied with vodka, violated, and kept prisoners. The indignant chiefs sent reminders to Kolomin that hostages were given him as guarantees that Russians would not harm their people, and they asked for immediate redress.

Kolomin had little time to argue, for Konovalov and Balushin inaugurated a reign of terror that showed that this outrage had been but a beginning. Balushin went from village to village tributary to St. George, beating the chiefs, taking furs by force, seizing girls, and warning them all that they would again be visited if they continued to trade with Kolomin. Nothing had been seen like this since the earliest days of the first trading ships on the Aleutians. Almost immediately Fort St. George was cut off not only from its fur-trading business but even from sources of food. Balushin's men lay in wait for Kolomin's men and beat them whenever they were found wandering far from the fort.

For a long time Konovalov tried nothing so violent as all this against the Shelekhov men, but Molokhov at Fort Alexander was deeply disturbed, especially at the rising resentment among the Indians. Kolomin pleaded with him to make war against Konovalov, but Molokhov feared the consequences of letting the natives see Russians shoot one another and in any event could not engage in any action so serious without the approval of headquarters at Kodiak. There were strong rumors, he told Kolomin, that the new chief just arrived that summer, Aleksandr Baranov, had secret orders to take command soon of all rival fur companies and put them under government supervision.

Kolomin hesitated to attempt the journey to Kodiak. It was December, ice floes made canoeing dangerous, and the crossing from the Inlet was in the open path of the Pacific's winter gales. But a fresh outbreak of cruelties decided him at last to try. Some of his men began deserting to Konovalov.

Weeks later he returned, changed in his attitude and filled with contempt for this Baranov he had seen. What could a rich merchant like Shelekhov be thinking of, to send such a coward? Baranov had carefully taken down his deposition and had then said that all he could do with it was to send it to the commander of Okhotsk! Saying he was finished protecting the Shelekhovski, Kolomin without further argument went over to Konovalov's command.

There was the wildest rejoicing at Fort St. Nicholas. Kolomin's men were received like brothers, forgiven in a great celebration. Everyone suddenly seemed affected by the new spirit—or rather the old, for this was a return to the unrestraint of an earlier day; Kolomin's men and Kolomin himself, long given to peace and a decent, almost religious outlook, went wild with excesses too.

The effect was disturbing at Fort Alexander. The men there wondered if they had been fooled when they heard such wonderful things about Baranov. Samoilov deserted to Konovalov, who began skirmishing in earnest against Molokhov and molesting the villages tributary to Fort Alexander.

The natives, incensed beyond endurance, began beating council drums, somber warning of trouble ahead.

5

The Sea and the Kolosh Strike

IT was spring at Kodiak. The *St. Michael Archangel* stood
ready to put out to sea. Confusion on the beach—shouted
farewells, last minute messages for loved ones at home,
wailing Aleut wives, children crying with the contagion of a sorrow they could not understand. Seventy-five men, their duffle-
bags stuffed with ivory curios and other souvenirs, were going
home. Botcharov was one—Baranov had decided to keep old Izmailov instead—and Delarov another. Furs to the value of three
hundred thousand, eight hundred rubles, were in the hold.

Baranov, in full command at last, threw himself into his plans
for the summer of 1792 with furious energy. Only one hundred
and thirty men remained to him at Kodiak and he had but four
months in which to do it all; yet he planned not only the greatest
drive on sea otter ever known but the building of another outpost,
on Prince William Sound.

His plans were drawn to the last detail. Twelve hundred Aleuts
would be the infantry of his advance. To the elders he had sent
requisitions for a fleet of six hundred bidarkas, each to be manned
by two men, to be levied according to the size of each village and
assembled at Three Saints Bay by May 15.

Naturally the elders were disturbed; some wanted to drive
harder bargains, and one by one they came to argue. Baranov,
learning how to handle these people, sat long hours through the

interminable discussions and explained his reasons over and over again, carefully refraining from showing the slightest impatience. And always the elders eventually agreed when they understood that they would be paid so much iron for each skin and that a Russian would accompany each artel of canoes. The Russians were enthusiastic over the plan, for they were going into new regions rich in furs and each man stood to receive half the catch of the artel he commanded.

Then he got his first taste of the futility of making plans for the conquest of this country. One night in April the ground gave a seismic heave previously unparalleled even on oft-shaken Kodiak; at sea there was a frightful roar, the ocean gathered its force, and a tidal wave swept up over Three Saints village. The waters rushed into the Aleut dugouts, toppled over the Russian buildings, almost sank the God's Friend at her anchor. On receding, the waters carried away most of the canoes, dozens of struggling bodies. In the half-light of the northern summer night the scene was one of sad confusion. Baranov worked furiously to help carry the half-drowned women and children to higher ground.

In the morning the Aleuts wailed for hours bemoaning the anger of the sea gods. Then they sank into an apathetic stupor. Baranov was frantic lest they fail him. He himself must set the example. Peremptorily he gave orders to move the entire village to Chiniak Bay on the eastern side at once. There was high ground there, and timber. This calamity could never be repeated there. Three Saints Bay must be abandoned.

No one argued. Even old Izmailov, sobered by the tragedy, hurried to take the first contingent of men in the sloop and set them at felling trees.

Baranov himself led the way at the new place with an ax, working with prodigious energy. His prompt decision to turn a tragedy into an improvement in the situation for the betterment of all, and his own example at hard labor, had the right effect on his men. He was accepted as leader and obeyed promptly. Somehow, the kind of men he had love perversely the man who can make them work.

He knew that the work could never be finished before the time to start his great drive. He hoped only to have the walls up, ready for roofs, which could be put on later in the summer when they returned. He planned a better village than the old. The harbor, although narrower, was deeper and better protected. An eminence guarded the entrance which could be crowned with a blockhouse and some cannon against outside attack. Back of this he laid out a neat square along which to range the cabins, bunkhouses, the blacksmith shop, commissary, bathhouse, and other necessary buildings. In the middle he planned a tall flagpole. He decided to call the place St. Paul harbor.

About May 10, he halted work to turn his attention to the summer's drive. Many Aleut villages had suffered also in the tidal wave but he insisted that his agreements be kept and succeeded in getting a force of four hundred and fifty bidarkas. They began to arrive, now, straggling in in groups of tens and twenties. He called a council of his men. There would be three main commands—two of two hundred canoes each, under Demid Kulikalov and Igor Purtov, to hunt exclusively; the third command, of about fifty bidarkas, would be his own, to explore Prince William Sound and begin building a fort, if the right place were found. Izmailov would go on ahead in the armed sloop to select a rendezvous on Nuchek Island.

Now bidarkas were arriving so fast that the beach before St. Paul was black with them. The Aleut hunters slept on the sands or stood and stared curiously at the Russians' half-finished settlement. Every available woman had been pressed into service to give the canoes last-minute examinations for punctures or cracks in the walrus hide, which they repaired with whale gut soaked in candlefish butter. Baranov walked among the crowds, bawling orders, assigning his Russians to their commands, dispatching the artels to Nuchek.

His own group was last to leave. Clad in kamleika, wooden rain hat strapped under his chin, on his feet soft sea mukluks, Baranov kneeled in the forward hatch of his canoe and drew the flap of walrus hide, fastening the canoe to himself, tight with the draw-string. His paddling companion in the rear hatch was ready. They lifted paddles and were off.

Two hundred miles they paddled, crossing Shelekhov Strait to the mainland, the scenery growing ever grander and more rugged until it seemed that God himself could design nothing to surpass it, until their canoes crept between Kenai Peninsula and Montague Island and they entered Prince William Sound.

On all sides, chains of mountains thrust peak after snowy peak to the skies. To the left stood the rugged Kenais; ahead, the brooding masses of the Chugach Alps rose sheer from the water's edge, covered with snow almost to their bases. Montague Island itself seemed a stark mountain chain rising from the sea. Everywhere cataracts rushed over jagged precipices, draining unnamed glaciers, filling the keen, sharp air with the low bourdon of thunder and changing the deep green of the unfathomable waters to a whitish hue.

Finally they sighted the rendezvous at Nuchek Island. The *God's Friend* rode comfortably at anchor, the beach in front of the dense forest was covered with drawn-up canoes, fires for cooking food burned cheerily, and the eleven hundred men talked in groups or lay on the sand and got some rest against the long ordeal ahead. Everyone was impatient to be off. At dawn next morning Baranov gave Purtov and Kulikalov their last orders. They were to draw maps of the good bays they saw, make friends of strange chiefs, and give them the copper coats of arms to show foreign shipmasters that they were Russian subjects. Then the four hundred bidarkas moved off to the southward like a gigantic flock of huge two-headed teal.

Then Baranov felled trees to make a few huts and a breastwork for a temporary camp and prepared to look about him. Izmailov, who seven years before had poked about here, believed Nuchek to be the only place sufficiently protected against bad weather and unfriendly natives for a fort; but Baranov impatiently sent him to investigate some small islands while he explored for himself.

His first impression of awe soon wore away and he saw that Izmailov might be right. This was a pleasant spot. The forest was dense, and many of the trees were tall enough even for ship's masts. The air was alive with birds—hundreds of rufous humming-birds hung poised over the spiny devil's-club; the stellar jays, crows, and ravens quarreled in the spruce, while the sparrows and thrushes went happily about their business in the thick undergrowth of salmonberry and huckleberry. Spring grouse fell easily to quick shots and the white-cheeked geese could almost be knocked over with clubs. In the interior were said to be many red foxes and a rare species of black-striped bear.

But none of this completely answered the food question for a post. For some reason fishing was not good here, and Baranov knew that fish must be the main diet in wintertime. He wanted to look at the mainland and at Montague Island before deciding.

With his interpreter at his side and a force of about ten at his back, he began inspecting the main shoreline in search of native villages, traveling in a baidar with one of his falconets fastened in the prow.

They encountered the hunters of a small rival trading company, who seemed to be ready to pull their galiot off the beach where she had been hauled up for the year; but the visit was brief and courtesies did not go beyond exchanging a little gossip and some tobacco.

Going on, they found a few villages of Eskimo stock, but at the southern end the dominant blood was Chugach and, at the upper, as on Cook's Inlet, Kenaitze—but with differences. These Kenaitze had acquired something of the rugged strength of their surroundings in their attitude and appearance. The gaze of their jet-black eyes was steady and unwavering, their lips were strong and firmly set, their noses aquiline enough to give them a faintly Roman bearing. They were as good at hunting as at fishing and despised the fish-eating Aleuts. Many of their customs, including that of living in long, communal dwellings, were borrowed from their fierce neighbors to the south, the Kolosh.

The sight of white men was neither new nor welcome to them. Almost every European trader and explorer who had ever come to these latitudes had put into Prince William Sound—certainly Captain Cook, at least two exploring Spanish vessels in years gone by, as well as the ships of Captain John Meares. All, of course, had claimed the place. Even after a decade the treatment accorded them by Meares was remembered grimly by the natives. Like all American natives, these looked upon all members of a tribe or race as collectively to blame for individual wrongs done. Moreover, news of what was happening on Cook's Inlet had been carried in detail over Kenai Peninsula and it was not of a kind to make them trust whites the more.

Baranov cursed the quarreling on Cook's Inlet. He had tried to tell Kolomin, when he had come to Kodiak the previous December, that the best he could do was to send his deposition to his friend Koch at Okhotsk, that he had no authority to interfere with other traders and furthermore had not the means at hand. Now he was hearing about Konovalov on all sides. Few of the villages received him with much courtesy, some were actually deserted on his approach, and all listened with indifference or contempt when he tried to tell them he was the great Nanuk come to be their over-lord and protector.

An exception to this general inhospitality was made by a portly old chief who had authority over four or five Kenaitze villages and a weakness for talking. But even his friendliness was scant at first.

The chief's dwelling was at least fifty feet long and built of enormous logs; perhaps ten families dwelled communally within it. All cooking was done over a fire in the center and smoke escaped through a hole in the bark roof. In order to light the gloom, flam-ing candlefish were impaled on the beams supporting the roof and their smoky glare redly illuminated the rooftrees, the carved and dyed food bowls, and the women squatting on the wooden ter-races to watch the visitors enter. The air stank of burning candle-fish, freshly cut cedar, cooking, and offal. Baranov and his men were offered boiled halibut, caribou roasted in ashes, and cranberries in candlefish butter, but their host preserved an attitude of aloof dignity.

He recounted the grievances of his people against the whites, told of the rough ways of the fair-haired traders on the ships, and boasted that some ten years before they had successfully retaliated. A ship at anchor had sent six of her crew ashore to get water and they had captured them all, sending them as slaves to interior villages.

The Russians looked at one another when this was translated. Every hunter had instructions to keep ears open for rumors of white captives. Among others, the French explorer La Pérouse had lost men on this coast a decade before. Baranov offered to ransom the captives, and the chief, his greedy eyes glinting, agreed to send for them.

Baranov formally presented the chief with the imperial arms on copper plate, explaining through the interpreter that it only had to be shown to foreign shipmasters in the future to guard the possessor against harm.

Instantly the chief's attitude became one of respect and a desire for conciliation. He took the square of metal as a mark of peculiar favor. Among the Kolosh it was a custom to exchange, whenever questions of tribal solidarity had been satisfactorily settled, large, flat pieces of beaten native copper. Inadvertently the Russians had capitalized on an important and significant ritual. And here was copper that had even more meaning than among the Kolosh. The chief indicated that he would listen closely to what Baranov had to say.

Baranov told his oft-repeated tale that he was the great Nanuk of the Russians, but that far away lived another leader, the tsar, so great that even Nanuk must be subject to him. He told of the tsar's great ships, his many guns, his huge villages, his mighty communal dwellings of stone, his thousands of men ready to do his fighting. The chief seemed to be impressed. It was important, he admitted, to have this tsar on his side, but he had been fooled in the past. The English had a somewhat similar tale. Besides, if Baranov had so much authority, why did he not stop the disorders on Cook's Inlet?

This was a ticklish point. Baranov was ill-prepared to answer. He did the best he could with the reply that if the chief would send hostages to his new fort and trade with him regularly, his protection would be extended against such men who did evil deeds because they were far from home.

The conference, by this time, had been going on for hours, with long pauses after each question before the appropriate answer was phrased. It was evident that the chief was not altogether satisfied with Baranov's answer about the Konovalov men, yet he seemed attracted.

His questions took a personal tack. Had Baranov a wife? How long since he had slept with his wife? The chief clucked with sympathy at hearing the answer. That was very bad for him, he assured Baranov. Oh, he had a woman at Kodiak who slept with him? The chief waved her away with scorn as of no consequence —an island woman! Now the chief drove his bargain. He would give Nanuk his own daughter to be his wife. He waved a hand and shouted. There was scuffling and movement among the women in the shadows and finally a figure in a white deerskin garment was pushed forward to be inspected. The girl came walking into the circle of firelight unabashed but keeping her eyes modestly to the ground. She was perhaps seventeen and was beautiful in the strong way of her people. Her nose was firm and straight, her cheekbones high, her lip was disfigured with no labret. There was none of the squat island figure in her carriage. Her hair, though coarse, was long and fell to the firm breasts beneath her deerskin garment.

But Baranov was in a quandary. This was the first chief with whom he had approached a satisfactory treaty. There would be many more such conferences, and many more offers to cement the alliances by the same method, some undoubtedly more important than this. Was he wise in tying himself up so soon? His hesitation irritated the old chief and it took some explanation to mollify him again. Nanuk had a Russian wife at home, he was told; he had to think this over.

Seeming to understand, the old chief—*Grigor Razkazchikov*, Chief Grigor Storyteller, the Russians dubbed him—subsequently let Baranov have twenty men to act as guides in exploring Montague Island and also produced the six men held as slaves.

They were an emaciated, heartsick lot whose eyes hardly lit even at seeing rescuers. The Russians were puzzled; they were very dark of skin and spoke a language that sounded like nothing the Russians had ever heard. Whence could these six have come? Baranov paid their ransom, took them to his Nuchek base, where he prepared to leave at dawn for Montague.

Next day's weather upset his plans. A gale blew in from the Pacific chopping up a dirty sea very dangerous for bidarkas. A day later things were no better. He cursed the delay before he realized that his luck was in reality better than he thought.

Into the comparative safety of Prince William Sound came creeping a seventy-five-foot schooner with an obviously injured mast seeking anchorage off Nuchek Island as her leadsman sounded the bottom. She flew the British flag. Baranov was excited. Could this be the privateersman Cox? They watched her approach from behind their screen of brush. The crew seemed dark of skin and many of them wore turbans. Soon they made out the roman letters of her name, *Phoenix*, Calcutta. The old hunters were positive she was a trader despite her open gunports and bristling armament, and Baranov could not control his eagerness to see one of Britain's famous vessels. He quickly ordered the whole canoe fleet deployed around her in the manner of natives crowding to trade, then put out himself in a canoe, trusting to his Aleut rain hat and kamleika to conceal his true identity until he was ready to reveal it.

He saw captain and mate issue hurried orders on the approach of his massed strength, the brown-skinned crew run to raise screens of bullock hides around the deck, as protection against flying arrows. At the single opening left astern the captain appeared and made motions for the canoes to come forward one at a time.

Baranov swung under the stern, grasped the ladder thrown down, and clambered aboard.

Instantly, he perceived she could only be a trader. Everywhere on deck, on display, were piles of brass junk, boxes of beads, bundles of clothing, cans of powder, a few old muskets. The captain seemed a friendly sort and the mate a short, thick-set man with a very handsome Irish countenance and a roving, curious pair of eyes. Baranov removed his hat to show his hair. Captain and mate stared in astonishment. Baranov explained in Russian who he was but the captain shook his head and countered with English, not a word of which Baranov knew. Spanish, Portuguese, French were tried. Communication seemed impossible except by signs until the captain tried a very bad German, whereupon they laughed in relief and shook hands. It was years since Baranov had spoken German but he learned now that he spoke with a couple of Irishmen, Captain Hugh Moore of the India trade and Mate Joseph O'Cain, better known in certain ports as Honest Joe, the Irishman from Boston.

Baranov was hustled off to the cabin where a turbaned Bengalese boy they called Richard was ordered to bring liquor and food. They talked all night. But they could have saved some of their breath, for dawn found the weather still dirty and it remained so five days, which meant that Baranov could give his conscience the best of reasons for standing by to help Moore repair his mast. Of course, he offered his force to fell the necessary timber and help the crew set it anew. He showed Moore the six ransomed slaves.

"Malays!" exclaimed the captain. Baranov made him a present of the six, who after ten long years thus had a chance to find their way home again.

But most of those five days were spent in the *Phoenix*'s cabin being served drinks by the amiable Richard. It is astonishing how much information can be traded back and forth in an unfamiliar and halting language when all are starved for news. Baranov soon threw reticence to the winds when he saw these men readily answered his every question. He told Moore he had been afraid he was the privateersman sent to murder them all and was immensely relieved to hear that Cox had died at Canton. Moore was astonished to realize the poverty of the Russians, when he got their story. The rumor that they were strong in the north and becoming ready to menace Pacific trade he dismissed now as fantastic. He saw them in their true light, as traders operating on the slenderest of means and with little more than an almost unbelievable bravery as an asset.

He and his kind approached the natives of this coast only with the greatest caution, the stoutest of little ships, and the utmost in armaments; the Kolosh further south were too prone to try to seize every ship they could. Moore had wandered this far north off the beaten track feeling he was indeed adventurous; and now here was this man poking about in canoes and armed only with muskets and falconets that should long since have been in museums.

He was fascinated by Baranov's almost complete ignorance about many matters he considered common information as contrasted with the man's evident intelligence. Baranov's ignorance about navigation, for instance, seemed incredible in view of his distance from home; moreover he knew little about California, the extent of Spanish possessions, the routes to Canton, the position and importance of the Sandwich Islands, or the part played by the British companies in the fur trade. So he told Baranov about Kamehameha, king of the Sandwich Islands, a very intelligent native who welcomed foreign ships, encouraged his people to learn navigation, and let them sign on ships for the experience. Moore pointed to Hawaiians among his own crew of Lascars.

The sea otter, Moore said, abounded on the whole coast all the way to California. Indeed, he explained, the journey this far north had not proved particularly profitable and they would have done better to stay around the fifty-fifth parallel, where they could have obtained five skins for every one they had found up here—a point that naturally deeply interested Baranov. They would have done better merely to trade with the Franciscan missionaries in California where, although trade to foreigners was legally not permissible and hunting otter prohibited, the missions, being dependent on Mexico for everything, were chronically in want and willing to sell skins for trade goods, a practice largely winked at by the authorities because of sympathy for the missionaries. Of course, Moore went on, your ship was technically liable to seizure, but on the whole the trade was safe, provided the crew behaved itself.

Baranov was consumed with envy. To be free, like this, to have a vessel like the *Phoenix* at one's own command! True that she would not be a complete solution to his problems; his furs would still have to be sent through Siberia; no Russian ship could yet enter Canton. But Shelekhov was working on that, and even a couple of cargoes of that Sandwich Island's taro and pork would satisfy much. Closely he listened to everything, and was deeply intrigued to hear that at Nootka Sound, where the English put in with the Spanish, Captain John Meares had built a vessel large enough to sail to Canton. He had done it with Chinese coolie labor, Moore said.

When on the fifth day the gale abated, the mast was set anew and there was little left but to say good-by, Baranov had acquired a very accurate picture of the status of the Northwest trade from the English viewpoint. He knew that it was not he nor his force they feared but the Yankees, who had come to the coast to trade for the first time not three years before and yet were already sending twice as many vessels as their rivals.

By way of farewell and as an expression of his deep gratitude to his new friends, out of his poverty Baranov gave them five silver foxskins and several kamleikas of intricate workmanship. As a return courtesy, Moore gave to Baranov the Bengalese cabin boy, Richard, who knew some English and could function as Baranov's interpreter as well as his personal servant.

Soon after his new-found friends had gone, he left his main body at Nuchek to hunt sea otter and pressed on to finish the job of exploring Montague Island with sixteen Russians, the twenty Kenaitze guides and as many Aleuts in canoes and one large baidar in the prow of which he had his falconet. He was learning how fast a summer can be frittered away with nothing accomplished.

He found a bay, felled trees for a breastwork and temporary camp, posted the falconet to guard the entrance, and appointed sentries before nightfall. Behind them brooded the high snow fields of Montague's two great mountain ranges.

In the morning those snows attract mists which billow in from the sea just before dawn like thick rolls of cotton, making the summertime half-light worse than the darkest night. The five sentries chose this hour to doze off.

Suddenly assailants fell on them with a series of frightful yells and jumped inside the breastwork to slash at the prostrate bodies with their long knives. They wore helmets and breastplates and carried wooden shields. Their faces were covered with grotesque masks which simulated the raven, the bear, the killer whale— exaggerated, frightening representations with huge tusks and terrible, staring eyes. Their attack was systematically conceived and carried out on orders from a general in the background. When the Aleuts recognized their assailants as Kolosh they let out frightful wails of despair and threw themselves on the ground, useless for further fighting.

Baranov had taken off his wet clothes to let them dry, was sleeping only in a shirt and wrapped in seal-skins. He jumped to his feet at the first shriek and sprawled over a log as a spear pinned his shirt to the wood. In the swirling, dark-gray mists, only shapeless forms could be seen struggling. Shrieks filled the air, groans, exultant yells, orders in the Kolosh tongue. He found his musket, leveled it at a figure with the head of some abominable bird coming toward him with a cutlass, and pulled the trigger. The Russians grouped together like cornered rats. But they had firearms and soon the breastwork was cleared enough to bring the falconet into position. The gunner Tumakayev set the match. It roared and the Kolosh dived for the protection of the forest.

The whitening mists showed the sun was rising. Baranov prayed for full daylight. What were the Kolosh doing here? Showers of arrows fell on them from the forests. The struggle lasted two hours. There was another rush from the Kolosh and another. Tumakayev and Baranov worked like demons over the little cannon.

Suddenly there came a rattle of musketry from out to sea. A hush fell over the battle. The Russians held their breath. Could Izmailov be near by with the sloop? The Kolosh general in the forest shouted a hoarse order, his main body sprinted for the beach. "Look," screamed a Russian, pointing to the beach. The retreating Kolosh were dragging off several of the Kenaitze hostages. Baranov was responsible for their safety. He ordered a charge and tried to lead a sortie over the breastwork, but he was driven back by the arrows from the trees. The mists suddenly lifted from the waters. The Russians cheered. A baidar was coming, paddled furiously by the men left at Nuchek. The Kolosh general shouted his last order, the rest of them escaped to the beach, pushed off their canoes, and were fired on from the Russians' baidar. Two or three bodies toppled into the water and the Kolosh canoes left behind them a long wake of blood; but their sharp-prowed craft quickly got out of range and disappeared down Montague's shore.

On the beach nine Aleuts lay slashed to death and fifteen were badly wounded. Four of the Kenaitze hostages were captured. The hunter Kotovschikov lay dead and Naspelov was dying. The only satisfaction was a number of dead and wounded Kolosh.

At first the latter refused to speak but the remaining Kenaitze showed how to break their stubborn silence. After their feet had rested a few minutes in the hot coals of the fire they said they were from Yakutat Bay and thought they had attacked a Kenaitze camp. They intended no real ill will, they insisted—it was not supposed to have been an important raid. But the Kenaitze felt they were lying, and after further persuasion the Kolosh admitted that the Yakutat Bay council had declared a war of reprisal on the Kenaitze for various misdeeds and that they were the vanguard of more than ten war canoes that could be expected any day.

The information gave Baranov an unexpected advantage. He could tell Chief Storyteller he had averted a Kolosh attack. He read the prayers for the dead over his fallen men, buried them, and started for Nuchek. On the way, however, his Aleuts told him something which again lowered his spirits. The four Kenaitze had been captured because they had rushed out to greet the attackers under the impression that they were their own people. This would indicate that Storyteller had planned some kind of surprise of his own.

Baranov was grim when he confronted Storyteller. The old chief pretended to be in a towering rage because Baranov had lost the hostages he was pledged to protect. "He says," translated the interpreter, "that your failure breaks all agreements between you. From now on they are privileged to kill any Russian they meet."

"Tell him," said Baranov to the interpreter, "that inasmuch as he broke his agreement with *me*, by secretly planning to attack me himself, that I am the wronged one and that I now feel free to kill every Kenaitze. Tell him I am astonished to hear of such treachery. I came here with only the most earnest wish for peace and desire to help the Kenaitze people. I have just borne the brunt of an attack intended for them and have saved many of his people by the sacrifice of my men. I have proved myself honorable but he has proven a liar and a schemer. Then say I refused his daughter at first because I wished to test his honor. Now I know the truth."

Blunt, rapid speech was disconcerting to these savages. The chief became involved in his protestations of innocence and friendship for Nanuk. Nanuk accordingly drove his advantage, demanded proof, got Storyteller to promise a hundred canoes and two hundred men for the summer's hunting fleet the following year. When the fort they intended to build on Prince William Sound was finished his village must bring the fort food and trade only there with furs. Nanuk would see how he behaved before considering taking his daughter. To everything Storyteller assented.

The conference over, Baranov went on to other villages to find

somewhat better receptions, but so many questions about Konovalov were asked everywhere that he knew he would have to
thresh that whole matter out soon. Meanwhile the bidarka fleet
began returning. No casualties had been sustained but Purtov
and Kulikalov had only a thousand skins—very few in view of the
size of force and effort expended. The Aleuts had feared this in-
cursion into the Kolosh country southward; despite their massed
strength, they had stubbornly hugged small bays and inlets and
had had to be constantly driven into the wider expanses of water
and shoreline by their Russian artel masters. The method was
sound, Purtov believed, for they had sighted extremely rich otter
grounds, but only the accompaniment of an armed vessel in the
future would give the Aleuts enough confidence to hunt freely.

It was late in summer when Baranov, on the *God's Friend* navigated by Izmailov, put into Kuchekmak Bay and saw the palisades
and gate of Fort Alexander for the first time and met Vassili
Molokhov. He was uneasy. So little had been done this summer,
despite his plans to accomplish so much. Few furs, a disappointing
number of tribes made tributary, not even a site yet picked for a
Prince William Sound fort; he had not had time to return to continue exploration of Montague Island. After looking into the
Konovalov matter here, he decided, he might keep his main body
on Nuchek Island to build the redoubt and send but a small force
home to finish St. Paul.

Molokhov showed him their stronghold. Conditions had grown
steadily worse, he reported. Kolomin had become as bad as any of
them, Samoilov had been made next to Balushin in authority. Now
they had two forts and superior strength; they made every effort
to cut the Shelekhov men off from their tributary villages, stopping their fur trading and cutting off their food. Molokhov sent
out his men only in gangs. Once a party of two Russians and forty
Kenaitze had been waylaid, the Russians left tied to trees, and the
natives taken to Fort St. Nicholas where they were beaten. To
make matters worse, Konovalov had received a supply ship from

home bringing supplies and still more men. This last caused unrest among Molokhov's men. Traders were always jealous when their rivals got comforts from home and they got none. He strongly counseled abandoning Cook's Inlet to the Lebedev-Lastotchkin Company. Too many hunters; the sea otter was being exterminated. A few months more and there would be none for anybody. But Baranov could only refuse. He certainly could never report to Shelekhov that, far from establishing new outposts, he had closed the only one there was. He decided to have a talk with Konovalov about his reputed powers to exercise exclusive rights on the mainland.

At dawn he set out, a fleet of canoes at his back, for Fort St. Nicholas on the Kaknu River, fifty miles up the inlet. At length he sighted the palisades through the forest trees and the two galiots, *St. George* and *St. Ivan*, pulled up on the beach. Armed men leaned on their muskets, awaiting them, among them Konovalov and white-bearded old Samoilov. Balushin was not in evidence.

Baranov was received with contemptuous ridicule and insults. There was nothing to discuss, Konovalov said. Baranov had only to understand that the islands could be his but the mainland was the exclusive territory of the Lebedev-Lastotchkin Company, by right of governmental grant. To the demand to see such orders, Konovalov only laughed, saying they were in proper shape and he would produce them when it suited him to do so. Tauntingly, Konovalov added that Balushin had left that very morning to build a fort on Nuchek Island on Prince William Sound. He added a warning to keep well away from that section if the Baranov men did not want trouble.

Baranov returned to Fort Alexander deeply disturbed and dejected. He knew Konovalov's kind too well to put the slightest trust in them ordinarily, but one thing they seldom dared make light of was the government. Had Konovalov indeed been given exclusive privileges over the mainland? Anything could happen among the merchants with their constant intrigues. Had Koch been removed from command at Okhotsk and replaced by some bribe-taking timeserver more friendly to Lebedev-Lastotchkin than to Shelekhov? Perhaps Shelekhov had fallen into some terrible trouble with Petersburg—everyone in Irkutsk had wondered how long he would escape. But why was he, Baranov, at least not told? Shelekhov owned shares in the rival company, following his old policy of having a finger in every pie. Could Lebedev-Lastotchkin order the Shelekhov men excluded from the mainland without Shelekhov's knowledge?

He was at least certain that Konovalov spoke the truth in saying that Balushin was building a fort at Nuchek. They had probably watched him, waiting for him to leave Prince William Sound, then immediately moved in. Old Storyteller would probably switch his allegiance the minute he understood Baranov had been outwitted. Baranov's summer had been largely a failure.

Into his dejection broke exciting news. From Kodiak came word that a vessel had just come there—a new vessel, just built at Okhotsk, skippered by an Englishman and sailed by five more Englishmen!

Baranov lost no time urging Izmailov to take the *God's Friend* to Kodiak.

6

---◆--◆-◆---

"Yakov Egoryevich Shiltz"

WHEN the decrepit *God's Friend* crawled into St. Paul harbor and Baranov saw there a brand-new, schooner-rigged little packet named the *Eagle* and met the English who had built and sailed her, he forgot that nothing had been done in his absence to finish building St. Paul and ordered the greatest *praznik* so far known in those parts. Buckets of the new vodka supply were poured into the fermenting kvass, meat was roasted in the square, packages of tobacco were again passed out. Two of the new men brought guzlas; music sounded in Russian America. Out of the Aleut dugouts the shy, giggling girls were pulled and made drunk and pushed into the circle of a hundred and fifty dancing men until they, too, caught the contagion and laughed and shrieked with the rest. Supplies, news from home, reinforcements, a new ship!

Guest of honor was the tattooed, red-haired English skipper who had brought a vessel across the Pacific in the unprecedented time of six weeks. Privately the Russians thought him the ugliest man ever seen, but they toasted him again and again because he was English, which meant he could do anything, and because his pronunciation of Russian made them roll on the ground with laughter. "To Yakov Egoryevich Shiltz!" they cried, which was their rendering of the name of James Shields, and each time Yakov Egoryevich answered by jumping to his feet, raising his own cup high, and shouting, *"Spassibo, spassibo, tovarishchi!"*

Why James Shields had decided to put the distance of half Europe between himself and England is a mystery no longer solvable. Able with his hands, skilled in shipyard crafts, dowered with a certain belligerent self-assurance and business shrewdness, he and five other compatriots with records as obscure as his but also with the stamp of the sea on them first appear to fame on the rolls of the army regiment stationed at Ekaterinburg, Siberia, where in a short time Shields rose to a commission. Shelekhov heard of him, asked him to build a small but fast vessel along modern lines at Okhotsk. The *Eagle* finished, Shelekhov proposed that Shields sail her himself to America to teach her type of navigation to others and, after laying over at Kodiak the winter, to return in spring with all furs. On the way he was to drop at Unalaska thirty-odd new men to take possession of that strategic way station on behalf of the Golikov-Shelekhov Company. Shields was agreeable to everything, especially when he discovered that nobody but himself could sail the *Eagle* and he could again stipulate the employment of his friends and hold the merchant up for a fee that made Shelekhov writhe because he had no alternative but to pay this independent Englishman.

And so Yakov Egoryevich was at Kodiak, at a praznik at which even Shelekhov was gratefully toasted and which lasted until dawn before the last man dropped off to drunken sleep, the last Aleut girl had been carried to the bunkhouses, and Shields had been solicitously put to bed by Baranov.

Baranov hurried to open the batch of mail brought him and digest the news from home brought also by word of mouth. Nobody had heard of any special powers granted the Lebedev-Lastotchkin Company. As far as anyone knew the situation at Okhotsk was the same. Koch was still in command, Shelekhov was still wealthy. Koch wished him well and said he would find a few comforts in the stores sent by his friends. His brother's crabbed handwriting expressed his intention of carrying on in the Anadyr, promised to see his family was cared for, and hoped that the personal comforts Aleksandr Andrevich had ordered by the *St. Michael* had reached him in good condition.

He kept Shelekhov's long letter for the last. It began with much important gossip. Jacobi had been replaced as governor general, Europe's troubles continued to occupy St. Petersburg's attentions, and his cherished schemes, including the one to open Canton to Russian ships, seemed no nearer accomplishment. "The French have incited the world to war against them," he wrote.

Due attention had been paid Baranov's request for a priest and the matter was being discussed. A station would be established by men dropped by Shields at Unalaska; one Popov would be its chief and answerable, like Baranov, to Okhotsk.

Then the letter got down to business, urged more exploration, and said:

"We send you now enough iron, rope, and sailcloth to build another ship which, under Shields' training, you must begin to build, at the same time laying keels for two others. Push the construction far enough this winter and learn enough from him to dispense with further assistance from a trained shipwright." Then there followed clear instructions to send Shields back the following spring with all furs: "Everything you need (for shipbuilding) not in this shipment will be sent you at the next opportunity. Have the Aleuts pick oakum, make rope, sew sails, and help the blacksmith. . . ."

Baranov was excited. Orders to build a ship! The magnitude of the task did not immediately occur to him, for he knew nothing of shipbuilding. The Englishman Meares had done it at Nootka Sound; it had seemed simple, the way Moore told of it. With Shields at hand, and the supplies Shelekhov spoke of on the way, what would prevent his building one large enough to make California and the Sandwich Islands?

But when he talked to Fyodor Rodionov, the supercargo who came with the *Eagle*, it did not take long to discover that either somebody had made a bad mistake or Shelekhov's order to build a ship was just a phrase. What chandler's supplies were aboard were adequate only for the upkeep of the vessels they had, and totally at variance with the statements in the letter. There was little iron, no copper or brass, less calking, only a few barrels of tar. Even Baranov could tell at a glance there was too little of everything. The only item in quantity was rigging, and most of that had seen use before. Rodionov, who seemed an honest if not too forceful character, swore the orders had been filled exactly according to specifications.

Baranov understood, then. It all was just another sample of Shelekhov's inability to keep from exaggerating everything. Not satisfied with being able to brag about the packet he had built at Okhotsk, he wanted to say he had ordered his man in America to build more ships. In contrast with his grandiose talk was the fact that he had been ungenerous even to niggardliness with everything that had come in the hold of the *Eagle*—not just with the ship-building materials, but with supplies of all kinds. What was sent would hardly pay the arrears of debt to the Aleuts for their summer's work. Then came a discovery that sent Baranov into a towering rage.

The invoices plainly showed "One large box for A. A. Baranov." He knew what should be in that box—the personal possessions he had not been able to collect before leaving Siberia, creature comforts he had ordered, such as good vodka, a little wine, some especially fine tobacco and tea, no doubt similar gifts from friends, some civilized clothing of which he stood in sore need. But a search from prow to stern revealed no such box, nor any package of any kind consigned to A. A. Baranov. Rodionov wrung his hands under Baranov's angry upbraiding but he could give no explanation of its disappearance—unless it had never been taken on at Okhotsk or dropped by some mistake at Unalaska. Bitter disappointment such as only a man can feel who desperately longs for some change from his savage surroundings filled Baranov's soul as he stalked off to find Shields.

Of course Shelekhov did not mean him to build ships. The necessary supplies could not be sent until at least the following summer and by that time Shields would be gone. It was all written for some prying official eye, so that someone might whisper, "They say Shelekhov is even building ships in America!"

He knew now why the instruction to send Shields back was so clearly worded. The Englishman's services must be costing the merchant plenty. Well, he, Baranov, would use him! He would actually build the ship which Shelekhov, in his scorn, considered simply a boastful dream! He asked Shields to teach him, and the Englishman agreed.

But even their preliminary survey showed the task all but impossible. In all the colony the only tool was the ax—there was not even a saw. There was precious little iron and what there was was due the Aleuts. There was little oakum, little tar, nothing with which to make paint. Moreover, Shields pointed out, the timber around St. Paul was neither of the right size nor quality and they would have a hard time launching a large vessel even if one were built in that harbor.

"Then let us look elsewhere," said Baranov.

Taking the *Eagle* out to sea, they cruised along the Kodiak shoreline, then crossed Shelekhov Straits and skirted the mainland shore that Baranov had traveled that summer. Here Shields grew more interested, for the timber was taller and of a different quality. He noted, too, the high rise and fall of tide, suitable for launching a ship, for along here the exposed flank of Alaska Peninsula receives the full brunt of the Pacific's pulse. He finally pronounced the timber on Montague Island to be what he would select and sighted a small inlet on the mainland that would be ideal for shipbuilding. Baranov named the place Resurrection Bay. Here he would build his ship. But first he must consolidate his position at Kodiak Island.

Baranov now dismissed Konovalov from his mind and concentrated on the plans filling his spare time and the needs of St. Paul village. He was satisfied that Konovalov was merely a troublemaker and contented himself with sending Molokhov a reinforcement of twenty men to help keep the peace and with the intention of writing to Koch in spring all about the crimes committed on Cook's Inlet.

He drove his men hard to finish building St. Paul as he wanted it, as a preliminary to his shipbuilding. Before the rainy season closed down in earnest he had the satisfaction of seeing his flagpole in the square, good cedar shakes on all the cabins and bunkhouses, a strong little breastwork commanding the harbor entrance, and his own house with several rooms and a porch. Now he could institute a manner of living he believed more in keeping with his station. The walls of one room he decorated with his framed letter of commendation from Count Ostermann, items of Kolosh armor, and curious bits of native carving in ivory. Here he kept his diary, wrote his accounts, interviewed his men, and received their complaints. Another room he made into his dining room. It signified his degree of taste that he regretted having no chinaware, but felt he had to content himself with the colorful bowls and wooden boxes the natives wrought into strange shapes by steam. He loved to eat with a chosen companion or two, served in state by Richard, who had quickly learned to understand Russian. The feminine part of his establishment was still the Innuit girl that had been given him. She wore a kerchief over her head, now, and earrings, and softly spoke the pidgin Russian of the Aleuts.

The village finished, he refused to let the men rest or idle but kept them hard at work burning tons of wood to make charcoal and helping the blacksmith forge bolts and nails from the colony's supply of iron. When the iron gave out he sent the men scouring the shoreline of the islands for traces of old wrecks from which the Aleuts had not always salvaged all the metal. And he himself toured the villages to persuade the Aleuts to give up the iron they had, promising them to redeem it later.

The Aleuts were far from pleased, of course, and gave up their precious metal reluctantly, but Baranov was always able to talk them out of anything. The pile of iron that accumulated at St. Paul evinced the nature of the idea that busily occupied his mind —that a ship could be built from the resources of the country.

He imposed a tight discipline. Before the flagpole in the square he made the men parade on Sundays and holidays and stand at some semblance of attention as the flag was raised and Kuskov or some other subordinate read the prayers for the day.

He abolished gambling, forbidding even the possession of a pack of cards. He knew too well the propensity of the kind of men who volunteered for promyshlenik service to go into debt that would keep them in servitude to the Company for years. He would suddenly appear in cabin or bunkhouse when the men were idle, and quite openly look for evidences of gaming.

He promulgated a set of strict regulations for sexual intercourse with the natives. Venereal disease had appeared in the village, probably brought by some of the new men on the *Eagle*. The remedy of the times were mercurials dissolved in vodka. He banished many a man alone to the woods with a bottle of the stuff on discovery that he was infected.

He forbade prostitution but encouraged pairing off. If a man wished to take a girl, he announced, he himself would make the necessary presents to the Aleut father without charging them to the man's account at the commissary. If the man wished to change the girl he was required to convince the father why she was unsatisfactory and otherwise see she was taken care of before he could choose another. For her part the girl had to cook her man's food and sew his clothing in a satisfactory manner. When children came they had to be baptized, Baranov offering to make the customary baptismal gifts.

In the matter of liquor he imposed no restrictions, except against distilling. He always kept a vat of crab apples, rye meal, and cranberries fermenting with kvass-yeast. Any man off duty was welcome to as much of the stuff as he could hold. It was supposed to be a preventive against scurvy. Whether it was or not, Baranov knew the temperament of his men and their cravings in such a climate. He otherwise encouraged all the merrymaking he could. His appearance in the bunkhouse often meant the start of a song fest or a dance. He would clap his hands, call on the two musicians to strike up their strings, and soon he would be bawling the familiar songs of Siberia with the rest, the songs that are so nostalgically similar to the mournful ballads of the American frontier.

And all of it, especially the hard work, was exactly the right way to guarantee the liking of the kind of men he had. They liked discipline, providing it was just. He might have become as revered among his Russians as among the Aleuts but for the Izmailov clique.

That old navigator's nose had been out of joint ever since the coming of the English. Now he became very troublesome, publicly sneering and professing amusement at the inspections and prayer readings on Sundays, contemptuously refusing to appear, and inciting others to do the same. Baranov never pressed the issue against the old man but kept his thoughts to himself all winter the while he planned his ship, scoured the island for metal of every kind to be forged into bolts and nails, and even set men to work to digging rock he believed contained iron ore, which he tried to smelt, though unsuccessfully. And meanwhile he assiduously cultivated the Englishman's friendship.

This was not hard to do, although it made fearful inroads on the colony's supply of better liquor. Shields was convivial and loved to argue. Baranov, who could be talkative with friends, was also positive in his views. A queer intimacy sprang up between the two men that manifested itself in arguments that seemed at times to bring them almost to the point of blows, especially when Richard had served them considerable amounts of hot vodka punch. Baranov's plans for the ship were the most fruitful source.

His thoughts were taking shape to picture a schooner with three masts, two decks, a length of seventy-three feet in the keel, a depth of thirteen-and-a-half and a length of seventy-nine feet in the top deck—a vessel of respectable size, especially considering the means at hand. Shields, with reason, opposed the third mast and the upper deck as ridiculously unnecessary and Baranov became stubborn about it. The discussion rose to such a height on one occasion that Shields walked out of Baranov's house and swore he would not return. But he did.

And Shields taught Baranov navigation, a priceless gift and one that would release him for good from thralldom to the Izmailovs and Botcharovs, and in his heart he was deeply grateful. When winter eased off and the weather would clear for a few hours he took the *Eagle* out of the harbor, Shields beside him, while Izmailov predicted freely to the village that those two would surely pile up on a reef. But they did not and after a few weeks Baranov found himself taking the packet out to sea with fair assurance and giving orders to the crew with a British crispness he borrowed from his friend.

Throughout all this Baranov kept throwing out broad hints to Shields about the fortunes to be made in the fur trade, painting gaudy pictures of the numbers of sea otter that must yet exist in places never discovered, and telling how, in the old days, the skippers of ships used to come home with finds worth a quarter of a million because they dared penetrate where nobody else had ventured. But Shields never seemed to take the hint and expressed no desire to stay.

Each man began regarding the other as a queer mixture of great cleverness and abysmal stupidity.

During April, Igor Purtov, Demid Kulikalov, and other master hunters who had been sent the rounds of the Aleut villages to make the levies of canoes for the summer's hunt, came back with disturbing reports. "They refuse," said Purtov. "They will not venture again along the Kolosh coast without an armed ship as escort."

"Go back and tell them an armed ship will go this year," said Baranov.

Purtov, himself unbelieving, went back to the villages. Baranov was far too preoccupied to go himself. A fleet of canoes began gathering before St. Paul, but only one hundred and seventy of them—one third the previous year's levy. Purtov said he could do no better with the elders. "They are too much afraid we may be lying to them about sending an armed ship with them. And they are also disturbed that you ask for a fleet after taking all their iron without paying last year's hunting debts."

Baranov had to be content. He braced himself, now, for the time had come to tell Shields of what he had in his mind.

He began by begging the Englishman not to lose his temper but to hear him through. He wanted him to remain in the colony another year or two. He wished he would, this summer, convoy the bidarka fleet at least as far as Yakutat Bay and explore that site with an eye to its possibility as a future outpost; while he himself would take men and supplies to Resurrection Bay to fell timber, build a construction camp, and prepare shipways in readiness for Shields' return in late summer. Then they would spend the next winter together at Resurrection building the schooner.

Shields refused. Baranov offered him a substantial share. Shields refused again. He had had enough of Russian America, he said, and Shelekhov's orders were to return without further delay.

So Baranov had to play his trump. He informed Shields he was under orders to remain. Shields looked at him in astonishment and Baranov produced his written authority from Koch which placed "such navigators as the government may assign to your Company" fully under his direction.

Shields was furious. His first thought was that it was a trick of Shelekhov's but when Baranov convinced him the idea was his Shields' temper flared and he struck Baranov a blow which sent the latter reeling. In a moment they rolled on the ground "beating each other like a couple of peasants," as a witness described it. When they were finally separated both were in a sad state, with swollen eyes, torn clothing, and teeth of doubtful soundness. Baranov found his voice first. "You will obey orders, Yakov Egoryevich, or I shall lock you up in your cabin."

Shields swore he would never move a ship for Baranov in any direction but Siberia, and Baranov had to order him tied up and a guard put on the *Eagle*.

It was several days, during which summer work stalled, before

Shields would consent even to see Baranov again. But he knew he was caught. Baranov could easily prevent his escape to Russia and he saw clearly enough that Baranov's authority was official whereas Shelekhov's was merely private. He made up his mind to drive a hard bargain.

He did. Baranov, who realized this was a man priceless to him, conceded terms that would make Shelekhov froth at the mouth when he heard them—sea-otter skins to the value of more than two thousand rubles each season to each of Shields' four companions, an even larger salary to Shields, and two full shares for two years of all the skins taken from any new fur-bearing islands he might discover on behalf of the Company. To make sure his man would not escape Baranov stipulated that the payment would be paid at Okhotsk, by the commander.

They were terms well worth a couple of years of any man's time. If Shields made a good discovery his share could run into the fifty thousands. They shook hands on it and Baranov invited the sailor to his house for a drink on the contract.

An hour later Shields heatedly maintained that according to their agreement he could explore as far down the Kolosh coast as he pleased and Baranov insisted just as heatedly that for this year he had best go no further than Yakutat.

7

A Ship's Keel Is Laid

THAT attempt to build the three-masted schooner began the change in him that was to be apparent in the Baranov of later years. He was determined from the first but as difficulty after formidable difficulty presented itself to dissuade him his determination mounted to such a stubborn passion and almost complete disregard for consequences that the record after a time ceases to suggest adequate motive.

His admirers in later years wrote that he did it to demonstrate the resources of the country and from a patriotic desire to advance the Russian cause, neither of which sounds very convincing inasmuch as he demonstrated rather the poorness of his resources and almost wrecked the Russian cause in America.

The whole effort, in fact, almost cost him his reputation and his life and threatened to destroy the whole Golikov-Shelekhov Company. He could easily have foreseen what he risked. The facts of what happened are well established, though they lie in letters, heavy with the smell of preservatives, from which friendly hands have long since expunged the controversies and in old Russian books baffling in their contradictions of unmitigated praise and utmost condemnation. From those facts the truth seems inescapable that he was blinded by some personal desire for which the wish to cross Shelekhov was but the start and the thought of having a vessel at his command large enough to sail to Canton, California, and the Sandwich Islands the driving and ultimate idea. It was the summer of 1793. In two years more, when his ship would presumably be built if the whole thing did not prove an absurd impossibility, his term of service would be finished. Did he see himself breaking from Russia to satisfy his intense curiosity about the world in a vessel of his own, just as he had always broken from places and things grown too familiar? There is the barest hint in the record that Shields was involved with him in a plan to adventure in distant places, but it is all too bare to trust.

His troubles began when he drained the Aleut villages of their iron. It was most unwise at the time. Despite his three years in America he had not yet made a really successful drive on furs, the commodity that made the colony possible. Good relations with the Aleuts and a big fleet for the summer's hunt were advisable. Yet he allowed the *Eagle* to convoy out of St. Paul harbor but one hundred and seventy canoes, a fraction of the previous year's strength, without going himself to make the rounds of the Aleut elders, as only he could successfully do, to rally them to more support. Of course he was gambling on Shields' leading the smaller fleet into richer fur grounds than ever before, and opening trade with the Kolosh for the first time—but it was taking a chance. What but a doubtful sense of honor would prevent Shields from absconding to Canton with a shipload of furs?

Further, he kept the majority of the Russians from the hunt and sent them, with supplies, in the *God's Friend* to Resurrection Bay to start putting up a construction camp. They were furious. They resented spending the summer months, the best for catching otter in quantity, at hard, profitless labor; on the catch of furs depended their earnings, the sole reward for their hardships. Baranov had to drive them to the task with reminders of the oath to obey orders that they had taken before the commander at Okhotsk.

He felt confident of success, that every lack such as calking, pitch, and tar could be provided for, just as he had figured out a way to provide for iron. He would try the forest moss for calking, tap trees to get pitch, use whale oil thickened with ocher for paint. And there was the bare possibility that Shelekhov meant what he had written and would send shipbuilding supplies "at the first opportunity." The lack of hardwoods among the native growths seemed the most formidable difficulty but he meant to make the local mountain ash serve instead.

But he found calking, pitch, tar, and hardwoods the least of his troubles, once at Resurrection Bay himself. Food was far from plentiful. The tide was turbulent and fishing bad. Behind him rose high country that made hunting difficult. He had to detach an uncomfortable proportion of his force to keep the camp supplied. They faced the open Pacific, and the gales that often whipped up without notice hit them with full force. The mountainous waves, having gathered size before the full sweep of an immense ocean, struck the shore and washed into the bay high enough to tear away, again and again, their first attempts at putting up a way. The best stand of timber was over on Montague Island. He sent a force there to set up a logging camp and raft the lumber over the strait; the winds disintegrated the rafts and dispersed the logs all over Alaska Peninsula.

It was weeks before the first problems were solved. He left Fyodor Rodionov in command while he ran over to Cook's Inlet, not so much to see how Molokhov had fared during the winter against the Lebedevski as to investigate a vein of coal of which he had heard and with which he meant to repeat his experiments at smelting Kodiak's iron ore. Molokhov reported that there had been a few more encounters and the situation among the natives was very tense; the Lebedevski had gone inland across the peninsula as far as Bristol Bay and had raided villages. And as for furs, once they had taken out as many as two thousand sea otter yearly; now they had not taken two hundred.

Baranov brushed these immediate problems aside impatiently, sailed to the west shore, looked for and found his coal, extracted several sacks of it and returned to Resurrection Bay to find work at a standstill.

Amos Balushin had crossed from Fort Constantine, the redoubt he had built the previous summer on Nuchek Island, to Montague from which he had driven off the loggers at muskets' points and had put up a breastwork and planted armed men to keep them away. "They say," said Rodionov, "that they will shoot us wherever we stir on the mainland." Parties fishing for halibut had actually been fired on.

Baranov cursed roundly. He longed to have his men return Balushin's fire but he did not dare. Instead he ordered supplies of dried salmon to be brought from Kodiak.

The decision shocked and angered the men, who hated yukola and considered it a famine ration, which it was. Where was the strict disciplinarian of St. Paul who had made them drill on Sunday mornings and taken away their cards? Was he afraid of a little lead? But he did not explain.

Izmailov led the talking against him. Worse, the old man openly took his sloop to Fort Constantine on Nuchek Island and fraternized with Balushin. Baranov strengthened his decision to send him away, even at the cost of depriving himself of the sloop.

In August, when he heard that Shields was on his way back and felt that he could safely dispense with Izmailov, he ordered him to pick up what furs there were at Kodiak and start for Siberia. Izmailov was furious. He charged that Baranov was sending him to certain death on the Pacific in that wretched old sloop, but Baranov was quietly adamant. Izmailov then made up his mind to cause as much trouble as possible, and he did. At Kodiak he picked up not only the furs but his children by his various concubines and the offspring of other old hunters and made off with them. The outcry was terrific. Baranov had not realized the Aleuts could be capable of such anger and emotion. Only after he had promised faithfully to write and get the children back was some semblance of quiet restored.

Shields' reports of the summer's work were good. He had taken the fleet down to the vicinity of Yakutat Bay past the fifty-ninth parallel, but because the Kolosh stronghold there had appeared so formidable they had not entered the bay to explore. They had seen many otter coves, had had no major accidents, and had brought back a most excellent catch of furs. Shields himself had made no fortune, having discovered no new islands, but he spoke with so much enthusiasm of penetrating to the Queen Charlotte Islands the next year that Baranov hardly dared believe his good luck in that the man seemed contented.

The Englishman surveyed their efforts at Resurrection with pity and wonder, of course, but with him there things went much better. With so able a foreman, Baranov could turn to solving his other problems of material. He wasted days trying to smelt Kodiak's ore with the Cook's Inlet coal. It proved to be so highly charged with sulphur that some chemical compound he could not understand was formed instead of pure iron; it burned too fast and hot, and he knew no way to test for malleability.

Eventually he had to tear himself away and turn his mind again to such everyday problems as guaranteeing a food supply. He sent a message to old Chief Grigor Storyteller up the Sound in order to discover the extent to which Balushin had gained the allegiance of the villages. The chief came personally to visit with several of his people and brought his daughter with him. The union that Baranov had tried, by every subterfuge, to avoid could now be postponed no longer.

The canoes, painted gaily in token of the occasion, came bearing down on Resurrection Bay in a fleet and when they landed at the foot of the steep beach the portly old Indian executed a few steps of the dance of friendship, then gravely handed over his daughter. Baranov managed to summon the proper enthusiasm and ransacked the camp for miscellaneous junk as gifts and for food with which to entertain his guests. The girl stood apart during the long interchange between the men, her eyes fixed on the horizon, her mien contained and expressionless. She wore again the white deerskin dress and her hair was sleek and black with oil. The chief explained his haste in coming. Balushin, he said through the interpreter, had come across the peninsula portage from Cook's Inlet as soon as Nanuk had left the previous summer, and he had since built himself the fort on Nuchek. Balushin had asked for hostages but Storyteller replied that he would give them only to Baranov. Balushin then tried to take some women by force but Storyteller's men drove him off. But the old chief was worried. Balushin had charged that Baranov had no business on the mainland. Could Nanuk explain that?"

"Tell him," Baranov answered the interpreter, "that he must believe me and that Balushin is wrong. The proof that I have a right on the mainland is established by Fort Alexander and my presence here. Tell him the next time Balushin bothers him to show the crest on copper I gave him, the insignia of the tsar."

The chief thought the tsar was too far away, but when Baranov assured him that he himself would stand by, as friend and son-in-law, their promises of alliance were reaffirmed; and Storyteller agreed to have four of his villages hunt and fish for Baranov, and to keep him supplied with food at Resurrection Bay.

There was no telling how long the guests would remain and the men went on with work as best as they could. It might be days or weeks, or until whatever inner voice dictated the Indians' social conscience should tell them to go. In the meantime, no hint could be thrown out that they were in the way and that it was a hardship to feed them. The chief and his men stood or sat on their haunches for hours at a time and gazed somberly at the sweating men with axes cutting down whole logs into one plank, at the gangs cursing, shouting, and tugging in concert at the tackle and pulleys as the beams were swung into place, and at the forges burning charcoal day and night as the blacksmiths hammered incessantly at the ironwork. But they were not the embarrassment to Baranov that his "wife" was. He took her into his shack while his savage guests were with him, of course, for there was nothing else to be done, but he could not have her remain in this place for very long.

Cautiously he suggested to her father through the interpreter that he feared for her among all these men, and that she should return to her village and wait for him to install her at Kodiak as his consort when he could do so with fitting honors. To his relief the chief seemed to accept this. When the Kenaitze left she took her place in one of the long canoes without a word of farewell to Baranov or a backward glance as the lithe craft disappeared into the mists of Prince William Sound.

But all seemed well, for a day or two later canoes came bearing huge halibut and welcome carcasses of fresh-killed deer and caribou, shipments that thereafter appeared in plenty and with regularity. Baranov breathed a heavy sigh of relief. One by one every problem somehow found solution. There seemed no reason why he should not keep his force at work all winter after all. He left Kuskov to worry about St. Paul, where remained only the sick and those he did not want at Resurrection. Soon bad weather closed down communication between Kodiak and the mainland.

The men at first buckled down to the hard labor with a better will, determined to finish it and be done, but by November life in their exposed position was all but unlivable. The storms screaming in from the ocean drove cold rain in their faces and drenched their clothes with fury, and when the rain turned to snow their hands froze on the tackles and the ropes hung stiff with frost. Meals at the long tables became silent, sullen affairs when Baranov was present and seethed with discontented talk when he was not. It was revolting to go from such labor to the primitive food dished up by the cooks. A little tea or some vodka would have cheered them immensely, but there was nothing. Shields counseled giving up the task. The cost in terms of human comfort was certainly exorbitant. But Baranov refused to listen.

He listened, however, when Balushin discovered that food was being run down the Sound and cut it off by sinking the canoes by musket shots as they passed Montague, so that the cooks again had nothing to serve but dried salmon. Shields himself led the revolt. In fact after a meal or two of the unpalatable stuff he picked up his share and flung it in Baranov's face with the remark that he was returning to Kodiak, and at once, unless they had better food.

Baranov jumped to his feet, white with fury but he stopped himself in time when he saw his men's expressions. He would gain no sympathy by being unjust. Everyone was at the limit of his endurance. "You are right, Yakov Egoryevich," he said with difficulty. "I will go up the Sound myself."

He set off with a force of men, an interpreter, and the old hunter Galaktianov as his *peredovchik* of canoes. The hundred-odd miles to Storyteller's district proved hard going; until they could reach the lee of Montague they had to traverse a path swept by the full ocean gales, which necessitated their lashing the canoes together in order to ride the mountainous seas.

Past Montague they breathed more easily but a surprise volley of musketry sounded from shore and water spattered all around their canoes. "They'll sink us if we don't shoot back," yelled Galaktianov, but Baranov shook his head and dug his own paddle hard to escape.

They got out of range without material damage but Baranov knew his prestige with his men was seriously shaken. Balushin had made an attempt to murder him and he had not fought back.

When he called on Storyteller he found the chief very angry. "I have been kind and friendly to you," was the substance of his words. "You swore to be my ally; what have you done to prove it? This Balushin destroyed my canoes bringing you food and wounded my men; he raided one of my villages and succeeded in capturing fifteen of my people. You lied to me about that crest on copper having any effect on him; when I showed it he threw it on the ground and spat on it, he said you just fool people with such toys. Until you prove your friendship to me by driving such men out of the country, our agreement is at an end."

It was direct talk for an Indian and delivered without the usual circumlocutions or pauses for thought. Moreover, Baranov had been received without ceremony and offered but scant food.

He listened with deep thoughtfulness. It was suddenly all too plain that there was nothing of any effectiveness left for him to do but to clean Balushin out of Prince William Sound if he expected to hold the Shelekhov empire together. Actually it was falling apart. They were being forced from their foothold on

Cook's Inlet, prevented from accomplishing anything at Resurrection, and alienated from the villages friendly to them and thus from sources of furs. Even the Aleuts on the islands had grown sullen.

His own men would cheerfully go to war against the Lebedevski, and Shields and his sailors would be right in the forefront; his force was superior, he had the guns of the *Eagle*. Yet his heart quailed at giving the order. There was more to it than Koch's instruction not to interfere with other traders; the sound of such a battle would undoubtedly penetrate to the courts of Siberia and in that event he could expect to be left nowhere but in the lurch by Shelekhov. That wily merchant was probably having enough trouble with St. Petersburg without having the accusation brought against him that he sought to exterminate his competitors by violence.

In order to conceal his panic Baranov launched into a long harangue on loyalty and pleaded to have the food supply line kept open at least until spring, when he could best maneuver his forces against Fort Constantine. He made elaborate pretense of taking official action by writing the chief's complaints down on paper and having Galaktianov make his mark as witness, but Storyteller was unmoved. He knew Nanuk was not being honest, that he was only playing for time. He contemptuously agreed to let one village send him food, providing he could persuade Balushin to lift the blockade.

Baranov's visit to Balushin was futile. He found Fort Constantine a goodly palisade with imposing gates and he cursed himself for the caution which kept him from locating here first. Balushin and his men stood on the parapets looking coldly down at him, and refused to invite him in or have any discussion with him. Baranov appealed to him on the basis of humanity, saying that the men at Resurrection would starve unless the food lines with the Kenaitze were kept open. Balushin only laughed. Baranov, losing his temper, then threatened to bring "his new frigate" and blow them to pieces if Balushin's men did not cease their depredations.

The men on the parapet again laughed but Balushin stopped them with a gesture. He hawked deliberately, cleaned his throat, put his finger in his mouth, and expertly flipped out the mass of mucous so that it fell on Baranov's chest. A roar greeted his marksmanship.

Baranov was pale and trembling with impotent rage as he and his men silently re-embarked in their canoes.

Returning to Resurrection Bay he found work at a standstill. Dire necessity had forced the men to stop all labor so that they might fish and hunt the cold woods of the Peninsula for food. The story of Balushin's insult became known within an hour and from that time on Baranov could not have recalled the men to work on a diet of caviar. His authority was gone.

So it seemed almost a blessing when, in November, a party of Aleuts in bidarkas made the all but impossible journey across the stormy straits with Kuskov's message that he was unable to keep order at St. Paul. Here was an excuse for Baranov to get away; it was obviously bad for him to remain at Resurrection under the circumstances. The men would live without him. He placed Rodionov in charge and braved the open Pacific with the Aleuts.

They planned to hug the mainland until well within the straits, but the heaviest gale of the season hit them. They bent their backs as they kneeled in the canoes, they tied their kamleika hoods across their faces to keep their eyes from being cut by ice particles, they scudded, the canoes lashed together, miles out to sea, and then were beaten back to shore and landed, none knew where, on a bleak Aleutian rock, their canoes heavy with water. But the wonderful Aleut sense of direction saved them and after some days Baranov reached St. Paul harbor again, his knees sprung with kneeling, his eyes aflame with granulation, his clothing stiff with salt.

The moment he could distinguish people through the driving rain obscuring the village he knew things indeed had gone awry. Men scurried away instead of greeting him, as if to give warning to others. He staggered at once to the commissary. The shelves were almost empty. He crossed to the main bunkhouse. The few men lay about with a watchful air or greeted him doubtfully. The place was filthy, the air foul with wet Aleut clothes and the reek of stale tobacco. It was this odor that awakened him to certainty. He walked to the bunk where lay a hunter with a broken arm, a man who had given much trouble for insubordination. "Get up," he commanded. The man hesitated, then shrugged, got up, and stalked off. Baranov prodded the skins that served as blankets, fished out a five-pound package of twist tobacco. He was about to turn for explanation when someone sprang on his back and bore him to the floor. He felt a sharp stab in his shoulder. There was a cry as men sprang to his help and his assailant was sent with a blow on the chin spinning against the opposite row of bunks, where he lay with the look of murder in his eyes and a knife in his hand.

Baranov rose, holding his shoulder. He breathed with difficulty. "Twenty lashes," he said, when he could speak. "Not for attacking me but for robbing the commissary." His voice raised slightly with hysteria. He had had no sleep for more than fifty hours, except for fitful snatches on his knees in the canoe. "Twenty lashes. At Resurrection men work and live in the cold, building us a ship, while you lie here doing nothing—and robbing them of their comforts. I will leave this bunkhouse; I advise you all to return what you have stolen."

He staggered out into the rain again and made for his house. He cursed his lack of lieutenants that had made him place one so young as Kuskov in charge. He had been foolish to leave Richard at Resurrection, to enter that bunkhouse alone.

He found his house empty and depressingly cold. He hurried to make a fire in the brick stove, to light charcoal, blow it into a glow, and place it in the samovar. Where was the Innuit girl? He got his frozen jacket off and it fell to the floor with a sound like thin boards. He staunched the slight flow of blood from his shoulder; the man's aim had fortunately been bad. He half noticed the air in here, too, was heavy with stale tobacco smoke. He opened the tea box; it was empty. He was too exhausted to curse. The door suddenly opened and his Innuit girl rushed in. She saw him and stopped in surprise, then the color suddenly drained from her round, smooth face, leaving her looking like a Mongol powdered for a ceremonial. She shrank toward the wall in terror. Baranov knew his natives. "Who has been here drinking my tea, smoking my tobacco, and sleeping with you?" The girl sank to the floor. But his anger was spent; he could feel only disgust, with himself and everyone around him. The girl began trembling with violent fear, her eyes wide and filled with horror. He closed his teeth on his questions. He did not want to know the man's name. He might be tempted to order a punishment that would kill him.

She suddenly began to babble. It had been so lonely, with Nanuk gone continually. She was the only Innuit and the Aleut women had looked at her with unfriendly eyes. It had not seemed wrong at the time to invite someone who would be kind. . . . But he was not listening. He had pulled up the trapdoor in the floor and lowered himself with difficulty to the tiny cellar beneath where he had hidden some vodka he had made against just such an emergency. Twice his hands felt carefully over the damp, soft earth, then again and again, frantically.

He was ready to send any man to his death when he emerged from that trapdoor. Fortunately the Innuit girl had fled.

8

Canoes Against a British Man of War

H E passed the winter virtually alone in his house, drinking vodka he himself distilled and brooding over his short-comings, both real and fancied, and his discouragements. He dramatized his misfortunes until they assumed monstrous pro-portions in his eyes, a weakness in his character that was to develop with the years. In vain, Kuskov and others protested that they had done their best, that everything was neither their fault nor his, but he shunned all companionship. He began to imagine that he was decrepit of body, that his age crept up on him, that his limbs ached and his sight was blurring.

But when something was at hand to be done he shook it all off and went to work. In February, passage to Resurrection was again feasible but he grimly stuck to the necessary and remained at Kodiak to organize the best hunting fleet they had had so far. At least he would not return to Russia empty-handed.

It cheered him to visit the Aleut villages, probably because they were so easily persuaded to think him a very great person. Every-where he was met with feasts and smiles. He talked to the people as if they were children, not roughly as to slaves, as others did. They responded beautifully; no suspicions here, as among the Kenaitze, no devious double-dealing. And they were so easily handled. When he asked how many canoes the villages could furnish, the elders always ceased smiling and pulled nervously at their wisps of beard, thinking of the iron not yet paid back and the long journey into Kolosh territory, but they were always easily confused by argument, like children. He had always extended credit to them when they were in need, he said, and never pressed for payment. They gave in.

By April he had the promise of four hundred canoes without in return promising an armed ship as escort—he was not certain of Shields. Nor did he commit himself as to when the old iron would be returned.

In May the canoes began gathering before St. Paul as usual and were being dispatched off in artels to meet at Cook's Inlet, where Purtov had spent the winter. Suddenly a message came from there which made Baranov order the massed fleet to Fort Alexander without delay and himself go there as fast as he could.

Two British warships had entered the estuary claiming to be explorers.

When he arrived Purtov told him he had boarded the vessels with presents of fresh fish and had met the commander, a Captain George Vancouver. The larger vessel, a sloop of twenty guns, the *Discovery* under Vancouver, had arrived first, and had then been joined by the tender *Chatham* under a Lieutenant Peter Puget; whereupon the two had ascended the inlet and were now examining the shoreline.

But Baranov took no chances on their being something else, though Hugh Moore must have predicted Vancouver's coming. He massed the four hundred canoes around the fort in readiness for attack and waited for the English to make the first move. He kept informed hourly of their movements and let Purtov visit them again with gifts of fresh halibut in his name. He received a cordial invitation to come aboard but he resisted, mightily as he yearned to see the inside of a British warship, for he understood he would be asked to show his charts. Baranov was showing no foreigners his documents. Vancouver records waiting about for some time to see "Mr. Berrenoff," but finally he had to take advantage of a favorable tide and departed for the southward.

Baranov dispatched canoes after the vessels to watch what they did around Resurrection Bay. He was angry with Purtov because Purtov had revealed to the English the existence of his "shipyard" there, but to his relief they apparently missed the place in the fog and continued southward and eastward, for Nuchek Island.

His plans for summer were now behind schedule and he altered them radically. He would not ask Shields at all to take the *Eagle* to escort the bidarka fleet; the fleet would have to sail without her protection, and he so told Purtov, at the same time giving him orders to land at Yakutat and try to make a treaty giving them land for a trading post.

Purtov was of course dismayed but he followed orders, setting out to pick up at Resurrection Bay the Russians whom Baranov had detailed to his command for the summer.

When Baranov later beached at Resurrection and mounted the high ground to the camp it was with quiet, grim determination. Several of the Russians had refused to go with Purtov, saying they were doing no more work for the Company. Purtov had sailed on without them.

Baranov surmised at once, from long experience with his people, that a *soviet* had been perfected during the winter. The men had organized against him.

He surveyed, now, the once busy little yard. The forges were cold and rusted, the charcoal dump sodden and flattened by rains, the tackles hung idle, the hull stood empty. Men came quickly at sight of him, called by silent signals; evidently he was expected. They gathered in small groups with a tense, watchful air. Shields upbraided him angrily for not having announced the presence of English vessels in the vicinity and demanded the right to get in touch with them. Baranov, knowing that the vessels were by now far away, gave the Englishman permission to send a canoe to Nuchek in an effort to catch them.

From Rodionov, Baranov received a disheartening report. No work had been done since his departure. All the men had had to hunt and fish to keep alive during the winter, and since then one of them had talked the rest into standing together and refusing to do further work until they were given real Russian bread at all times, tea and tobacco. Balushin's men had paid them a visit and told them that Baranov had left for Kodiak so quickly the previous November because he had heard the place had been captured by Konovalov.

There was little to encourage Baranov as he looked at the group of men whose sullen, silent stares confirmed Rodionov's story of their insubordination. One was a former soldier exiled to Siberia for refusing to submit to military discipline; he had signed with the Company because it seemed a simple way to earn a living. Another represented the reason many Russians drifted into frontier life—habitual drunkenness. A third was a broken trader from the Ussurian taigá who could be clever with his hands and had a good brain but never failed to find chances to idle. There was hardly an honest peasant face among them, yet all knew life like this and this labor well—indeed, they had never known anything else.

Baranov understood perfectly he had lost face with them because of his evasion of the problem of Konovalov. He would never regain his authority until he had dealt summarily with that menace. But what could he do? He still dared not attack. Yet he could not continue to temporize.

At last he made his decision. Writing a note to Konovalov he commanded the latter to report to him immediately at Resurrection Bay, saying that he, Baranov, had just been invested by the governor general of Eastern Siberia with extraordinary powers to settle all disputes between traders in Russian America. Truth had failed him. Now he must try lies. If Konovalov came in answer to the note, Baranov intended to take him by force and hold him prisoner.

Days passed. Shields restlessly awaited an answer to his message to Captain Vancouver, who he understood was still somewhere around Prince William Sound; Baranov no less restlessly awaited answer from Konovalov.

Rodionov, the faithful Richard, and the few others who shared Baranov's secret were also nervous. The majority of the men were puzzled by the fact that Baranov hardly spoke to any of them, and even refused to see the spokesman whom they had appointed to discuss their grievances. They hung around the camp idly, waiting for they knew not what.

And then the event arrived, heralded by Konovalov who came striding into camp with several followers, all heavily armed and obviously ready to fight if fighting was called for.

In the brief parley that preceded the melee that followed Konovalov made it evident that he had come only after much debate between himself and his lieutenants. He had long expected some kind of summons, knowing the strife between the companies could not endure forever, but he had confidently expected also to prove that the Shelekhovski were the interlopers. It was a shock to have the summons come from his hated rival, but the governor general's name was one that had impressed him too much to ignore.

The camp was paralyzed with astonishment at his sudden appearance but quickly recovered its wits. Konovalov stared at the muskets leveled against him, at Baranov, then at the camp. But he was no coward. Not until several of Baranov's men lay on the ground bleeding profusely from cutlass strokes were Konovalov and his men subdued and tied hand and foot.

Baranov then ordered them chained to a wall and he threatened to lash any man helping them to escape. As soon as possible, he announced, they would be taken to the stockade at Kodiak.

Later the men gathered at the long tables at Resurrection Bay and waited, subdued and silent, for their food. The whisper had passed that Konovalov's capture had been effected at the order of the governor general. What would Baranov do next? They watched him emerge from his hut, walk toward them to his place at the table. They put down their unfilled plates quietly. The cooks gently hung their ladles on the edges of their kettles.

Baranov's remarks on that occasion have been preserved.

"My hunters," he began, "I thank from the bottom of my heart those who did the work entrusted to them. I am gratified to see the results of your labors after my absence. The work we do here is to the glory of our fatherland and the honor of the Russian people.

"But some of you saw fit to spoil it. You had meetings, conspiracies, plots. You divided into factions with grievances against each other and against me. It makes me unhappy that I must try to rule such men. What about the regulations made by the Company in the matter of division of work and reward to which we all subscribed and swore before the commander of Okhotsk when we signed the articles? Instead of remembering your oath you gave way to self-will. Your duties were defined in your contract and you knew what they were before you came. I have here a copy. I would like you to study it with me and ask yourselves: have you a right to refuse any duty justly assigned to you or can you with justice ask for food we haven't got or must save for emergencies?

"You know, the great Solomon said, 'Any town, state, or family that divides against itself shall fall.' Take a rope. No matter how thick it is, if you divide it into strands each can easily be broken. However, as long as that rope is whole a hundred men cannot break it. In our own literature a story is told of a Scythian prince who had seventy-five sons. On his deathbed he summoned them all for his blessing and asked each to bring an arrow, which he ordered tied into a bundle. He then asked if anyone could break the bundle, but no one could. Then he gave each man a single arrow which, of course, he easily snapped. Then he said to them: 'Remember that, my sons. As long as you are together you will be strong and invincible, and the glory of our race will endure to all posterity, but if you disagree and live in discord, as easily as you broke those arrows your enemies will exterminate you.'

"Now a man who knew nothing of Christ spoke that way—yet we are Christians and still you cannot pass a month without quarrels and complaints to plague your chief at every step.

"At home what sort of lives did you lead? Did any of you do anything much above herding pigs, or did any of you even have a bench to sit on except in the vodka shops where you spent most of your time? Here, however, you can become judges and prime ministers in council. Now I want nothing from you but a clear, short statement of any complaints you may have; if I see any means of helping you consistent with the general welfare, I shall. But I shall waste no time over orders to me or futile pretensions. Whoever has broken the law or the Company's rules will be punished according to his offense and the guilty may as well decide now not to try to implicate the innocent.

"Let us not listen to those who sow discord but keep strictly to the letter and spirit of the contract we signed. That is my advice to you."

That afternoon the forests again rang with the sound of ax blades on wood and the forges again glowed hot and red. The men shouted and sweated at the tackles and heavy timbers again began to move into place to make a ship.

And, shortly before sundown, a bidarka arrived with a note for Shields. Captain Vancouver thanked him for his kind offer of his services and regretted he could not turn back from his southward journey.

Once again life at Resurrection Bay moved in the pleasant rhythm of work.

9

A Ship Is Launched and a
Wife Taken

IT was early September, less than four months later, yet the ship
was ready to be launched. The bidarka fleet had returned;
Purtov had the biggest catch of furs ever made and had successfully concluded a treaty with the Yakutat Kolosh, having
fortunately encountered Lieutenant Puget, whose ship had protected them; and all the Russians of the colony had been a month
at Resurrection, readying her for the great event.

Their excitement transmitted itself by that mysterious tele-
graph which could in a few days convey a message of import from
Ilyamna to Sitka, and hundreds of stolid Indians paddled in from
Cook's Inlet, Prince William Sound, the Peninsula, and the islands
to stand about and raise hands to open mouths in surprise when
they saw what the Russians had built with so much cursing and
straining. Old Grigor Storyteller was there, of course, impassive
and imposing with the vast dignity befitting the father-in-law of
so great a man as Nanuk, but occasionally deigning to explain what
was happening to the other visiting chieftains. And, of course, they
all brought tribute in furs, for, since Konovalov had been taken
in irons to Kodiak, peace had redescended on the region and Nanuk
had become an awesome figure. He had waited all this time before
inflicting punishment on Konovalov and Balushin, Storyteller ex-

plained, in order to find out who among the Indians were really his friends, but when he was ready he struck.

Baranov had performed miracles of ingenuity. His idea of mixing the native moss with hot pitch for calking had proved sound. So had his use of mountain ash for hardwood. For paint his mixture of hot whale oil with red ocher from the iron deposits adhered admirably to the wood and proved to be waterproof. Of course he had not been able scientifically to control his colors and the hull presented a variegated patchwork of different reds. The vessel was bare only of cabins and deckwork. Shields finally convinced Baranov that carpentry of a sort beyond their abilities was needed for finishing, and she had best be sent to Okhotsk for her cabinetwork.

But she had three masts and two decks and stood seventy-nine feet long in the upper deck, just as Baranov had planned, and she was strong and sound and her lines looked true and reasonably fast. For her sails, all the canvas in the colony had been commandeered, all the tents, even the trousers and coats from men's backs and legs. An army of Aleut women sewed them with strong seal-gut thread into great sheets. Hence the sails, too, presented a queer patchwork, but that could be remedied with new canvas—when Shelekhov sent it.

And her name, Baranov decided, would be *Phoenix*. Some say he chose it to honor his friend Moore, others because she had indeed, like the phoenix, risen from little but ashes. Whatever his reasons, when Shields gave the signal and the blocks were knocked out from under her, he broke a precious flask of vodka over her bow and so named her, as she slid down the ways.

But their troubles were far from over. The rigging sent by Shelekhov in the *Eagle* proved even more wretched than they had first thought. Frayed ends had to be carefully spliced to make whole rope. Shields stormed and cursed at the inexperienced Russian hands who snarled the complicated system. But order eventually came out of chaos. The sails went up, filled a little; she slowly set before the wind. A gust blew, the sails bellied and tightened, and she moved toward Kodiak. A great cheer went up —terminated abruptly by a groan. With cracks like pistol shots the sails gave one by one, and then hung grotesquely, like dirty rags, around the rigging. All Baranov's curses were of no use. There was only enough canvas left to make a mainsail. They sewed it together, bracing it with what cordage they had, then raised it cautiously. It held. Baranov directed Shields to sail her cautiously to St. Paul Harbor. He detailed a few men to remain at Resurrection Bay to establish it as a permanent station, and then himself returned to Kodiak by canoe. The date was September 15, 1794.

At St. Paul, where she arrived in a few days in safety, there was a tremendous praznik in honor of the *Phoenix*. The first ram brought to Kodiak by Shelekhov when he established the colony was slaughtered and barbecued. "But he proved too tough to eat," Baranov wrote, "so we got drunk instead."

To keep the new peace on Prince William Sound he had had no alternative but to bring Storyteller's daughter to Kodiak. The Innuit girl he had taken in because she was neat with his clothes and acquiescent in bed; beyond those needs he had not been greatly concerned. To think of a tie which meant more seemed an annoyance.

But the Kenaitze girl seems to have been of a different sort, who, to some extent, at least, was able to adapt herself to her position as consort to the Russian Nanuk. Baranov draped a kerchief over her head to indicate his wish that she dress Russian fashion, which she seemed to understand, and he gave her a pair of rings for her ears as a small gift of welcome. With the rings and the kerchief the girl was savagely beautiful, with a dignity that was never to leave her even when she was an old woman.

He named her Anna Grigoryevna. He did not give her clothes to mend or immediately teach her to make his tea or cook his food. He told Richard to serve her as he would him and brought Aleut women into the house as servants.

That fall, perhaps under the salutary influence of his new

domestic situation, he could write in his journal that the colony looked forward to the most contented winter in years, with no unduly heavy labor ahead and the finest stock of furs ever gathered in a summer in the storehouses. He could record, too, his satisfaction at Purtov's having concluded the treaty with the Yakutat Bay Kolosh for a post; how safe it would be to put a colony there was yet to be proven, but it was a thrust to the south. There had been a few casualties; Botcharov's son, Ignatii, had fallen in a scuffle on the Purtov expedition. The world at large seemed at peace; Purtov had met also the *Jackall*, of London, whose master told him that Catherine was still empress at Petersburg, George III still king in England, that in France there were no more kings for the French state was now a republic, and that peace existed between Russia and England—welcome news to Shields.

His only major disappointment was expressed when he wrote, "No transport has come this year."

But even that disappointment was about to be lifted. Baranov was making leisurely preparations to have Shields lay the keels of two small sloops, each not more than forty feet long, on Yelovi Island out from St. Paul Harbor where the colony could keep busy through the winter without undue strain or leaving home, when someone on the hilltop let out a startled cry, "*Korabl!*"

Everyone dropped his tools and ran to see. There in the roads, standing in for the harbor, was a galiot, the speed of which showed that someone who knew the channel was in command. When her name could be made out it spelled, to everyone's amazement, *Three Saints*. But it was soon evident she was not the resurrected original but a very old and worn vessel of similar lines, probably renamed by Shelekhov after the one that had taken him to America and brought him back in safety.

Baranov dispatched men to the village to prepare a welcome and make the bunkhouses ready and himself ran impatiently to the wharf to be the first to greet the new arrivals.

He need not have hurried. She was heavily laden and her gunwales crowded with men; she would not be against the wharf in an hour, even with the sweeps out. He had plenty of time to get over his surprise and develop some new ones. On the poop the unwelcome figure of Izmailov could finally be identified as the skipper. And among the crowd at the gunwales getting their first glimpse of St. Paul stood eight or ten men unmistakably wearing the high conical hats and black cassocks of the higher Orthodox priesthood.

Izmailov made a great flourish of experience in getting in but he forgot a certain rock in the harbor and brought up against it with a dull crash. The galiot shuddered and heeled over sharply, throwing the people on deck in sad confusion. But the galiot righted herself, and by quick work with the sweeps Izmailov got her off, to hurry her against the wharf before she should fill from the hole in her bottom.

The mob on deck could now be clearly discerned and old faces recognized. There seemed at least eighty people aboard. They must have slept packed in like herrings. Four of the priests were archmonks, he could see, and one, a tall ascetic, wore the rich golden cross of hierarchical authority. The others seemed of lesser station, but monks too. All except one, who had a fair beard and hair, had long hair flowing to their shoulders and luxuriant black beards.

Baranov knew little about monks. He knew only they were something far different, a class apart, from the familiar Russian village clergy. These latter were typically ignorant and lazy. Monks, on the other hand, were often very literate and saintly men entitled to hold rank in the *tchinn*. Their celibate life served further to set them apart. But even the most informed about monks would have been hard put to guess what they were doing in Russian America.

The sweeps brought the galiot against the wharf and in shallow water just in time, for she settled on the bottom. The blocks were kicked out of the gunwales, the gangplank thrown to the wharf with a crash. The first, of course, to step ashore was the priest with the rich gold cross, followed by his clergy. Baranov kneeled with his Russians as the priest made the sign of the cross, gave thanks for their safe arrival on the scene of their future labors as missionaries, prayer for the merchant Shelekhov who had sent them here to open the hearts of the heathen to the pure gospel of Christ, and then solemnly invoked the blessing of God on Russian America.

The prayer finished, all rose from their knees and Izmailov presented His Eminence the Archimandrite Iosaph Bolotov of Valaam Monastery near St. Petersburg, and then, in turn, the archmonks Father Nektar, Father Makar, Father Afanassii, and Father Juvenal the fair one; an archdeacon, Father Stepan; two monks, Fathers Herman and Iosaph. Then there were their two servitors, men of minor orders. Father Nektar looked the intolerant kind; Father Juvenal's aristocratic face had the far-away look of the true ascetic; Father Afanassii was mentally strange. Of them all, the monk Herman seemed the most common of the lot. The cassocks of the others were all of fine cloth, their beards well kept, their hands soft and white. Baranov, unprepared for so large a number of guests, had his men take them to the bunkhouses, all but the archimandrite, for whom he ordered the salthouse cleaned as a dwelling.

There was still another vessel on the way, he learned, the *Catherine* under navigator Gerassim Pribylov, who had delayed by having to land cattle at Unalaska. On her were fifty-two more promyshleniki and also thirty serfs and their families, whom Shelekhov was sending as colonists, and the bulk of the supplies.

With the seventy promyshleniki arrived on the *Three Saints*, the *Catherine's* contingent would mean one hundred and twenty-two new hands. He needed them and was pleased. He wished, however, that he could make out the meaning of the coming of the priests and the serfs.

From the gossip he pieced quite a pattern together. Skelekhov had apparently been lately pulling some powerful strings in Petersburg and had secured the all but impossible permission to ship serfs out of the country; from Shelekhov's viewpoint they would presumably make perfect colonists as they would not have to be paid. As for the priests, the merchant had apparently made some incautious boasts to the Church of his pious intentions toward the Aleuts and had said he would pay missionaries' expenses. This was the result. The priests had had to lie over at Okhotsk several weeks before the ships could be readied and there Izmailov, Botcharov, and all the other troublemakers Baranov had got rid of had talked against him to Shelekhov and the priests, charging him with gross immorality, illicit distilling, vile treatment of the natives, and brutality toward his own men. This had naturally instilled into the minds of the priests a prejudice against him which was to add greatly to his difficulties.

Moreover, he learned, his exposure of the Lebedevski troubles to Commander Koch had caused a furor at Okhotsk. There was a new governor general at Irkutsk, a fact that somehow had given Shelekhov and Lebedev-Lastotchkin much trouble. The Archimandrite Iosaph, he was told, was supposed to have full authority to straighten out the controversy.

This promised a fine bit of trouble for Baranov! He had forged the governor general's order to put Konovalov in irons, where he still was. What would the archimandrite think of this?

As quickly as he could he invited Father Iosaph to his house. The priest came with his servitor and his letters. He was intensely surprised and incredulous when Baranov told him that Shelekhov had established neither school nor church there. He had been told that a great work had been started and that Baranov had been allowed to let it lapse. Shelekhov's boastful lies were further emphasized by the letter which Father Iosaph handed Baranov from the merchant—a letter obviously intended for eyes other than his own.

"I present you," the letter said, "with some guests selected by the empress to spread the word of God in America. I know you will feel as great a satisfaction as I do that the country where I labored before you and where you now labor for the good of Holy

Russia has in the presence of these men at last a hope of genuine future prosperity. . . ."

The letter spoke of the serfs, whom Shelekhov had bought of an estate. He was sending his former secretary, Polomoshnoi, in charge of them and they were to be established in a colony for agricultural experimentation at Yakutat Bay. Yakutat, from the reports Baranov had, was no place for agriculture. Kodiak Island itself was the best on the whole coast. But here were the orders to send them there, together with directions for building and governing the town to be set up at that place.

"Plan it from the beginning to look like a town," said the letter. "Do not let strangers who come think our people always live in filth and squalor, as at Okhotsk. Please, dear friend, plan it to be beautiful and pleasant to live in. Have public squares for meetings and gatherings. . . . The streets . . . must radiate from the squares . . . Public buildings, such as the church, the monastery, the jail, etc., must be planned and built in the style of big cities. . . . Dress the hunters in coats of military pattern . . . beat drums at daybreak . . . *Your work will be discussed and help create a sensation at court.* . . ."

Father Iosaph handed him another letter, his authority to mediate in the Konovalov affair signed by both Shelekhov and Lebedev-Lastotchkin. "We pray Your Eminence to ascertain the true facts. . . . If you think it is for the advancement of Christ among the natives to make a change. . . ."

Baranov made no bones of what had happened but plunged into a recital of Konovalov's crimes. He told of robbery against the Indians, the rape of their women, the contempt shown for official and imperial insignia. The story had its effect on the priest. Deeply shocked, he warmly approved of attempts to restrain such men. Then, the interview closing, Father Iosaph handed Baranov a small package. "A gift, Aleksandr Andrevich. I was told you would enjoy it and it seems to be necessary in this climate."

Baranov was deeply touched to unwrap a small flask of vodka!

Three weeks later the *Catherine* had not been sighted but Baranov almost hoped she would never come; he had his hands full enough with the efforts of the eighty off the *Three Saints* to adjust themselves to the country.

The stupid, the dissolute, the drunkards were common in Russian America, but most of them had had some backwoods or frontier experience that let them adjust themselves with little trouble to the life. But most of the seventy newly arrived promyshleniki were city men, convicts of the worst type, who had been offered some sort of reprieve if they served with the Company. They had come without the slightest conception of what would be expected of them. Some of them were without shoes, and even without adequate clothing. They were generally infected with venereal diseases and acted like insane men when they saw how easy it was to get Aleut girls. Baranov had to repress them with the harshest severity; ruthlessly he weeded out the sick ones and sent them to Cook's Inlet with what mercurials he had. The rest he put at hard work on the two sloops on Yelovi Island and additional shelter for the expected *Catherine*'s people.

The priests were of less than no help. Shelekhov had told them that he had sent three years' supplies for their upkeep but, of course, he had done nothing of the sort and they blamed Baranov for depriving them of what they had every reason to believe had come on the ship with them. In vain he protested that everyone lived humbly in America, catching his own fish and killing his own meat, that no one had time to wait on them, especially with the necessity of building all the new shelter. He tried consulting them on colonial affairs but they could never agree, even among themselves, and always rejected the practical for the ideal. He understood that Father Juvenal could draw architectural plans but found him unable to make suggestions for even a plain bunkhouse. When the archimandrite insisted that a church was more important than a building for the coming serfs, Baranov gave them all up.

It was November 6, and hope had been given up when the

Catherine was sighted, her mainmast and most of her rigging gone. Crowded to the gunwales as she was with humanity and her hold filled with cattle, sheep, goats, and chickens in pens for the serfs' projected colony, she reeked like a slave ship.

The hunters were no better than the first batch and as for the serfs, Baranov had not seen such people since he quitted old Russia and had almost forgotten they existed. He remembered seeing them hitched to plows with the very horses on estates or harnessed to pull flatboats up the Volga—men and women vacant of eye, slow of movement, and patient, representatives of the very bottom of a social system that bought and sold them like cattle. Polomoshnoi, Shelekhov's confidential agent in their special charge, was a young man of no force of character.

Baranov left the cargo checking to Kuskov and Rodionov with careful instructions to look out for the boxes addressed to him, and then hurried home to read the letters which he hoped would straighten out the fantastic pattern of events and intentions.

As he opened the bulky sealed envelope from his employer several papers fell out. He picked one up. "Complaints of the Navigator Botcharov against Aleksandr Baranov." "He manufactures vodka contrary to law . . . He is immoral—keeps a native girl . . . interferes with navigation . . . has done nothing about agriculture . . . lets everyone drink freely and grants many holidays." He picked up another. "Complaints of the Hunter Belonogov against Baranov." "He makes men work far beyond their powers . . . he is overbearing . . . dispenses cruel and arbitrary punishments. . . ."

These seemed in written form about the same sort of thing the priests had heard verbally in Okhotsk. Why was Shelekhov sending him copies? To show he had them?

He turned to the letter, which he saw was signed by both Shelekhov and Golikov's business agent, Polevoi. It was dated at Okhotsk that summer. He did not have to read far to see that few of his actions had pleased Shelekhov. The merchant seemed angriest with his exposure to Koch of the Lebedevski troubles; more so even than with the smallness of the shipment of furs on the *God's Friend.*

"... You, so noted for your resourcefulness and skill, seem to us like a lion frightened by mice—and very silly mice at that, from your own description. It would have been so much better to use a little diplomacy. Spending, say, three thousand rubles in judicious bribery would have stopped all that trouble . . . Please never send papers about such things to government officials; put them under seal and send them to us so we may use them as we see fit . . . Do you imagine your friend Koch will command here forever? . . . The net result of your dramatic and futile writing was that we had the devil's own time getting needed decisions from the government. . . ."

One of these government decisions was interesting. "We have been by decree awarded three hundred and thirty miles of land around each of our settlements upon which no rival may encroach. Your strength will henceforth lie in this new right and it should stop the gentlemen at Cook's Inlet . . . We shall say nothing more about this, knowing you will now act more boldly. Stick to what is required of you and we will thank you.

"In commenting to the government about insufficient men you also make a mistake; to end your dissatisfaction we send you 123 new ones. . . .

"What is all this about supplies? . . . On the *Eagle* we sent you enough to have kept ten companies going in former days . . . We are in the dark as to how all that cargo was used. . . ."

"We do, however, thank you for moving to St. Paul. . . ."

There was a long page of comment on his report of meeting and entertaining Captain Moore. "We are astonished at your brashness . . . Visits of foreign ships cannot be tolerated . . . We would not have let the ship go. Their trade with natives is thievery from us . . . It would not have been difficult to capture them with the help of natives . . . You should know better; you have read books and should know what to do in such cases . . . We doubt you would have had such friendly assistance had you visited Nootka or

California . . . In the future be bold enough to tell these foreigners they have no right to trade."

Instructions were clear to let the missionaries fend for themselves. "We have supplied the holy fathers with enough to last them three years if they are careful," (which was a lie). "Give them seeds from our own grain but nothing more." Of the real reason for sending priests there was not a hint, and regarding the serfs only a repetition of the order to install them at Yakutat in a colony devoted to agriculture, improbable as that sounded. But there was a great deal of space devoted to a criticism of Baranov's administration, about which Shelekhov seemingly had made diligent inquiry only of the sort of men Baranov had kicked out. "Don't listen to all the flatterers with whom we hear you surround yourself." There was no complaint about his having kept Shields but he was begged to get along with the Englishman without quarreling all the time, as he was reported to do.

The men who were checking the cargo on the *Catherine* gave him something more to think about. The invoices noted the contents of the boxes consigned to him—brandy, ale, several bottles of fine Bessarabian wine, a special keg of vodka, cigars, tea, special tobacco, and clothing—gifts from friends, mostly. But they were not to be found. The consignment of medicinal alcohol was missing too. By his fury and threats, he finally learned what had happened.

Old Gerassim Pribylov, the navigator, first broke into the stores not long after they left Okhotsk. Pribylov, once the finest and most daring navigator out of Okhotsk, discoverer of the famed Pribylov seal rookeries in the Bering Sea, had such an insatiable appetite for liquor that he had not had a ship for years. He had been drunk all the way across the Pacific. Because of it he almost lost the *Catherine* when unloading at Unalaska. The passengers finally compelled him to share it with them, and they all got drunk too. One night there was such a brawl aboard that in trying to broach a keg of vodka they drunkenly smashed it and it all washed over the deck and into the sea.

No wonder the galiot's mainmast was gone, her rigging in shreds! As for Baranov, in the four years he had been in America not one creature comfort he had sent for had ever reached him. He had never even solved the mystery of the box missing from the *Eagle*. And now all that fine wine he had meant to keep for special occasions, all that ale, that vodka, swilled down by these swine at sea, spilled, wasted, thrown away. The wonder was the *Catherine* had not piled up on some reef!

His thoughts as he turned to prepare for a winter with the priests, serfs, and the new men he had received were indeed far from pleasant.

10

Father Iosaph and Baranov Report

THE cold, hard winter of 1794–95 tended to make the Archimandrite Iosaph no fonder of Baranov. The priest's momentary approval of the man who had curbed Konovalov's licentiousness had not been enough to dissipate his resentment against the same man whom he blamed for the hardships under which he lived, and the godlessness which surrounded him. His fingers, used to the subtler offices of the altar, were rough and cracked from scrabbling on the beach for his food and cutting firewood. Such labor does not keep the hands as spotless as they should be for the Holy Sacrifice.

Everyone had suffered that winter. Everyone had known the pangs of hunger. Father Iosaph had charged Baranov with having withheld supplies. Baranov had told him that there were no supplies, that such food as he was to eat he must find for himself.

Iosaph had made a trip to Cook's Inlet to investigate the Konovalov troubles. Konovalov had been released from custody so that he might be heard on his home ground. Father Iosaph had gone there fully expecting to find Baranov had lied in every respect. Instead, the evidence was incontrovertible that terrible crimes had been committed by the Lebedevski and that Baranov had told the truth about them. No other decision was possible for Iosaph than to send them home for trial, but perhaps because he was loathe to let Baranov take immediate command of their forts, he granted them all the time they needed to close their affairs before leaving. Now the *Phoenix* was about to sail on her maiden voyage for Okhotsk, and Father Iosaph prepared a letter for her to carry to Shelekhov.

"My dear friend and benefactor, Grigor Ivanich," he began, "I can better feel than express the esteem and affection I cherish for you . . . During the winter many Kenai and Chugach hostages living here were willing to be baptized, but this has been my only pleasure. The Russians are a hindrance, not a help, to my ministry because of their depravity, which I find in startling contrast to the strong moral fiber of the untutored natives. Only with the greatest difficulty did I persuade a few of the hunters to marry their concubines; the rest would not listen.

"We do not even have a temporary church. Baranov said he would build a small one, eleven by twenty-eight feet, but the logs are still uncut. Hence I have absolutely nothing to report to the Most Reverend Metropolitan of St. Petersburg.

"I fail to find one good thing about the administration of Baranov. I do not know if it was your biting remonstrances or our arrival that made him so contrary, but I feel I must warn you that he is stirring up a revolt against you among the hunters and makes them sign quibbles against your authority . . . He lies about the true aims of the government.

"Starvation has stalked this place ever since our arrival. We cleaned out rotten dried salmon three years old to have enough to eat. Baranov refused to send the Aleuts to fish for us and told everybody he was not required to furnish our food. . . .

"The cooks are half-naked and barefooted. In addition to having to feed people night and day they must cut their own wood. We ourselves have to pack wood on our shoulders from the forest. But the chief manager doesn't have to do that. When he wants a kettle of hot water his henchmen in their haste chop corners off houses or take shakes from the storehouse roof! He never goes out of his house to see for himself how things are, as a manager should. He sits in his house, day and night, writing heaven knows what chicanery . . . He never tried to experiment with agriculture. I should like to raise a few potatoes and cabbages but we have not the right tools . . . We try to till the soil with sharpened poles. . . .

". . . He told the hunters they need not be ashamed of their evil ways, that he has instructions to be strict with the priests, to make them eat local food, to use them for all kinds of labor and so on. We help ourselves at the open table—digging clams on the beach. But Sir Baranov never feels hunger! Birds and seals are shot for his table! Deer meat is sent from Kenai. He always has milk. . . .

"Winter was cold . . . yet to me only did he assign a private dwelling."

This was the sorest of all points. The monks, used to their quiet cells and the gathering at stated hours to sing the holy office in choir, had only the bunkhouses for shelter. Three rows of billets, two hundred and seventy men in accommodations for far fewer. At night the wooden shutters closed tight to keep in the heat— and the odors! The reek of wet seal-gut garments hung to dry. At night Baranov encouraging the men to dance and sing for all they were worth, the floors shaking under the stamp of nearly six hundred booted feet, the rafters trembling with the roar of song. The men forgot the monks who lay in their bunks trying to read the office they could not sing in choir, the monks who wished to weep as they remembered the quiet peace and dignity they had aban- doned to come to this place. And when the native women visited the bunkhouses! Not a few had become prostitutes since the corning of the new men, growing wealthy under the shower of gifts, causing black looks and jealousies that sometimes erupted into quick brawls in which the men tore and hit until Baranov came running and sent them back to their places with cuffs and curses.

"The liberty that reigns here," the letter continued, "is of an al- most French licentiousness that gives me pause. As a subject it would make a book. I should write about Baranov's attitude in this to the Metropolitan or the Holy Synod but my regard for you prevents me . . . If he remains as manager there will be no change. I must admit he subscribed fifteen hundred rubles out of his pocket for the church building but I would rather give that back and have him manage better. You must not tell him I write these things. I do not fear him but I don't want to make things worse . . . His division of furs and trade goods is nothing but a swindle. . . .

"At first he and Shields had terrible quarrels during which they beat each other like a couple of *muzhiks* but now they are at peace and I like their peace even less. Several have told me that Baranov's henchmen have said: 'If we kill the archimandrite and Father Juvenal, we can crush the rest like flies.' But I suppose I should not believe every rumor.

"Last year when the English explorer (Vancouver) came to this region, Baranov gave him not only all particulars about our settlements but even a list of the hunters and their names. The English were kind and gave him presents but he behaved like a churl, climbing aboard their frigate and shouting, 'Tell your captain I've come to have coffee with him.' Naturally they were free with their coffee to make him talk."

The archimandrite closed with a rueful analysis of what he had found among the Lebedevski. "But we must remember the disordered state of the country when analyzing criminal acts." He closed with the flourish, "I remain, always, your friend who prays to God to give you good health. . . ."

The difficulties of that winter had almost driven Baranov, too, to the breaking point.

His greatest trouble had been with the serfs. The affair of the serfs had been a heartbreaking revelation of the depths of duplicity of which Shelekhov was capable. Years before, the Empress Catherine, to remedy some abuses in her empire, had issued a stern decree forbidding selling serfs into slavery in foreign lands or using them at any endeavor but agriculture. Shelekhov had bought this bunch from a bankrupt estate and got them out of Russia only on the sworn representation that he intended using them to found

an agricultural colony at Yakutat. The government, which knew
nothing of Yakutat, at length reluctantly consented but demanded
it be kept informed of the colony's progress. This, too, Shelekhov
faithfully promised. But through Polomoshnoi he sent Baranov
instructions to use the serfs at whatever work he pleased and send
them where they were most needed.

Baranov, horrified, refused point-blank to be party to any such
dangerous deception. He was amazed that Shelekhov could be
so daring. He, Baranov, was having none of his letters supporting Shelekhov's lies quoted around St. Petersburg. He told Polomoshnoi that the serfs would, as promised, found a colony to
attempt agriculture at Yakutat.

He had quartered the serfs in their own bunkhouse with Polomoshnoi in charge of them. They made trouble from the beginning over the unaccustomed diet of dried fish. Then, learning something about this America and the fact they were to be sent into a
region inhabited only by a particularly bloodthirsty and savage
tribe, they revolted, arming themselves with sticks and stones and
crying they would not go. Baranov had had to string a couple of
the leaders up in the square and knout them before they quietened
down.

Nor had the new "hunters" presented a much easier problem. By
Christmastime Baranov never walked about St. Paul unarmed or
alone but always with Kuskov, Richard, or Shields. He kept everyone hard at work on the two sloops and by spring they neared
completion.

To relieve the atmosphere, tense as that of a prison camp, he
went often to the bunkhouses of an evening and on Sundays to encourage innocent singing and dancing, to the vast disgust of the
monks.

These he had come to leave severely alone. He never listened to
their horrified remonstrances or explained that the colony had
ever, or would ever, be managed differently. He only waited for
spring to relieve the congestion and kept his own counsel. Between the priests and himself there raged the eternal conflict

between the two worlds of fact and ideals. There was not an inch of common ground for them except on Sundays, Saints' days, and the great feasts. On such occasions the temper and appearance of St. Paul changed miraculously. A solid piety descended on the colony. Before the improvised altar the archimandrite and his priests chanted the office, consecrated the holy bread, and were answered in song by three hundred voices thick with nostalgia. And behind the cross in the processions Baranov walked with bowed head and clasped hands.

Anna Grigoryevna became, except for his tried friends, his one unfailing source of pleasure. She had quickly picked up enough Russian to understand and be understood. He jealously guarded the seclusion of his home for her. And then there was Shields, with whom he had fought his way to a profound understanding and who now stuck by him without a word about going home. Shields carried on the real job of exploration incumbent on the colony, had taken the *Eagle* into the Bering and explored thoroughly the shoreline of Bristol Bay. He continued to teach Baranov navigation and that summer they planned to explore the Kolosh coast to-gether, Baranov intending to sail independently for the first time in the *Olga*, one of the new sloops.

Now Baranov, too, wrote his letter to Shelekhov, to lie in the pouch alongside that of Father Iosaph, as the *Phoenix* made her way westward.

"I will wait either for a change in your attitude toward me," he wrote, "or for the arrival of my successor who, I hope, will be trusted more than I am. Since coming to work for you I fear I've lost that which I value most—my good name. You had best find a successor. I am getting old and my senses are dulling . . . My energy is failing me. I do not feel equal to all your important in-structions nor do I think I have the ability to fulfill them. Quite aside from all this it hurts me to hear you give men drinks and draw them out to slander me. My conscience is clear. I have been guilty neither of negligence nor of misappropriation of your funds. Go ahead and gather from such as Botcharov all the notes and proofs you want; I will face them all. There will always be witnesses who actually saw things. You are not being honest with me . . . I know you're trying to injure me for some purpose of your own . . . I assure you that only the oath to guard the interest of the government and my instructions to advance the empire make me stay and spend my youth and energy. It was not our mutual agreement—many parts of which you broke.

". . . I read your recent letter with restrained politeness, seeing you consider me not a friend but a menial who may be expected to work only in his own interest and is not really worthy to manage this colony . . . I am going to answer every part of the letter with that blunt truthfulness to which I've always clung without fear of the strong and powerful.

"First about shipping furs. Sea otter are not caught here like cheap salmon but our field extends thirteen hundred miles . . . At Kenai hunting is poor . . . The passage to Yakutat is hard on the Aleuts. Imagine the poor devils making the journey both ways, thirteen hundred miles in narrow bidarkas, without sails and only by paddling. They cannot take many supplies so must endure hunger. They often perish in storms, for the shore offers no adequate shelter . . . in constant danger from their bloodthirsty enemies. These are the conditions under which they hunt! They do it but only by dint of constant vigilance on the part of the Russian hunters and you can imagine the state of mind in which they are. I would certainly have sent you more furs on the *God's Friend Simeon* if I could, as I say, scoop them up like salmon . . . I had only one hundred and fifty-two men. Of these more than half were busy at Resurrection Bay . . . There was almost a mutiny . . . I returned to Kodiak at the risk of my life. As for the details —well, it is long since you've sent enough paper and my memory for past offenses is bad.

"You sent orders to build a ship. I was short of steel, iron, hemp, calking, and even pitch and turpentine. I imagined you would keep your promise and send supplies, but when July came and no ship—what could I do? Further lower myself before my hunters and admit defeat? Besides, the Lebedevski outrages had to be taken care of. . . .

"You say enough goods were sent on the *Eagle* for ten companies . . . You can't compare this new order of things with the old days when the promyshleniki came with nine bags of provisions and forced the natives to work for them like asses . . . We pay for food supplies and give presents. I can boast that among all undertakings of this kind ours is the most fairly managed. I give not one extra thread to my favorite Russians, natives, or hostages . . . When you release me from my duties I assure you I will, if I am still alive, present you with a most complete accounting in person and one you will long remember. . . .

"You need send us no more ships; just return the *Phoenix*. There is not enough rigging . . . nor men capable of glorious deeds. Few are any good among those you recently sent. They owe so much they are in hopeless bondage and some have no clothes or shoes. With men whose souls are dead little can be accomplished. Where do you get such people? The *Phoenix*, complete with furs, comes to you. I hope you will recompense those who built her and are hard up, so that they will have heart for future exploits . . . The next time I ship furs, however, I come with them unless you change your attitude toward me and send me men capable of labor instead of parasites picked up just to round out a figure.

"If you get information from such incompetent loafers as Belonogov you must expect nothing good about me. It is true we dance and sing . . . It is not true we drink all the time . . . None but myself and Izmailov makes liquor unless without my knowledge . . . It is true I keep a girl . . . It is true I have not been successful with agriculture. I have never had time, have never lived in one place more than a summer, so I cannot brag about results. Carrots, potatoes, radishes, and turnips are grown. No luck with cabbages or barley. We had tobacco growing at Three Saints Bay but the tidal wave destroyed it. Peas and cucumbers never ripened. Perhaps the holy fathers will have more luck. . . .

"As for your rebuke on the subject of Captain Moore, you

astonish me. To me you show limitless greed and cupidity. How can you insult me by believing I would break the holy laws of hospitality toward the helpless as you suggest? Only barbarians do such things . . . I consider the French our enemies, but I refuse to take it on myself to repulse by force the English from places not yet defined by our own government as Russian soil—at least, not without an order more official than yours. . . ."

Together Baranov and Shields watched the *Phoenix* stand out to sea, old Izmailov in command, on her first trip to Okhotsk. Her sails were canvas brought by the *Catherine*, her deckwork was still to be put on, and she was still painted only to the water line; but she handled like the finest and bore away many hunters who had served their time, all the letters home, and more than three hundred thousand rubles' worth of furs.

When she had gone Baranov threw himself into his summer's tasks with energy, his winter's ailments disappearing in his eagerness to do some exploring himself for the first time. The plan was for Shields to leave first with the bidarka fleet and sail on possibly as far as the Queen Charlotte Islands—dropping Russians at Yakutat on the way who would start building shelter for the oncoming serfs; and then on the return trip meet Baranov in his sloop near Sitka in July. He, in the meantime, would have closed the Lebedevski forts according to the new concessions granted Shelekhov, and dispatched the Yakutat colonists on their way to Yakutat.

When Shields had taken his departure with the fleet, Baranov ordered Pribylov to ready the *Three Saints* and remained at Kodiak until he had performed the unpleasant duty of putting Polomoshnoi, the serfs, and their belongings aboard. To accomplish this, Baranov had to call on qualities of brutality of which he had not thought himself capable. The serfs had to be driven aboard almost with clubs. They cried hoarsely that they were being taken to certain death at Yakutat, but he was adamant. Aboard, too, went Father Juvenal to lend his knowledge to helping plan the settlement. Pribylov said he wanted no priest aboard to bring him bad luck, but Baranov knew the old drunkard was more likely to do his duty with Juvenal about.

The galiot sailing at last, Baranov set the *Olga*'s sails out of St. Paul Harbor, navigating her himself on his first long voyage, with Richard the Bengalese and Ivan Kuskov as companions and only crew. At Cook's Inlet he poked about a day or two, glorying in his independence and investigating further the region's coal deposits, until a message reached him that sent him with all speed to Nuchek Island on Prince William Sound. Konstantin Samoilov and twelve other Lebedevski men had been caught in an Indian raid, tortured, and killed.

On Nuchek he found more than an uprising. Father Juvenal and others supposedly on the way to Yakutat were stranded on the beach. There had been a serious mutiny on the *Three Saints*. The serfs had taken one look at the savage grandeur of Prince William Sound, successfully revolted, and threatened to hang Polomoshnoi and all of them if forced to penetrate such a howling wilderness further. Pribylov had put Father Juvenal off and turned back to Kodiak.

Baranov by bidarka sent word to Kodiak promising the direst punishment and ordering Pribylov peremptorily to take the serfs to Yakutat at once. Then he looked into the matter of the murders.

At Fort Constantine the Lebedevski hunters received him with relief. Ragged, poverty-stricken, worried because they had not had a supply ship for three years, and torn with internal dissensions, they begged to be taken under his protection and control.

But Baranov was not ready to discuss this. The thirteen dead men had been kept for his inspection. Months before, it developed, Samoilov and these men had raided an interior village of the Kolchanes and had taken away some women. The Kolchanes had retaliated by killing them all; Samoilov, the old promyshlenik, had been crucified and his genitals torn away. "He will not again taste of our women," the assailants were reported to have said.

Baranov was worried about leaving so important a death unavenged. This man had once been chief at Kodiak; he was among the earliest of the promyshleniki. But with Shields away and the *Three Saints* in difficulties he was virtually powerless. Besides, the Indians had meted out only justice, horrible as it was. Nor could Baranov afford the time. Before returning to Cook's Inlet he told Father Juvenal and the rest to wait where they were for the *Three Saints*.

He wasted little time with Konovalov but showed him the new authority to control everything within three hundred and thirty miles of Fort Alexander and ordered him out of the Inlet, giving him until the following summer to close his business. He paid no attention to Konovalov's threats to bring him to justice before the governor general at Irkutsk, but hurried on to the south. If he failed to connect with Shields his venturing alone past the fifty-fifth parallel might prove a foolhardy experience indeed, especially if he got caught in the fall gales off that coast.

He had clear sailing down the bleak shoreline past Prince William Sound and when he sighted hoary old Mount St. Elias, landmark of Yakutat, he turned in. The moment he landed on the island in the bay, he found the men Shields had dropped fortified behind breastworks and must have wished he had kept on. There was no sign of the *Three Saints*, Polomoshnoi, or the serfs. It was plain that Pribylov had disregarded his message—or more probably they could not get the serfs back on the galiot at Kodiak. However, the men told him it was as well that the settlers had not come, because the Kolosh at the village at the head of the bay swore they had given the Russians no permission to have a fort and generally manifested a most unfriendly attitude.

Baranov, ignoring all warnings about the extreme treachery of these natives, ordered everyone to arm and accompany him ashore at once.

Had he been in less of a hurry, what he saw when approaching the village might well have given him pause. It was an imposing place of tremendous communal houses with strange heraldic devices over the doors and flanked by carved idealizations of beasts, men, and gods, those mute testimonies to pride of clan and sept and past tribal history, thoughtlessly called totem poles by white men.

The men were giants in physique. With their conical skulls shaped in babyhood and facial paintings to show their kinship to the living things of sea and air they could, when their attitude was unfriendly, appear terrifying in the extreme. But Baranov approached them truculently and demanded that the chief see him at once or suffer dire consequences.

"I am Nanuk of the Russians," he explained without the usual preliminaries that indicate polite conversation among all savages, when he was finally seated in the "old man house" of the Yakutati chief. "Once your people attacked me on Montague Island; they saw me shoot and shoot straight. Last year I sent my lieutenant, Igor Purtov, here to treat with you as a friend instead of inflicting the punishment you deserve. You told him you sold us ground for a post. Now what are those lies I hear?"

"I told your man he could have the island," admitted the chief, sullenly, "but I withdrew the gift before he left because I discovered you will not sell us guns and powder."

Purtov had told him about the long controversy over this point. Baranov had given strictest orders that no guns, powder, or shot must be sold to a single native; the fact that he had done that with the Siberian Chukchi was the reason he had been forced to come to America. "When you show you can be trusted," answered Baranov, bluntly, "my own distrustful attitude may be different." He also refused to give a single hostage. "Which is it to be—peace or war? Must I bring my fire-ships here to help you decide?"

He stood in the greatest danger of his life. The Kolosh could easily have seized him to hold for a ransom of more powder and shot than they could ever use. But he gave them no time to think, to deliberate together as was their democratic wont. His irritation and impatience communicated itself to them as evidence of his strength and lack of fear. He learned how to handle the natives of the mainland coast, that day; they were cursed with some of the habits of his own people. He got his deed to the island.

During the potlatch they gave in his honor he raised a pole in the midst of Yakutat village to the top of which he nailed the Russian flag. Bravely it flew in the face of the grotesque symbols of totem and taboo against the background of glaciered mountains with St. Elias snowy in the distance.

Returning to the island in the bay, he paced off foundations for the buildings to be set up. Then, telling the men left to continue building, he boarded the *Olga* again with Kuskov and Richard, and turned the little sloop's nose southward.

A magnificent panorama greeted the eyes of Baranov, Richard the Bengalese, and Kuskov the clerk as the little *Olga* plowed the swells before the breeze past four hundred miles of bare Alaskan coast leading to Sitkan waters. They saw the flanks of Mount Fairweather and Mount Crillon rise sheerly and boldly fourteen thousand feet into the air from the sea. Past Lituya Bay, rich in sea otter, past Icy Cape they continued until they sighted Mount Edgecumbe, landmark of the Sitka region. They picked their way through the intricate network of bays, fiords, and estuaries, some of them tiny passageways between grim rocks, some magnificent sheets of water mirroring more snowy peaks than they could count, exploring and seeking the rendezvous Shields had designated. At times the little boat seemed in the open seas; again, she entered a canal whose lofty walls of syenite and granite shut out the daylight and against which her rigging scraped. Many feathery cascades fell to churn the sea into white bubbles. The shores were thick forests of gigantic cedars, spruce, and fir, never touched by fire but protected from that scourge by the blanket of wetness that overlay everything. Between these forest giants was a tangled mass of ferns and bushes, almost impenetrable without an ax. And all around them, as the *Olga* nosed her way into this green and blue paradise, the sea birds rose in fearless clouds, the islands echoed with the hammerings of woodpeckers, the owls called insolently, and the ravens seemed to mock their timidity.

At length they located the sound where Shields was to meet them. Here and there on the journey they had sighted stragglers from the bidarka fleet but nowhere had they seen the main body. In a little cove, wherein a constant fog would protect them from surprise, they beached the *Olga*, stretched nets for fish, and rested from the incessant roll of the sea.

Here the big trees were perfect for shipbuilding, the tides apt for launching ships, the harbors ideal for defense, and the sea otter plentiful. The grandeur of the place seemed to demand some ritual, some gesture of the sort observed by explorers and discoverers the world over. Baranov chopped down a small tree and fastened a crosspiece midway to the top. This cross he set in the ground in the presence of Richard and Kuskov, and at its foot he buried the copper crest of the Romanovs.

When neither Shields nor the main body of the fleet had appeared by mid-September they knew they could remain no longer. The advancing season was already putting forth its warnings. They indeed encountered gales which they bucked at great cost in anxiety and exhaustion. Abreast of Yakutat, Baranov wanted to enter, deeming it safer to remain there the winter if the weather did not abate and wishing in any event to see what had been done, but the wind was against him and his skill was unequal to tacking into the bay. He tried it for a whole day, his booms slewing about and his canvas cracking like pistol shots, and finally he concluded there was nothing to be done but continue homeward while the wind at least was with them. If it veered they knew they would never successfully land their sloop on that coast.

It was a battered, famished, and thirsty trio who finally thanked God with the sign of the cross for the welcome sight of St. Paul Harbor in the midst of an October storm.

The *Eagle* was safe in the harbor. Shields had been to the Queen Charlotte Islands and had looked for them on the way back, but Baranov had arrived too late and they had missed each other in the bad weather. And beside the *Eagle* lay the *Three Saints*, still at anchor. Polomoshnoi reported that nobody could control the serfs. Even now, he said, they were hatching a conspiracy to seize a vessel in which to return to the Asiatic coast.

For the second time that year Baranov had a revolt to punish. He ordered the ringleaders seized, strung up by the thumbs and lashed until unconscious, and then deported to outlying districts. The rest he told sternly that they might expect the same thing if there was further trouble and that the following summer they could expect to go to Yakutat if it had to be at the points of guns.

It was with a grim feeling indeed that he looked forward to a second winter with the serfs, the priests, and the men. His one consolation was that Shelekhov must be arranging to find his successor. After what he had written, he must surely be relieved the following summer.

11

An Empress Dies; a Child Is Born

IN May of 1797, twenty months later, Baranov was still in
America. Not a word from Shelekhov. Indeed, for three
years there had not been a ship or a word from Russia, not
since the priests' arrival, nor had the miserable remnant of the
Lebedev-Lastotchkin Company—Konovalov, Balushin, and Kolomin were long since gone—received any either.

The past twenty months had been marked by few incidents out
of the ordinary. The previous summer, Shields had found Nootka
Sound empty and deserted and the only foreign shipmaster he encountered had been a fellow Englishman, a Captain Barber. Was
there some catastrophe of war in Europe, so to clear the seas?
One morning old Pribylov was found dead in his cabin, which left
Shields the sole experienced navigator. He hurried to finish the
training of two of the most intelligent men, Kashevarov and Medvednikov, so that they could at least navigate the *Three Saints* to
Yakutat and get the serfs out of St. Paul. Baranov was determined
he would not endure either their presence or Polomoshnoi's longer
on Kodiak.

Shields had again set out with the bidarka fleet and an advance
force to drop at Yakutat. Again the serfs were loaded with all their
gear on the galiot and again she set out, but this time Baranov
followed her in the *Olga,* prepared to spend his summer building forts and blockhouses for the settlement there.

The entire episode of the serfs had been something to move the heart to deepest pity. When they were finally disembarked at the island in Yakutat Bay where they would thenceforth live they were too broken in spirit to care that they had been made to penetrate the wilderness at last, and that it was as full of possible terror and death as they had feared. There, a few miles from them across the bay, in the village whose grim totems they could see above the trees, lived a people whose chief pleasure was murder of people they did not like. The serfs went heavily about their tasks of cultivating the soil.

The *Three Saints* was wrecked on her return trip; Medvednikov's skill was not great enough to get her safely back.

Though that fall brought no ship or news, things were a little better at St. Paul. The serfs were gone, the new men had gained experience. They built a little church at last, Baranov donating fifteen hundred rubles to the colony's five hundred for it, and the little steeple housed a brass bell they had all helped cast. Its good ring gave the village a fine Russian feeling, but the church had the effect of making the clergy remain together instead of dispersing as missionaries. Father Herman, who was very fond of children, began a school and Fathers Makar and Nektar learned the island tongue at long last and preached vigorously to the Aleuts; but otherwise they fell back on their old monastic habits of life they were supposed to have abandoned when they left Valaam, and spent hours singing the office and examining their consciences.

Shields, like the rest, marked time that winter. He had grown used to America; it was more exciting than Siberia. He would be a rich man when he returned to Russia, with his share of furs piling up on the Company's books, but he was willing to amass more. He also seems to have hated to desert Baranov in his great need for trustworthy navigation. He cheerfully went about preparing to convoy another bidarka fleet to the southern coast.

Then Baranov made a discovery that threw him into a mood of profound gloom and invested his isolation with a feeling of ominous fatality. He was about to face the bitter conflict of all whose native women bore children. He found that Anna Grigoryevna, in silence and with as little wish to disturb or annoy him as always, had been pregnant for several months.

Would he go when his chance came, leaving his own child behind according to the inflexible rule which he invariably enforced on his own men, a rule which even Father Iosaph upheld as wise, or would he reconcile himself to permanent exile? If Shelekhov had only relieved him when he had agreed to! Here was another reason for cursing the wily merchant.

True, it was still possible for him to harden his heart, if he had a chance to leave; according to the Kenaitze people's ways the child belonged to the mother's clan and no one would misunderstand if she reappeared in her father's village with it, together with presents enough to make her independent for the rest of her life. But his soul revolted at the thought of letting his child be brought up as a savage, although there seemed no alternative. He could not take Anna Grigoryevna to Russia, for his wife was alive, nor could he take the child from her.

The priests were deeply incensed by this new advertisement of Baranov's indulgence in the universal habit of taking a native woman. At mass and other religious observances Baranov always stood behind the processional cross, as secular leader of the place. One Sunday morning when it was Father Juvenal's turn to preach, his references were pointed and unmistakable. "The description of the man to whom I refer," thundered Juvenal, his ascetic's eyes flashing and his incisive voice lashing out like a whip at Baranov, who stood in his place behind the cross without a word, "lies in Holy Scripture itself. 'My heart showeth me the wickedness of the ungodly, that there is no fear of God before his eyes. For he flattereth himself in his own sight until his abominable sin be found out. The words of his mouth are unrighteous and full of deceit. He imagineth mischief upon his bed and hath set himself in no good way. . . .' "

But Baranov never replied publicly to the priests.

On June 13 of the old Russian calendar, Anna Grigoryevna bore her child, a boy. He was dark, with thick hair and his mother's fine features. Baranov named him after the saint whose day it was and, following the custom, after himself—Antipatr Aleksandrovich.

In July, Baranov was still at Kodiak and it was well that he was, for a ship came, an old vessel, the *Alexander*. She brought few new men and no supplies, for she had been delayed for months by accidents and her passengers and crew had consumed everything, but the burden of her news made everyone forget what she lacked. One communication, from the bishop of Irkutsk to the archimandrite Iosaph, ordered the priests dispersed from Kodiak and sent to outlying districts for more missionary work. The second note came from Natalya Shelekhova.

Shelekhov was dead, wrote his widow. He had died two years before, in 1795, and lay buried in the courtyard of the convent in Irkutsk. She was her husband's chief heir, but the Company affairs were in a very bad state, no more money could be spent at present, and Baranov must remain in America until released.

The crew of the transport reported that the *Phoenix* still lay at Okhotsk, with little done to finish her decks and cabins. The Golikov-Shelekhov Company was insolvent—that was the gossip throughout Siberia. The merchants of Irkutsk had found Shelekhov's sudden death a fine time to unite against his widow and try to break the company. Old Golikov was unable to help in the financial crisis because he again was in difficulties over money with the government and his fortune had been seized pending an investigation. This left Natalya Shelekhova to carry on the fight alone except for the young merchants who had married into the family and shared the inheritance.

But what a funeral Shelekhov had had, he was told. And the monument that now stood over his grave! In white relief against gray marble was depicted the story of the colonization of America. There were relief maps of Alaska and the Aleutian Islands. A plaque recalled Shelekhov's orders to his navigators. The representation of the three vessels he built formed a frieze—the *Three Saints*, the *Archangel Michael*, and the *God's Friend Simeon and Anna His Prophetess*. The sculptured figure of Shelekhov himself raised bas-relief hands over the unnumbered thousands of Aleuts he had supposedly made into Christians. And running all around the base was a long poem declaiming the merchant's great deeds as an explorer and discoverer of new lands in America. This poem, the tale wound up, had cost a great deal of money and was written to order by none other than Gabriel Derzhavine, former court poet to Catherine the Great.

But there was still greater news. Catherine the Great was dead, and her son, Paul I, was tsar. This was a surprise, for all Russia had expected that Catherine's son would never be emperor, for he was thought mad. It had been thought that Alexander, her grandson, would accede to the throne. Paul hated merchants, it was whispered, and he had been heard to say he would recall all dwellers in foreign countries.

And finally, Europe was indeed torn by general war. In France there had risen a Napoleon Bonaparte who fought everybody. Tsar Paul had declared his enmity for republican France.

Baranov at once prodded the priests into activity toward obeying the Irkutsk bishop's order. Only two or three and their servitors need stay at Kodiak, he decided. The rest could minister to outlying stations. Father Juvenal chose to go to the Ilyamna people, in the mainland's interior west of Cook's Inlet. Baranov warned him that those people were very primitive and not notably friendly, but Juvenal had had enough of natives tainted with white men's ways and wanted to preach to an unspoiled people. Baranov shrugged and arranged for his transportation, then himself left on his summer's rounds in the *Olga*.

On the Inlet he saw to building a palisade and blockhouse on the west side for a small new station, and on Prince William Sound he finally took possession of Fort Constantine, the old Balushin stronghold. As usual he spent the summer ax in hand.

Old Storyteller had of course been overjoyed at the birth of his grandson and throughout the region the Indians swore fealty to Baranov and promised to send more canoes than ever with the hunting fleets—even the Copper River Kolosh were impressed and sent the willow wands, symbols of peace.

Baranov was late returning to Kodiak and brought the *Olga* through weather that let him know that if he ever got home he was at last a first-rate sailor.

By October 25 everyone had ceased scanning the horizon for ships any more, so the electrifying cry, *"Kor-a-bl!"* almost caused a riot. It was the long-looked-for *Phoenix*, complete with new cabins, new men, a generous holdful of supplies, and a mixed collection of good and bad news.

Confirmed were the death of Empress Catherine and the accession of her son, Paul. Father Iosaph was called to Irkutsk to be consecrated a bishop. Shields was ordered to rejoin his regiment in Russia, probably to engage in the great war. Natalya Shelekhova had been successful in regaining control of her husband's interests and had affected a union of all the fur-trading merchants into the United American Company. The new company answered Baranov's plea for navigators and sent by the *Phoenix* three graduates of the cadet school at Petersburg, headed by Midshipman Talin, and a veteran merchant skipper from the White Sea, Herr Podgasch.

The first letter Baranov opened, dated July 30, was from the directors of the new United Company: "In reading this you will no doubt wonder at all the signatures, among whom you can count many sincere friends. You will be glad to know the reason:

"Natalya Shelekhova notified you May 23 of the new corporation being formed at Irkutsk. She has mingled her interests with the others so as to form one firm, the United American Company.

"Our shareholder Emilian Larionov sails to Unalaska to be manager there. He will take up with you personally or by letter the resolutions arrived at by the United American Company . . . He knows our plans for the future. We would like you to co-operate with him in their development . . . We would write you at greater length but all this has just been accomplished and we must dispatch the note by courier to Okhotsk at once . . . We only add we want you to remain as our chief manager. In fact we beg you to remain . . . However, if you are still determined to leave, please turn over your duties to Larionov. We grieve to suggest this and we say it only to avoid misunderstandings that might arise due to the enormous distance between us . . ." The names of thirteen Irkutsk merchants signed the letter.

There was also a letter from Emilian Larionov, who had disembarked at Unalaska. Larionov was friendly and praised Baranov's accomplishments. The new United Company, he said, contemplated great things and this union of merchants meant less wire-pulling than in the old days. In Petersburg plans had been going forward to form a vast company with powers similar to the British East India Company's. Empress Catherine had died before it was approved and since Tsar Paul's accession no one knew what would happen to it and they could only wait and hope. Finally Larionov admitted that although he knew he was supposed to take Baranov's post if he wished to leave, he did not feel equal to the task and also begged Baranov to remain; the writer was content with his limited sphere at Unalaska, where Baranov could call on him for help if the need arose. As a token of his personal esteem, Larionov concluded, he sent as a gift several cases of fine vodka and also forwarded a certain box consigned to Baranov five years before on the *Eagle*'s first voyage, which Larionov had found sitting at Unalaska.

A third letter, doubtless from his brother Pyotr, told him that the glass factory, which, it was hoped, would support Baranov's wife and children, had gone to pot of recent years. Because of this and a bad debt of twenty-two thousand rubles that proved uncollectible, some of the credit on his furs had had to go to the support of his family. In the Anadyr trading venture Pyotr still held his own and maintained the business, but a partner named Belonsev he had taken in had decamped with three thousand rubles. Baranov's wife was far from well and was growing old. His daughter Afanassya was about to marry a government secretary named Vassili Belayev. Their sisters Avdotya and Vassilissa were well; Vassilissa had a grown son named Ivan Kuglinov who wanted to go to America to be with his uncle Aleksandr, but Avdotya had never married. Pyotr had had an argument with the Okhotsk commander's office over some of Baranov's bills for personal supplies and they claimed he owed five thousand rubles. The Lebedev-Lastotchkin Company had instituted damage suits in the courts against Shelekhov's estate and Baranov was named one of the defendants with the possibility of being fined thousands of rubles.

In view of this news, there was only one answer to give. If Baranov did not wish to die a pauper he had best return to Russia at once.

". . . and my business affairs in Russia, while they may not seem much to you, are in bad shape," he replied to Larionov, in a letter for transmission in spring. "What with the interests on my debts, payments to my wife, litigation by the Lebedev-Lastotchkin Company, I should get out of here. My money is evidently being frittered away in incompetence and if I remain I am likely to lose what little I have saved . . . But of course I cannot just get up and leave; the Company's interests are too closely involved with our country's affairs. So I wait for you. The place has made me old before my time. My health has given out, my senses dull. I should like to be relieved before I must return only to spend my days among Siberia's helpless, old men."

12

The Sin of Father Juvenal

IT was the following spring, the spring of 1798. The *Phoenix* was leaving, with Baranov's letter of resignation; Father Iosaph was on board on his way to his consecration as bishop, and Shields was going too. Baranov was heavy-hearted at losing Yakov Egoryevich, who had been his closest friend for six years, his most able lieutenant, and who had taught him more of value to him than any man living.

The village bustled with preparations. The usual number of hunters first prepared to go, and then with tears in their eyes showed up to re-sign for five more years, cursing because their children held them. The priests were holding many ceremonials of farewell for Father Iosaph. But Baranov could take no part in any of the active preparations. During the winter he had given a praznik in honor of Father Iosaph's appointment which came to an ignominious end when Baranov fell and broke his leg. Then later, as he sat immobile in his living room, his injured leg on a chair, Anna Grigoryevna, passing by with the samovar filled with hot water had stumbled and upset the contents all over him, burning him badly.

And the praznik had affected little rapprochement with the priests. Father Iosaph believed the *Phoenix* should wait for him at Okhotsk while he went to Irkutsk for consecration and returned, and Baranov, of course, did not believe the occasion important enough to hold up the schooner that long, which shocked the fathers.

But he managed to get to the wharf, with help, for all the fare-wells, and watched his beloved schooner leave.

He returned to his house. At least there he had found peace. Antipatr grew steadily more healthy and sturdy; like all native children he was invariably good-natured, talking, laughing, or playing when invited to do so but quiet when neglected. Anna Grigoryevna, too, held him—indeed with a stronger bond than ever. Her young body had brought him a happiness of which he had thought himself long since incapable and her kindness and devotion to him were excessive. It made him burn with wrath to see how mother and child had to avoid the priests. Well, Father Stepan had gone with Iosaph, and Father Makar had also left to be dropped at the western Aleutians as a missionary, leaving only Nektar, Herman, the mentally unstable Afanassii, and their servi-tors.

But they were still able to make things uncomfortable for him, as he was later to discover. Unknown to Baranov, Father Makar had persuaded some Aleuts to join in a written protest which was on its way to Petersburg. And now another element entered into future troubles. Of the four young naval cadets who had come the previous year, three had gone back with the *Phoenix*, but Mid-shipman Talin remained. Talin was a vain, strutting, pompous youth who represented the worst faults of the Russian class sys-tem of the times. Having almost failed at the Petersburg cadet school, he had taken service with the Golikov-Shelekhov Com-pany just before Empress Catherine's death, when she granted the Company the right to hire navigators of naval training who would consent to join; he had taken the employment because it was one way of gaining the experience he so badly needed. But he was from Petersburg, which was enough to make some people listen to him, and his natural arrogance was increased when he found his grade of midshipman, low though it was in the *tchinn*, or order of ranks, still the highest in the colony.

He soon began pretending he knew more than he did about the situation in the capital. Actually he probably knew no more than the rest—that Tsar Paul disliked merchants and had been heard to say he would turn the Russian colonies in the Pacific over to the navy if he did not actually recall everyone home. At any rate Talin created considerable unrest and several hunters came to Baranov to ask what would become of them; Baranov of course answered that they would know something as soon as he did and meanwhile their job was to carry on. Father Nektar, however, believed Talin, and Baranov, though as usual he paid little attention to gossip, began to be aware that Father Nektar was preaching to the Aleuts that they had not much longer to work for the traders.

However, when the time came to make the levies for the summer's hunting fleet the Aleuts as usual formed their artels, infuriating Nektar. Talin meekly took orders to convoy the fleet in the *Eagle* and when the parties had left, a measure of peace, as usual in summertime, descended once more on the colony.

Baranov decided to remain again at Kodiak for the summer. The skin was almost healed on the burned places but his leg was still stiff. However he moved quickly enough when hurried news came from Molokhov that they had a real Indian uprising on their hands; the new station established the previous year on the Ilyamna shore had been surprised, destroyed, and the people massacred. It was astounding news in view of the seeming good feeling the previous summer.

Baranov sent Molokhov at the head of an armed force to investigate, but the force had hurriedly to veer to the defense of St. Nicholas, where the attackers next converged, and reached there just in time to save that fort from burning and massacre. The last of the Lebedevski were glad to pile into their ancient galiot, the *Ivan Boguslav*, and get out of America for good.

As Molokhov chased the attackers into the forests, Baranov made the rounds of the villages and found to his dismay that down on the southern coast the foreign traders must lately have been disposing of a great many guns for furs, for several of them had traveled hand to hand all the way to this region. The chiefs were disturbed. If their enemies, the Kolosh, got such goods, they wanted them too. Two or three of the head men were so insolent in their complaints that Baranov had them arrested and sent to Kodiak to be put in the stockade. He examined the guns he found. They were mostly wretched old fowling pieces of Massachusetts make, but even so they were guns. It was apparent that something would have to be done about that situation along the southern coast, and quickly. But he refused point-blank to consider the natives' plea for guns among the Russian trade goods. Baranov had never forgotten the experience in Siberia that brought him to America.

Some of the attackers were captured, tied to trees, and knouted as an example to the others; a few more were sent to Kodiak for imprisonment. He put his own men in charge of Fort St. Nicholas and sent Kuskov to take command at Fort Constantine on Prince William Sound.

Disturbing rumors had also been filtering through from the Ilyamna side, whither Father Juvenal had insisted on going deeply into the country. The priest had come by the previous year, Molokhov said, with his books, vestments, and supply of wine for the holy service; the Indians in the vicinity had pleaded with him to stay on the Inlet, saying they had long been friends with the Russians and deserved their priest more than the Ilyamnas. But Father Juvenal kept on. The Kenaitze had refused to guide him further than the opposite shore and there he had plunged into the forest alone. For a year nothing was heard from him.

Then the boy Nikita, a son of an Ilyamna chief who had been a hostage among Russians and knew the language, appeared with the priest's diary and an extraordinary story.

"The priest appeared in the village of my father, who is named Shakh-mut," he related. "My father's brother Kot-le-wah had met him on the trail. The people were suspicious, for they had had much trouble with the Lebedevski, but I translated the story of the priest, which was that he had not come to trade or take anything from them, but to make a better people of them.

"So he was told he could remain, and, until a house could be built for him, he could live in my father's house and have the use of one of my father's four wives. Father Juvenal's manner at this was very strange, and all wondered why he refused. Then Father Juvenal preached, and I translated as well as I could. He told them about the Christ who died on the cross to save us, and my people were deeply moved that God should give his Son for them.

"I was given to the priest as his companion when his house was finished. He baptized me in the river and all were curious to see if I would live afterwards. I answered that I had seen people live a long time after Russian baptism, and they were impressed.

"Winter came on. Nobody could understand why the priest cut his own wood with an ax, or why he sewed his own clothing. When the sun showed certain times of day he would fall to his knees wherever he stood and remain for many minutes with bowed head. The girls of the village felt it a shame he should live alone and many offered themselves to him, to cut his wood and sew, but he pushed them away with indignation and told them such offerings were very wicked.

"Because it was such a strange thing for a man to be able to withstand women and yet the priest was able to, my father Shahkmut was deeply impressed and so were many others who were baptized. When the priest told me to say it would give him much pleasure if he would be baptized, my father consented to come and receive instructions.

"I was fearful of what would happen when my father found out the truth. I knew that to be baptized he must give up all but one of his wives. Besides, he thought baptism meant making him a Russian. I told him it did not mean making him a Russian but only a Christian. 'What is the difference?' my father asked. 'The priest says baptism will make me a better man, and what better people are there than Russians? They know how to keep food all winter

hit him and he fought back. I was sick to my
pushed him down. When they drew away fro
lay on the ground and blood streamed from

"Someone—I don't know who—drew a k
him as he lay there, and buried the knife to
then stepped back. The crowd watched, s
several minutes, the blood streaming from t
then to everyone's horror he seemed to want
fell back, stricken with awe. He put his hand
lifted himself, slowly, to his feet, then stood th
trickled down his beard, smeared his face, and
black cassock. I saw his lips move and he cla
God, come to my assistance. O Lord, make h
them be confounded and ashamed that seek m

"Suddenly the crowd yelled with fury and
this time with knives. And when they had t
apart they threw the pieces into the lake. I di
had run to his cabin to save the book he seeme
the book in which he wrote every day. I kn
which Russians give to writing by the hand, an

Father Juvenal's diary gave further details o
had been visited upon the soul of the priest—

". . . September 25: With trembling hand
currences of the past day and night. Much ra
the disgraceful story untold, but I must overc
write as a warning to other missionaries who n
Last night I returned at the usual hour to my cel
In the middle of the night I awoke to find mys
woman whose fiery embraces excited me to su
fell a victim to lust before I could extricate m
regained my senses I drove the woman out, but
be very harsh with her. What a terrible blov
recent hopes! The people, of course, will hea
God is my witness that I have here set down th
of anything that may hereafter be said. . . ."

long, they live in better houses, they have all the guns they want
and big boats.'

"I found it impossible to explain the truth to my father and
Father Juvenal's instructions I could not always translate accu-
rately. I came to love Father Juvenal. He was very good to me.
Two orphan boys came to live with us, given Father Juvenal by
an old woman who did not want to see them starve, and Father
Juvenal was always kind to them; he never kicked or cuffed them.

"The day came when my father was baptized with a slave and
one of his wives. The whole village came to the creek to see the
ceremony, and afterwards there was much feasting.

"The next day the trouble started. My father sent word that
he felt so much better already that he was sending his three other
wives to be instructed, too. Father Juvenal knelt in the little room
he called his cell and prayed for a long time. He told me, then, he
must find some way of postponing the ceremony until he could
make sure his doctrine was clear.

"Then—I don't know how it happened—one morning the village howled with laughter. The night before one of the girls of
the village had crept into Father Juvenal's cell and got into his
bed with him. The three of us boys were sleeping in the other
room and we heard him say something—then there was silence
for a long time—after which he screamed like a madman that she
had made him fall and he drove her out of the house with a stick.

"The next morning he did not come out of his cell for a long
time, and when he did he seemed like a man who had lost his senses.
His eyes were wild and staring, his hair was disheveled. 'Nikita,'
he said to me, 'I have committed a terrible sin. May God have
mercy on my soul.'

"He was afraid to go into the village though I told him everyone
would consider it only a joke. My father rocked with laughter
when he heard that one of the girls had persuaded him to be a
man, and went to see the priest to ask why the baptism of his
wives was delayed, but the priest's attitude made him angry. He
could not understand why the priest would not look him in the

face or talk. Finally he said roughly th
tized at once—that he would order the
Juvenal said nothing.

"The feast started. Father Juvenal sta
out eating. When he came out his eyes
again, and he told me he was going to
truth, that I must translate exactly wha
Father Juvenal entered my father's ho
people. My father laughed and signaled
by the fire and partake of food, but Fat
and told my father, 'Shahk-mut, you ar
put away three of your wives and live
was so frightened I translated correctly
understood, was very angry. 'Why can't
and say what he means?' he shouted. 'V
woman touches him, he feels desire, too.
house.'

"I brought Father Juvenal some foo
kneeled in his cell. I told him he must g
brother, Kot-le-wah, had convinced my
and a fool, proved by the fact that he sa
one wife is wrong. Kot-le-wah, you see, h
Father Juvenal's vestments. While I was
brother came into the house with ivory o
le-wah started to take the vestments dov
Juvenal with a cry tried to protect them,
with the club.

"I waited until my father and his br
bathed the priest's wound and he came
I told him. 'You are in grave danger.'

"But he only smiled, that strange sweet
when he had not eaten for days, and wall
The women saw him and laughed. It made
on them with harsh words. They could n
but his tone was insulting. A circle forme

A later entry: "I am laughed at wherever I go, especially by the
women. It will take great firmness to regain my lost prestige and
that of the Holy Orthodox Church. I have vowed to burn no more
fuel in my cell all winter—a mild punishment, indeed, when compared to the blackness of my sin!"

Still an earlier entry told of the man's stress of soul: "August 8:
I dreamed I was stretched out on a narrow ledge of rock with heavy
seas beating up on both sides. I felt perfectly safe, however, and
made no effort to rise. All at once I saw St. Innocent of Taurus
standing at my feet and I dreamed he asked me to make room for
him to lie down too. Crossly I answered, 'Surely there is not room
for both of us.' At that there came a terrible voice from the sea
saying, 'Who are you and what have you ever done that you
hesitate to make room for a martyr?' Then I dreamed I rolled off
into the sea. This dream disturbed me very much when I remembered it. I walked up to a rocky place and there kneeled on the
sharp stones to pray and ponder the meaning of the dream."

Leaving the bitter tragedy behind him, Baranov prepared to return to Kodiak, for the summer was spent. He and Richard sailed
alone; Kuskov remained behind, in command on the sound. Foul
weather hit them and again they had trouble. When Baranov was
finally helped aboard the wharf at St. Paul it was with more than
a touch of fever and a throbbing leg. He went back to bed at once
and without immediately asking about the success of the summer's
hunting fleet—usually his first care.

Later he received Igor Purtov's reports of the summer's hunt
thoughtfully. The Eagle had convoyed them eight hundred miles
to the south, yet trade had been very poor. Yankee vessels the
previous year had visited the coast in large numbers bringing hundreds of guns which the shipmasters had bought cheaply from
their government after their revolution against the English; these
they sold dearly to the Kolosh who, in their eagerness to acquire
the arms, had hunted the coast bare of furs.

Again the necessity of occupying that Sitka region presented itself to Baranov. But there was nothing to be done about it just then; Baranov had never felt less like occupying any place but his bed. Years of abuse of body were at last taking their toll. His leg, though mended, ached incessantly and he coughed constantly.

When he finally recovered he continued to remain in his house, feeling complete disinclination to move about the colony. His faithful men told him that things had been happening, that Father Nektar had been going about from village to village, preaching openly against the Company, but he brushed the news aside impatiently. Neither did the gossip move him—that Talin had been heard to reveal that he had papers commanding him, as a naval officer, to take charge of the colony soon, for the naval men were coming on the *Phoenix*.

To a delegation of hunters who came to see him and ask if it was true that he hugged his house because he knew some awful truth about the end of merchants' rule but was afraid to reveal it, as Talin now was charging, Baranov only replied as he had the previous year, that when he knew anything they would know it too. The delegation left, shaking their heads; if anything was about to happen to the Company they wanted to prepare for it, perhaps to move their families elsewhere and engage in farming.

One day as Baranov sat in his house his friends burst in to say that Talin had called a meeting of the whole colony at the bunkhouse, ostensibly—as highest in official rank—to give the oath to the new tsar but in reality to depose Baranov.

Leaning on his cane, his joints aching, Baranov hobbled out of his house on his cane. The meeting had overflowed into the village square and the entire village listened to Talin haranguing them in a high voice from a stump. Father Nektar and his assistant clergy stood near by as if lending him moral support, their bearded faces unsmiling and grim. Things indeed were serious. The revolt against Baranov had broken out. The breeze blew Talin's words disjointedly toward Baranov.

"By this time the merchants' company is dissolved. Baranov knows it and withholds the news from you. When I left St. Petersburg I had orders to wait until this year, when the naval officers would come to take command. To prepare for their coming, I will now take command of the colony and all will signify their acceptance by taking the oath to His Imperial Majesty, Paul Petrovich—"

The crowd was suddenly conscious of Baranov's presence and parted uneasily to look at him. Talin stopped. Baranov stepped forward and stared around him. His old and best men were here. This was no gathering of malcontents. There stood Medvednikov, Tarakanov, Shvedzov, Purtov, and Kulikalov. One of them broke the silence. "We want the truth, Aleksandr Andrevich."

Baranov whirled on the speaker. "The truth? The truth is that I am chief manager here until you see something in writing to the contrary. What have I to do with rumors and talk? If this man"—pointing to Talin—"knows something, why has he never come to my house to tell me? I want no more of these meetings. You are ready to listen to anything because we have no sugar, tea, or tobacco. If you came to this country expecting to live like princes—"

His voice had warmed, almost to the old fire, but suddenly he stopped to stare around him again. The faces of his men were hard. Baranov was not riding roughshod over them this time. They waited, but Baranov's eloquence had died. To everyone's astonishment he stared at his feet and shrugged. "*Nitchevo,*" he said. "Who does know the truth?"

The crowd reacted excitedly. Talin seized the opportunity. "Russians!" he cried. "Look at him—he is afraid!" But before the meeting turned completely against Baranov a faint cry came from the hill in the distance.

"*Kor-a-bl!*"

The crowd was suddenly silent. The cry was repeated. The people broke and ran for the hill. "Russian colors!" jubilantly cried those who reached the hilltop first.

Hours later the ancient galiot *Zachary and Elizabeth* cast anchor before St. Paul, and Baranov was lifted aboard to see on the poop his old enemy, Botcharov! Forgotten were the old differences and they embraced like brothers, one with relief at the successful end to a journey full of mishaps and delays in an unseaworthy tub and the other with joy at his delivery from a winter full of discomfort.

That night bread, vodka, tea, sugar, and tobacco were again dispensed from the commissary. That night again there was high praznik, the bunkhouses ringing with the song from two hundred happy throats, the tinkle of guzlas, the stamp of booted feet, and the shrill laughter of Aleut girls thrown high in the air by the dancers. For in addition to the creature comforts brought by the galiot was the last news from Russia that all was the same.

And Baranov sat in the midst of it all and directed the singing and dancing. His cane lay forgotten in his house and his joints no longer ached.

The priests and Talin stayed in their houses without a word.

13

·•-◄

Sitka Is Bought with Blood

SPRING again, the spring of 1799. At St. Paul village the
winter had passed in cheerful content, for there had been
luxuries enough and the new men whom Botcharov had
brought had kept busy building another new sloop at their small
shipyard on Yelovi Island, out in the little harbor. Nobody had had
the time or the inclination to listen to Father Nektar or Midshipman Talin.

As for Baranov he had seldom passed a happier winter. Now his
objective was to plant a colony on Sitka Sound without fail by
the following summer. He would start the work and have it ready
for Larionov to finish when he arrived on the *Phoenix*, which
would surely pick him up at Unalaska when she brought the new
bishop. His administration would end in honorable accomplishment for himself.

It was imperative that the Russians move to that rich spot and
control it without delay. In another two years, judging from the
reports sent by Kuskov from Prince William Sound, the Yankees
would have a firearm in the hands of every savage. Writing his
report which Botcharov would take back to Siberia when he sailed,
Baranov noted:

"It's safe to assume that in the last ten years the English and
Americans have sent to that region (Sitka) ten ships annually and
we may also assume each carried away an average of . . . two

thousand skins. This, during a six weeks' season, would come to twelve thousand—or let's take the smallest estimate say ten thousand pelts . . . At the current Canton price of forty-five rubles apiece this amounts to four hundred and fifty thousand rubles . . . And such shipments to Canton have a very depressing effect on our own market . . . If we want to prevent the ruin of our business by the English and Americans some such step must be taken. Above all, it is imperative that we move nearer them to watch their actions . . ."

There had never been a more opportune time for such a move. Due to the Napoleonic wars neither English nor Spanish were at Nootka Sound or at any other permanent settlement anywhere on the coast nearer than San Francisco Bay, more than two thousand miles away. Baranov had the largest complement ever at his disposal for summertime duty—almost two hundred and fifty men. He had Talin and Podgasch as navigators, two sloops, a packet, and a galiot. When the *Phoenix* arrived there should be still more men and a schooner.

In May he issued his orders to the colony. Founding Sitka would be the only major task that year. Podgasch would leave first in the *Catherine* with heavy supplies, and wait at Yakutat. Talin in the *Eagle* would pick up all available men at the mainland forts. There would be no hunting fleet this year but the Aleuts must gather as usual, proceed to Fort Constantine, meet the canoe fleet Kuskov would have ready there, and then go on down to Yakutat. Baranov himself would follow in the *Olga*. Only skeleton crews of Russians would be left at all other posts. From Yakutat the massed force would move on Sitka.

Father Nektar was almost beside himself with rage when he heard that a force of seven hundred Aleuts, their arrears of debts paid by Baranov, were willing to go to Sitka. Talin, who had sulked in his cabin all winter, returned Baranov's written order with an insulting question. What did Baranov mean by dispatching ships and otherwise trying to command navigation? Where did Baranov get the idea that he, a merchant, could give orders to anyone of rank? Didn't he have any understanding of his position? To this Baranov wrote an extended reply addressed "To Gavril Terentyevich the noble gentleman, Midshipman in the Navy, this humble report of the colonial manager Baranov. Dear Sir: "I suppose I have to explain as you request why I, a trader without rank or noble descent, manage all the matters of the Company here as well as give orders regarding navigation. I enclose for your information Secret Orders 18 and 19 from the commander of Okhotsk . . . Now, I never challenged your knowledge of navigation; I merely notified you what trips and surveys you must make this summer for the benefit of the Company and the government. I am therefore asking you either to send me a written refusal or to comply with the instructions as drawn up by me. If you have some special instruction from the high government, or from the Company stockholders, please prove it so I may not remain in doubt. With humble respects, I remain the obedient servant of your nobility, Aleksandr Baranov."

Talin knew better than to send a written reply to this. His answer was oral. "Tell Baranov that if he so much as sets foot on the *Eagle* when I'm in command, I'll have him hung from the yardarm." And, in order that Baranov could not bar him from the vessel, he lost no time in slipping the packet's anchor and setting sail for no one knew whither.

That left the *Catherine* as the only ship with any real capacity to hold materials and supplies, but Baranov sent her on nonetheless and, after taking leave of his child and Anna Grigoryevna, he and Richard boarded the *Olga* and headed for Prince William Sound after the huge fleet of canoes.

Arriving at Fort Constantine, where Kuskov had been in command all winter, Baranov found almost two hundred more bidarkas ready to go. Yet in spite of this careful carrying out of orders, Kuskov was opposed to the attempt to colonize Sitka then. All over the mainland, he said, the natives were growing insolent and restless. They understood, at last, that Russians, too, could be murdered, and bad feeling and truculence were growing, what with

Yankee guns passing from hand to hand up the coast. It was not safe to weaken the northern garrisons. But Baranov had gone too far to be dissuaded. Leaving Molokhov as usual in command at Fort Alexander and placing good-natured Rodionov at Fort Constantine in Kuskov's place, the immense line of bidarkas set out from Nuchek toward Yakutat, five hundred and fifty canoes all told, escorted by the *Olga*—more than one hundred Russian men, several bringing their wives for permanent occupancy of a new home, and some nine hundred natives. In all the promyshlenik advance to its next foothold comprised over a thousand souls.

Bad luck seemed theirs from the beginning. Crossing the narrow inlet out of Prince William Sound south of Nuchek Island, where even a moderate wind stirs up the strip of sea to boiling fury, a squall suddenly met them and before Baranov's eyes thirty of the frail canoes were engulfed.

Every canoe that was still afloat at once began battling to make shore. The Aleuts did not need to be told that the sea gods were angry that day. Baranov and Kuskov had to cast anchor, for the beach was too shallow for them to come close in, and join the rest by throwing out, with great difficulty, their shoregoing canoe. The offshore breeze almost swamped them but by twilight willing hands pulled them both, drenched to the skin, onto the beach, where they camped for the night.

About midnight the camp sprang to its feet, startled by the dread Kolosh ululation ringing in its ears. The Aleuts with cries of terror made a break for the forest—straight into the arms of the enemy.

Baranov ordered them back, but it was too late. The Russians were alone with their Aleut wives to load their muskets for them as they fired at the yells and the flashes from the Kolosh guns. Baranov knew that if they could hold out for an hour or two they would have no more fear that night. The Kolosh method was to attack and, if victory were not complete almost at once, to retreat.

The battle did not last long. In an hour the woods were suddenly silent, indicating that a very small force had caused the disturbance. Baranov commanded quiet for a time longer, then softly and cautiously called the Aleut survivors by name; most of them proved to have hidden themselves in the driftwood.

The rising sun revealed a sea rippled by only a slight wind. As they resumed the journey southward, thirteen empty bidarkas remaining on the sands indicated that twenty-six people were dead or captured. With the sixty who had been drowned, eighty-six had already been lost before the actual attempt to found the Sitkan colony had even begun.

A day away from Yakutat the *Eagle* was sighted tacking back and forth apparently aimlessly. Baranov raised and lowered his flag in signal but the packet's boom veered and she steered away from him. One of the Russians in a canoe was ordered to ask Talin for a supply of water, and a quarter hour later Baranov, through his telescope, could see Talin laugh and give some answer. The answer proved to be, on the canoe's return, "Tell Baranov that if he wants water I hear there is plenty at Sitka."

With that brutal and insolent reply ringing in his ears, with eighty-six of his men left behind him dead, Baranov sailed on in the *Olga* to Yakutat.

Here he found matters about as bad as his enemies would have liked to represent them. Fear of the Kolosh across the waters of the bay had made Polomoshnoi keep the palisade high and the wooden fortifications strong. But aside from that, Yakutat was in a state of fright and chaos. Seven of the serfs and thirteen of the hunters had died of scurvy—sufficient indication of the small amount of greenstuff grown at Yakutat. The plain truth of the matter was that agriculture was impossible; one cannot plow fields in continual fear. The serfs had quarreled incessantly with the promyshleniki, asking that they be allowed to become hunters too. Polomoshnoi had taken to getting drunk alone in his hut and neglected to keep the peace. When Baranov arrived everyone crowded around him, gesticulating and crying to have his wrongs listened to.

For a day he held court, listening to each side, trying to make some sense out of the interminable and conflicting charges, counter-charges, and complaints. As a result of the hearings he deposed Polomoshnoi and put one of the older hunters in charge.

He then resumed the business of proceeding to Sitka. Podgasch had brought the *Catherine* safely to the rendezvous where she lay quietly at anchor. Medvednikov was sent on ahead to pick a site for the settlement and to build a temporary camp to be ready on their arrival. Then the whole flotilla set forth—the bidarkas, the galiot, and the sloop.

It was July 18, when Baranov sighted the peak called Mount Edgecumbe that he remembered as marking Sitka Sound; a few hours later he saw the long island fronting the sea where he had once camped and the sound reaching inland toward the innumerable waterways of the interior. As they steered cautiously inside, a flash of white on shore attracted them. It was Medvednikov waving a shirt. They beached before the temporary camp, but Baranov at once expressed dissatisfaction with the site on the grounds that it was too exposed and not high enough for a commanding fort. All that morning, he cruised about in the *Olga*. One place struck his fancy—a rugged knoll atop which no doubt all the surrounding region could be seen. Unfortunately the Sitka Kolosh had had the same idea and had long since occupied it. The long line of solemn totems could be seen plainly, grim in their vivid colors against the green forest, warning others off as effectively as if the grotesque birds and beasts depicted in colored woods had spoken.

Deciding that Medvednikov had chosen the best place after all, Baranov returned to the beach where the canoes were arriving by the dozens every hour and before which the *Catherine* was anchored. Axes were fetched and they soon began to ring on the trees. Then all sound stopped as if on signal and a tense silence fell on the forest. A file of twenty or more Sitka Kolosh warriors had stepped out of the woods and stood, with folded arms, watching them. The Aleut women whimpered and drew close to their Russian husbands. Even Baranov was impressed by the appearance of these natives.

They were, in physique, culture, and leadership, the aristocrats of the Northwest Coast. Beside them their Yakutat brethren to the north seemed merely pettishly mean. Tall men, well over six feet, their muscles rippled beneath their naked bronze skins like those of a panther. Several of the twenty warriors wore short beards two or three inches long; their long, coarse, black hair was drawn into knots at the backs of their high, conical skulls, powdered with goosedown and surmounted by single black-and-yellow feathers. In their ears they wore iridescent shells and over their shoulders were thrown blankets of woven mountain-goat wool edged with ermine. Their attitude seemed neither threatening nor disapproving; it was merely silently questioning.

The interpreter whispered in Baranov's ear the name of the leader—Ska-out-lelt, chief of the Sitka *kwan*, a distinguished-seeming man of perhaps forty-five. A fine, brown woolen toga was swung over his shoulders in such a manner as to give his powerful arms free play. Several of his men carried guns and powder-horns of English and Yankee make. Baranov signaled silently to the interpreter, who stepped forth.

"This is the great Nanuk of the Russians, of whom we spoke last year."

Ska-out-lelt turned to one of his own chiefs to answer. The interpreter turned to Baranov after the few spoken words.

"Ska-out-lelt says there is no use trying to trade. A Boston ship has just left Sitka Sound."

Baranov stepped forward to make a speech. He came here to live and not merely to trade, he said. He was the assistant to the great emperor who was ultimate lord of all this region. This emperor had sent him to build a village where they could trade with and help their fellow subjects, the Kolosh, against aggressors. He had heard that foreign ships had sometimes done evil things to them. The Russians would stop such practices. To prove he came in friendship he was willing to pay whatever price for a site they asked.

The strong faces of the twenty natives remained perfectly immobile during the translation. Their eyes did not seem to perceive that these Russians possessed guns, clothes, copper, and iron—things they coveted. Who were the friends of Sitka *kwan?* Friendship was a complex affair, something guaranteed by more than a word. From Yakutat on the north down to Cape Flattery and almost to Puget's Sound the Kolosh nation existed in a complex federacy linked together by intricate ties of blood, marriage, and shamanism. Who were these people who spoke so lightly of entering this order, hallowed by a tradition so old that no man could remember its beginning?

Yet at the close of the harangue, after the proper interval of silence had passed following Baranov's speech, Ska-out-lelt said to the interpreter, "Ask Nanuk how much he offers."

So Sitka was bought in the ancient coin of beads, brass, and bottles.

An hour later the tents were being pitched, the sound of axes again echoed from the sides of Mount Verstovia on Sitka Sound, and the Aleuts busily put out in their canoes to hunt otter alongshore.

By Easter Day of the year 1800, Fort St. Michael was almost finished. All winter the thousand men had worked in the pouring rain, keeping the axes ringing, the forges glowing, the saws filed. The name was chosen by popular vote.

There could be no doubt it was the finest structure on the Northwest Coast. Surely it would withstand any siege! The stout beams hewn from whole logs held the upper story two feet out from the lower, and two sentry towers gave the most indifferent marksman direct aim at whoever might try to set fire to the timbers. The basement underneath the building measured seventy by fifty feet. And around a great square comprising not only this central stronghold but kitchens, shops, and bunkhouses stood a strong, high palisade of logs.

And none too soon was their defense finished, for the candlefish had begun to run in the sound. This might mean that Baranov's men had all the food they needed but also it meant that the Kolosh for miles in the interior gathered in the villages of the archipelago to replenish their own supply.

All remained far from well in the relations between the Russians and the Kolosh. Baranov learned from the interpreters that Ska-out-lelt of the Sitkans had been severely censured for selling land to the Russians, in the councils of the allied Kolosh tribes, the Chilkats to the north, the Awks, and the Hootznahoos. Politics were being played; Ska-out-lelt's nephew, a young chief named Kot-le-an, desired the chieftancy of the Sitkans and intrigued against his uncle, urging this act of friendship to the Russians as a reason for deposing the aging man. And Ska-out-lelt, it was reported, yielded to the pressure and was ready to revoke the bargain and permit the massacre to start.

Although Baranov pretended unawareness of all this, he never relaxed vigilance, keeping a substantial proportion of his garrison on sentry at all times. On Easter Day, because it was long since his men had seen anything of splendor or ceremony, he ordered a simple wooden cross made and planted in front of the fort, the flag raised, and a drill with several small cannon before the flagpole. As the guns were wheeled into position a crowd of Kolosh who had been watching suddenly vanished into the forest. A few minutes later it was excitedly reported to Baranov that an interpreter had been seized and carried off to Sitka *kwan* as a hostage and that the Sitkans were arming.

He said nothing and went on with his preparations for the ceremony. The men lined up at attention, all those with muskets out in front. Baranov bared his head, Ivan Kuskov stepped forward with the book and read prayers for the day as the flag was raised.

At the petition for the health of the tsar the little cannons boomed and the men shot their muskets off in the air.

As the ceremony proceeded the Kolosh massed at the edge of the clearing and watched with expressions of puzzled animosity. There must have been at least five hundred of them. When the ceremony was finished Baranov told his men they would go straight to the Sitka *kwan* to demand the return of the interpreter. He instructed them simply to follow him and obey orders and threatened to flog the man who fired before he gave the order.

It was an act requiring the utmost boldness. Nevertheless his heart had plenty of time to grow faint as he saw into what he led his men. Runners had arrived ahead of them with news of their coming and as the Russians stepped between the rows of grim totems fronting the long houses, the massed strength of huge, silent Kolosh grimly fingering their weapons outnumbered them at least twenty to one. The utmost silence prevailed. The very air was tense. One false move and they would have been fallen upon without a chance to avoid capture or death.

Baranov's bearing, however, indicated he felt none of this. He stopped boldly before the largest house he could see. Beside the door stood two warriors, henchmen of old Ska-out-lelt. Baranov ordered the main body of his men to fire their muskets into the air when he dropped his hand. At the same time two Russians with the men under them were to rush the two warriors standing by the door and seize them. Just then Ska-out-lelt stepped out of the doorway. Baranov dropped his hand. The women and children screamed at the heavy volley. On the steps eight or ten Russians struggled to tie the hands of the two captive warriors. As Baranov had calculated, the rest of the Kolosh, including Ska-out-lelt, watched the struggle silently, offering their men no help. In a few minutes the two lay on the ground, tied hand to hand. The Russians had two hostages for the one held by the Kolosh.

The coup, simple as it was, worked perfectly to ease the tension. The Kolosh were always impressed by feats of bravery and ingenuity. Ska-out-lelt smiled and invited Baranov into his house, served him food and haggled over the exchange of the hostages. The Russians departed knowing they had gained a measure of admiration from the Sitkans.

April wore on, building was finished to the point where Baranov could safely leave, and although he was worried that he had had no word from the north since the previous fall, he stayed on at St. Michael in great curiosity to see the Yankee shipmasters. Most of them wintered at the Sandwich Islands, he understood, and started for the Northwest Coast by March. And he had correctly been informed, for now they came, one after another. First he saw the *Jenny*, commanded by Captain Jonathan Bowers, then the *Rover* of Captain Davidson followed by Captain Dodd's *Alexander*, Captain Swift's *Hazard* and the *Alert* under Captain Bowles—nearly all veterans of one or more trips to "The Coast," and all from Boston.

Baranov, accompanied by the invaluable Richard, visited each skipper as he arrived. Traders the world over recognize their kind, and moreover his approach was always friendly and disarming; consequently he was for the most part entertained as well if not as bibulously as at Captain Hugh Moore's table. Indeed some of them professed horror at drinking rum and in other ways were unlike Moore—they were very granite-faced and businesslike.

Deeply concerned over one item in which these skippers freely traded—firearms—he never failed to register a protest when the friendly footing had been established; but the answer was usually the same—a refusal to stop the sale. They had traveled 15000 miles to sell these guns, the Yankees replied, and were not turning back now.

However, he discovered a new worry that almost overshadowed this concern when he heard of the prices the Yankees paid for furs. Two yards of broadcloth, a gun with ten cartridges, or four pounds of lead and powder—for one otter skin! For an especially fine bundle these Yankee shipmasters would even sell the small falconets and cannon they carried for their own protection. The Russians usually bought a skin for a few pounds of old iron.

Otherwise he got along with the Bostonians in perfect accord. He questioned them and they answered readily with almost every detail about their business; he found little change in procedure since Captain Moore's day except that the British, in their preoccupation with the Napoleonic wars, seemed to have lost the supremacy in Pacific trade to the Bostonians.

He understood that the causes sending them so far from their home in Massachusetts were identical with those that sent his men so far from Siberia. Just as St. Petersburg drained the gold and silver of Siberia and left only furs as the economic basis for all trading, so had London long drained Massachusetts. That commonwealth, since it had established its independence along with the other American colonies, had to have trade. Salvation came to it in the discovery of the secret that the furs of the Northwest Coast would buy goods of the Chinese. Within two years after the discovery, by 1790, the Boston-Sitka-Canton-Boston route was a fixed course.

Baranov realized that he and these men were the spearheads of forces both reaching out desperately for economic life. It was up to them individually to growl over the spoil or share it in peace, for the reward was large and important to both sides.

He had perforce to admire the Bostonians' vessels and found them better adapted for their purpose than Captain Moore's had been. The most successful were strong brigs sixty-five to ninety feet long, small enough to navigate the intricate waterways yet large enough to withstand the furies of the open sea, copperbottomed for tropic waters, skillfully navigated. The passage around the Horn from the eastward, Baranov heard, was more dangerous, difficult, and attended with more hardships than any other in the world. On their way they broke voyage at least once —at the Sandwich Islands, where King Kamehameha was as friendly to them as he had been to the British.

For cargo they brought copper, bolts of red and blue "duffils," scarlet coating, chisels, pea jackets, Flushing greatcoats, buttons, blankets, beads, and hundreds of old muskets bought cheaply from the American government as useless relics of the Revolution. Curiously—and providentially—that ancient medium of aboriginal barter, New England rum, was absent from most of those early bills of lading.

But they had achieved less success in peaceful relations with the Kolosh than had Baranov and depended more on a show of force. Every vessel, besides being heavily crewed, carried six to twenty loaded cannon and blunderbusses on swivels, and every man was armed with several pistols and a cutlass. Hardly a trip was taken, the shipmasters said, without a battle at some point where they stopped; the Kolosh were treacherous and aggressive, especially where the British had been.

They told him of a certain notorious Captain Henry Barber, an Englishman, whose practice was to let the Kolosh aboard ostensibly to trade then to seize the lot and hold them for ransom in furs. Wherever this Captain Barber had traded there had been trouble in after years. Along the Queen Charlotte Islands several ships belonging to different skippers had been seized and burned, and the crews held as slaves in remote Indian villages.

Another difficulty which the Yankees made lay in the fact that they sold their furs at Canton for prices lower than the Russians asked at the Chinese border.

"Our only remedy would seem to be," he wrote, "the establishment of a customs house . . . by which we could also enter Canton at a saving of 20 per cent. The Americans say they could get a price higher by 20 per cent if our shipments to Siberia were discontinued . . . Some solution must be arrived at. . . ."

Summer. Baranov prepared to leave Fort St. Michael. Four hundred and fifty were to be left as a garrison—four hundred Aleut males, about twenty Aleut wives of various men, and thirty Russians—the pick of his oldest and most trusted men, such as Tarakanov the handy with tools, Tumakayev the gunner, the Kochessov twins. Medvednikov he made commander with old Nakvassim as second. On them he impressed his orders, the gist of which was to remain friendly with Kolosh and Yankee alike, but not for one second to weaken the guard or relax vigilance. Then, after dispatching the three hundred canoes under Kuskov carrying five hundred Aleuts and Kenaitze back to their island or mainland homes, he followed in the *Olga*.

The events of the next few days, had Baranov been at all given to superstition—which he always professed to scorn—should have made him believe his luck was up in safely establishing Fort St. Michael. Hardly a day out of Sitka, two hundred Aleuts of the homegoing bidarka fleet died within a few hours of eating a strange black mussel they dug on a beach where they camped the night. Their throats swelled, their abdomens seemed to burst with agony, and they died despite the frantic efforts of the Russians to give emetics of gunpowder mixed with sea water. Baranov knew that that finished all chance of fur hunting on the way that summer; the survivors were stricken with complete apathy. He let them go straight to their homes, not thinking, perhaps, that the occurrence would finally stamp the idea of Sitka as an evil thing on Aleut minds.

Arriving at Fort Constantine on Nuchek, he further heard that the *Eagle* had gone down off Montague Island with Polomoshnoi and, worse, eight of his best Shields'-trained sailors and twenty-two thousand rubles' worth of furs. Talin, however, who sank her while cruising about for his own enjoyment, had escaped and was alive at Kodiak.

Rodionov, giving the climactic blow, added that the *Phoenix* also had probably been lost. They thought so because the Japan Current had been washing up boxes of church candles and bricks of Manchurian tea—and the *Phoenix* had certainly not arrived at Kodiak that year, with or without the new bishop. Rodionov wound up the sorry list by saying that Fort Constantine had sustained another native attack that winter and that Molokhov on Cook's Inlet also had had much trouble.

Baranov wearily took the *Olga* to the inlet to see Molokhov, who told him the natives had grown completely un-cooperative and were saying they would furnish no more canoes to Baranov's fleets. Molokhov sensed something organized back of it all—and it seemed to stem from Kodiak Island. This made little sense, for the Aleuts would not initiate revolts. The hand of Father Nektar was plain.

Despite his immediate surmise that something was happening on Kodiak which badly needed looking into, Baranov paused there only briefly, without opening his mouth about the probability of the *Phoenix* having been lost, to pick up a carpenter who had helped work on his beloved schooner. He then put out to sea again to explore the beaches as far eastward as he dared, to look for further evidences of the loss.

He found enough to make him weep—enough wreckage to make the tragedy a certainty. It soon became apparent that the wreck must have taken place a good thousand miles away, and much earlier in the summer, calculating as best he could the speed with which the Current would carry the objects he found; yet he kept on, hoping against hope to come upon survivors. He bore no personal love for Bishop Iosaph, but a priest was a man of God.

Back over the path by which he came to America he beat, examining beach after beach, scouring inlets and estuaries, calling out and listening for answering shouts, finding kegs of cheese, bales of sodden bread, boxes of more church candles stamped with tiny crosses, until the autumn gales threw rain and spray in their faces with savage fury and warned them to return home before it was too late. He hoped to make Unalaska, to find out whether Larionov had been on her, but at length he realized that pushing further was madness.

Turning back, his arms aching on the tiller and his heart heavy in his breast, he enjoined strictly on his crew the utmost secrecy about their fears. No use loosing another wave of mourning atop the one from which St. Paul must have just recovered.

14

Anna Grigoryevna

IT is easy to believe in God—even the somewhat stern God whom Father Nektar preached—on the Aleutian Islands. The wonders of His creation often take place before your eyes; islands appear and disappear with the semblance of miracles. The fires of hell are plain enough in the smoking peaks and the frequent convulsions moving the earth underfoot. And in summer when the fogs sometimes lift it is easy to invest the glimpse of blue heavens caught briefly with palaces of agate and chalcedony. As for everlasting life, it was a startling thing to the Aleuts to understand that they need not fear death but could have life forever by just accepting baptism. Inasmuch as their vague gods little cared what anyone did, they felt they could hardly lose by accepting.

Father Nektar and his assistant clerics worked like beavers all that summer. Their hearts filled with holy joy at the dozens who came for baptism. Even mainland natives came from the most distant places to watch the Russian shamans perform in their church with their robes, hats, candles, incense, and altar. As for the singing, only the Aleuts' high color as they listened and occasional hands lifted to mouths in token of astonishment betrayed their inner excitement.

Having mastered the Aleut tongue, Father Nektar had learned at last how to coax in the lost sheep. In the simplest terms he could find he went over and over again the main tenets of his faith—the

Creation, Fall, Redemption by the blood of Christ, Life Everlasting. He traveled from village to village, preaching. When the *Phoenix* came back with the new bishop he would be able to lay at the feet of his superior a land completely won for Christ.

Father Nektar might have become a great missionary if he could have separated Christ's tribute from Caesar's, but he had conceived such a mortal hatred for that man Baranov, a hatred almost holy in its intensity, that his hands clenched when he heard his name. Immaterial to him that Baranov was willing to let his work alone if he would let Baranov's. Nektar had been thankful for the long months Baranov stayed away at Sitka, for it meant the perfecting of his plan to give the bishop, in addition to a spiritual domain, a material one free of Baranov's influence. Talin had nothing to do with any of it any more. Father Nektar saw Talin in his true light, now. Talin remained in his cabin drunk, these days; the colony knew that his wanton joy-riding the previous summer was what had lost the *Eagle* and several lives.

There was plenty to feed Father Nektar's anger. Many Aleut villages were empty of men because they were away with Baranov; some Aleut wives wailed the funeral songs in advance, when they heard their husbands had been levied to go into the Kolosh country. And when the bidarka fleet returned that summer with its sorry record of deaths from eating poisoned mussels, Nektar preached the complete overthrow of Baranov.

One of the enlightened material contributions of Father Nektar was to urge vaccination against smallpox, a scourge of the native tribes. It was done in those days by passing a thread infected with the pus of a previous victim through an incision in the arm. Naturally he got at first but few volunteers to try it, until he approached the Kenaitze prisoners whom Baranov had confined to the stockade for their troublemaking on Cook's Inlet. They were willing and as a reward Nektar got them released from custody and taken on his rounds as examples to show they were still alive and moreover immune to the disease.

Unrest swept Kodiak. There had been no supplies for a long

time. Baranov remained absent. The village elders wondered when their pay for their peoples' service and for all the deaths would come in. Nektar exultantly pressed the advantage. "Refuse to work for Baranov," he thundered in his sermons. "Throw the traders out!"

At St. Paul his eyes fell on a woman who to his notion was the living symbol of all he hated. She kept close to Baranov's house but sometimes she passed through the village with her little son, going after water or to pick berries, walking straightly and proudly, dressed in red silk kerchief and close-fitting woolen dress that showed her firm breasts, earrings pendent from her ears. The Aleuts saluted her respectfully, for she was Anna Grigoryevna, Nanuk's wife, but she seldom answered; Nanuk had told her to remain aloof from the colony and besides she was a mainland woman, above the Aleuts in her own estimation.

Anna Grigoryevna was desperately lonely. In fall she often went to the beach and gazed anxiously for sight of the *Olga*, looking across the sea to the mainland where her people lived. At home at this time of year the boys would be noisily undergoing the purification ceremonies, the women singing long, involved tribal songs as they preserved candlefish oil into butter, the shamans painting masks for the Winter Plays. Nanuk came home at last, but with a worried frown and was immediately off again, she knew not whither.

The preaching, the singing at the church, the baptismal ceremonies attracted her strongly, and she was curious. What she heard she understood. This God of whom she heard was not unfamiliar; the mainland people also knew a supreme being called *El*, who was also all-powerful, had created everything, and had a son who sometimes interceded for people when his father chastised them unduly. As for the talk of saints and guardian angels, the shamans also taught that everyone has a *yeik* who follows him at all times, guarding him from evil.

But all her contacts with the priests had been most unfortunate.

A lay brother once had seized little Antipatr and shaken him angrily, calling him a child of sin. Once when she had entered the church intending only to stand in back, with the unbaptized, the same servitor had had her put out.

She was surprised, then, to have Father Nektar suddenly turn his attention to her and, with as much kindliness as he could assume, urge Christianity upon her. She was eagerly willing. But when he explained that she must leave Nanuk she was puzzled. Who would take care of him, mend his clothes, comfort him on cold nights, rub his shoulders with vodka on the places he said hurt the most?

The priests were getting used to talking in simple terms. Anna Grigoryevna was told she could do Nanuk's housework but must not get into bed with him.

This puzzled her more. She understood the priests considered her a bad woman because she associated with Nanuk and lived in his house. Now the priests said nothing about leaving the house but only forbade something she considered relatively unimportant. Anyway, who would sleep with Nanuk if she did not? Someone should.

But the priests were adamant and she left them in deep perplexity. Here was some remote logic she failed to grasp. Had Nanuk deceived her in some way? Had he led her into some life shameful to the ways of his people?

But they would not let her alone. She was told that little Antipatr could not be allowed to go to Father Herman's school, that she was a bad woman and set a bad example to the colony. "If you are afraid of Baranov, he will not be here much longer," she was told. "Then what will become of you?"

"I will return to my people," she answered.

But still they would not let her alone. She felt cornered, frightened. She wished desperately that Nanuk would return. She became an object of execration in the village because she refused baptism.

Baranov returned late in the season from his exhausting trip looking for remains of the *Phoenix*, ill with worry and strain, and again took to his bed without more than a cursory investigation of affairs at St. Paul. Silent, preoccupied, for a long time he hardly noticed that his wife was tense and worried too. But suddenly he discovered the truth, that the civilization into which he had brought this once-savage girl had forced problems on her also.

He had assumed that a child, if one came from her, would bring him heartaches, but it had never occurred to him that the woman would also cause her share of them; he had always taken it for granted that when the time came for parting she would return to her people unchanged and without regrets. Now, he suddenly saw how impossible that was. She had changed, she wanted to accept the faith of his people. What could he do? Let her be baptized and then put her away because he had a wife in Russia? What, then, would happen to his alliance with the native tribes on Prince William Sound, on which his living with this girl was the bond? Her people only in that region remained wholly dependable. Yet it was also too plain that she was a human being with a soul. Baranov believed it a sin to refuse baptism. Moreover she was the mother of his child, his only son; she had been loyal, gentle, and kind. Though but a scant twenty-two she moved with a grace and beauty that would have done credit to anyone of his own race. What right had he to tell her that she must continue a savage, that she could not know Christ?

He cursed for the ten-thousandth time the fact he had not, long since, been relieved to go home. His job brought him as many personal problems difficult of solution as his material ones.

His resentment against Nektar was natural enough. The priest could very well have left his woman alone. Remembering the hint of Molokhov on Cook's Inlet that some sort of trouble stemmed from Kodiak Island he began investigating at last, and was incredulous at what he found.

There seemed to be a plot afoot for a rising to murder all the

Russians. This seemed too fantastic for even Father Nektar to think up.

He might have liked to debate with the archmonk and thresh out what he had to say about Aleut slavery. But he was silent. Who could judge of freedom or slavery in countries white men exploited? From what he had heard, things were no better in India, California, and South America. In the old days the early Russian traders came in ships with the gatherer of *yassack*, the tribute in furs for the tsar, and theirs was one long history of oppression and abuse. Empress Catherine had finally abolished the custom of taking tribute from natives and instead had given the trading companies the privilege of putting Aleuts to work.

Baranov always paid his Aleuts, sooner or later, and his Russians took identical chances with them in the same canoes and the same forts. In many cases whole villages were empty of men for whole summers, true. But, he told himself savagely, St. Michael had been built so that the Aleuts would not have to make such long journeys, and when he had enough Russians he would gladly dispense with the Aleuts. Of course the whole enterprise was in the long run a scheme to enrich a few on the guts and blood of a subject people, but was he St. Petersburg to change it?

As always, he waited for intriguers against him to make the first move. Talin still kept to his cabin, the priests went about their business with apparent disregard for him. On Christmas Day, Baranov went about the colony with as much geniality as he could assume to wish everyone well. Then came New Year's Eve, the last day of 1800.

They were enjoying one of those rare Aleutian winter interludes when the rains miraculously cease, the sun shines faintly enough to turn the background mists into iridescence, and the rich grass of the moor shimmers like green fur. It was a holiday, of course. Baranov, Richard, and Podgasch took a jug of vodka to the bunkhouses and the shout passed through the village that the chief manager was treating. Soon the building was full. Now Baranov rapped for order.

He announced that the previous summer he had received word that the Company planned on possibly abolishing the old method of working on shares, na paik, and substituting the straight salaries for all employees. "Before I write my spring reports to Irkutsk, I would like your opinions."

It was a much-debated subject, popular with few, and discussion was very heated when suddenly Father Nektar, Father Herman, and the other clerics burst in with Talin, their flushed faces showing they had been running. "What are you discussing?" Talin asked peremptorily.

The hunters looked away from the incompetent naval stripling who had lost the *Eagle* but Baranov answered him, calmly, with the truth.

"What right have you to decide such government matters?" asked Talin. "You are just a simple citizen. I order this meeting to disperse."

Baranov knew immediately that the priests and Talin had rushed in here because they had expected to find him talking of something else. He was on the track of the real intrigue, he surmised at once. Something was about to happen. He bowed ironically to Talin. "Very well, Excellency." He looked at his men. "You heard the order from this nobleman. What are you all doing here?"

The faces of Talin and the priests flushed at the roar of laughter from the men.

New Year's Day, the day following, Baranov took a glass of tea on the porch of his house in company with Podgasch and Richard. The fine weather continued. Suddenly, up from the beach came a crowd of shuffling Aleuts headed by Father Nektar in full vestments. Like an avenging monk of old he strode, like a fighting priest of Kiev leading an army against Tartars. Baranov's friends rose in dismay but he quietly told them to keep their seats.

"We have come to tell you," said Nektar when the crowd had reached the steps, "that next spring neither the Aleuts nor any other tribe will furnish men or canoes to hunt for you."

Baranov continued quietly to sip his tea. He understood now

why Father Nektar and Talin had been so disturbed the previous day—they feared he had had wind of this meeting and might prepare the hunters against it. He could discern several village elders in the crowd but addressed Nektar. "Do you not realize, archmonk, that the right to use these people is given us by law? Stop our activities and I assure you your actions will be brought to the government's attention as a charge of treason."

Nektar did not flinch. He knew that God is just and that His punishment would surely be inflicted on this man. Baranov singled out the St. Paul elder. "Have you lost your senses, grandfather? It is long between now and *cagáligim tugidá*, the Hunting Month, and before then your people will come to me for supplies many times. I assure you they will go hungry if you listen to this man's foolish words."

The elder looked sly. "A ship will come this year to pay us?"

Baranov almost smiled. It was at least partly the old trouble—payment on time. Nektar broke in harshly. "These people have made me their spokesman. They will stand no further oppression." His voice gathered fury. "And I will not rest until you are brought to justice for your murders and punished with at least fifty lashes!"

Baranov felt Podgasch's hand on his arm but he was too experienced in these crises to lose temper. He laughed. It was Nektar who lost his head. "Anyone setting the example you do," he said, his voice trembling with rage, "in keeping a woman and having children by her should be barred from the church and the sacraments."

"I know of no law sanctioned by the tsars to that effect."

"It is not the tsar's business but God's. Henceforth you will not walk behind the processional cross in God's house. If you so much as enter it I will stop mass until you leave." And Father Nektar signaled the Aleuts to disperse and stalked off.

The archmonk kept his promise. The following Sunday amid great tenseness on the part of the congregation, Baranov took his place as usual as secular leader behind the processional cross in the church toward the building of which he had given fifteen hundred rubles. When Nektar and his clerics walked out of the sanctuary carrying the holy books and saw him, they immediately turned back and closed the gates to the altar.

Baranov turned quietly to the congregation. "Go back to your quarters. There will be no services today."

Immediately, with a handful of hunters Baranov slipped out of St. Paul to descend on village after village to ascertain the full extent of Nektar's damage. It seemed considerable. In each place they found the elder fled at their approach and the Aleuts sitting in sullen rows and refusing to speak except to say, as if by rote, that they would furnish no more bidarka fleets.

For the first time Baranov felt uneasy. This firmness of decision did not square with the Aleut character. Had religion effected some deep and fundamental change in them?

They finally caught one elder before he could wriggle away. Frightened by Baranov's proximity he babbled out the whole story. Yes, the elders of Kodiak and Afognak Islands had been called together, on an occasion when the prevention of smallpox was preached and the Kenai hostages were present. Father Nektar had also made them all promise to stand firm against Baranov in the future. But after the archmonk had left the Kenaitzes had thickened the plot by proposing a simultaneous rising of all natives, on the islands and on Cook's Inlet and at Prince William Sound, to take place as soon as Baranov left again in spring for Sitka. All the Russian holdings were to be seized but the Russians were not to be killed—only cast adrift.

Baranov had the key at last to the mystery put forth by Molokhov that summer. As he retraced his steps back to St. Paul he took hostages from each of seven villages—it was years since hostages had been taken from the Aleuts—and when he got back to St. Paul, he also arrested the elder there. He confined them in the bunkhouses and then waited for someone to make the next move.

During Baranov's absence on this errand the storm in Anna Grigoryevna's soul had been beaten up anew. She had been persuaded to come to Father Nektar's house, and now they surrounded her, questioning her relentlessly. How long was she to continue setting this bad example? Was she going on forever denying Christ? "Is it the boy who keeps you back?" asked Father Herman, who dearly loved children.

Anna Grigoryevna had fallen to her knees. Head downcast, for a long time she could only nod or shake her head to each question. Finally she burst out wildly, begging them to let her alone. Yes, she wanted to know Christ, to be a Christian.

"Then it must be the boy holding you back," said Father Nektar. "If so, remember the word of God: 'If thine eye offend thee, pluck it out.' Do you know what that means, my child?"

But at that moment, just as Father Nektar felt he was about to deliver a soul white-hot into God's hands, one of the lay brothers burst into the room with the news that Baranov had rounded up seven village elders, including Elder Peredovchikov, and was holding them prisoners in the bunkhouse.

Nektar sprang to his feet and, followed by his clerics, ran from the room.

Anna Grigoryevna, left alone, rose from her knees and staggered from the house. *"If thine eye offend thee . . ."* She found her house deserted but for little Antipatr. She snatched him up and ran from the village toward the sea where rocky cliffs looked down into the harbor. Below them the surf ran at the base of the jagged volcanic rocks, swirling in angry white.

The boy screamed as he was thrown but nobody heard, for the surf pounded like thunder and overhead the wheeling gulls themselves screamed like children.

Baranov stood in the doorway to the bunkhouse facing the angry monks. The village, sensing trouble, crowded into the square. Baranov looked for Talin and was disappointed not to see him. The great naval officer was sticking close to his house, leaving it to the monks to battle alone.

Father Nektar summarily ordered Baranov to deliver up the

hostages, threatening to order out every Aleut on the island against him if he refused.

This was what Baranov wanted to hear. He told Father Nektar he was guilty of treason and ordered his hunters to surround the priests and confine them in the stockade.

The hunters moved to obey but in the scuffle the priests were allowed to escape, to run into the woods. "Let them go," said Baranov. "A night or two in the forest will not harm them."

Then two grave-faced Aleuts came up from the harbor, bearing an inert little form which they had found, they said, on the rocks when they were hunting seal. In panic Baranov looked at his son's pupils and felt for his weak pulse. Thank God! The boy was alive. Quickly, kind hands took the child to care for him and Baranov questioned the Aleuts. Had he fallen? Could he have fallen? Neither appeared likely. Where was Anna Grigoryevna? Pieces of her story came out from enough witnesses to make a pattern.

Grimly Baranov ordered the priests rounded up.

Days passed before that was done. Some had found sanctuary in various Aleut villages. Baranov ordered his hunters to bring them before him. He informed them bluntly that thenceforth they would keep their hands off the colony's secular affairs and confine themselves to their priestly functions or be placed under arrest. Father Nektar replied that no mass would be said as long as Baranov was present. Baranov, his patience at an end, ordered them all put into the stockade.

Easter, time of greatest rejoicing on the calendar, came and went without the comfort and color of religion to give it meaning. The priests stubbornly paced the stockade. Anna Grigoryevna had not reappeared.

But even had the priests chanted the most jubilant mass the pall of gloom hanging over the colony might not have been dissipated. Supplies had often been low but now they were nonexistent. Many had not tasted sugar or tea for a year and almost all wore fur or leather next his skin. This was 1801 and there had been no ship since 1798. Everyone felt there was little use in working further; why just pile up furs in a storehouse, when they bought no comforts? The Aleut strike was broken but no one planned a hunting fleet. There was nothing with which to pay them.

Suddenly, on May 6, the now unfamiliar cry of "A ship!" galvanized the colony. But when the telescopes revealed the fact that she was a Yankee, Baranov ordered the guns manned and the little brass cannon on the knoll were wheeled into position. As she tacked warily into the harbor, Baranov heard his name called with a strange accent and, peering through the telescope, recognized the handsome face of Joseph O'Cain, who had been first mate to Captain Moore on the original *Phoenix*. The *Enterprise* was from New York and now O'Cain was mate to Captain Ezekial Hubbel. Soon Baranov was aboard eating the first good meal he had tasted for years, while the Irishman told him of his adventures, through the invaluable Richard. After he and Moore had left the North, he said, he stayed in California for a time, got on the good side of the governor, was much attracted by a Spanish beauty, and thought of settling. But life was too slow, so he went back to the sea.

It turned out that O'Cain had an interest in the cargo of the *Enterprise*. Always on the lookout for ways to outwit his competitors, and having heard at Sitka that the Russian colony had not had a transport for years, he immediately thought of coming to trade his cargo to Baranov for furs. O'Cain had convinced Hubbel that the journey to Kodiak would be a wise gamble inasmuch as if they could persuade Baranov to sell them furs, they would arrive at Canton a full two months before their competitors, who would still all be trading on the Coast. He ticked off the items they had for sale: molasses, rum, sugar, flour, tobacco, canvas, guns. . . .

O'Cain's proposal posed a difficult problem for Baranov. This visit bore every evidence of the intervention of Providence, but he had no authority to trade with foreign ships and none whatever to make purchases in the Company's name. He could, of course, buy on his own responsibility and trust the Company to consider the circumstances, but he knew very well that some selfish share-holder in Irkutsk could easily ruin him for life by disclaiming the responsibility.

On the other hand it was now fairly certain the *Phoenix* was lost and if no other transport arrived this year his enemies could walk off with the place. Also he knew that if he did not buy the muskets, O'Cain would sell them to the Aleuts and the Kolosh, and this was no time to have armaments increased in those quarters. As for sending O'Cain off to Unalaska for Larionov's approval, he was not even sure Larionov was alive, and besides, that would mean weeks of delay for which he was sure these men would not stand.

Finally he offered two thousand prime red and silver foxskins for the entire cargo. O'Cain demanded sea otter instead. The legend has it that after a long wrangle they agreed to drink it out. If either O'Cain or Hubbel could hold more rum than Baranov, payment was to be in sea otter. If Baranov outdrank the two Americans he was to pay in fox. Richard was ordered to stay sober as a witness and judge of the contest.

Over the mess table the brass lamp swayed with the motion of the ship at anchor as they drank glass for glass and talked. Baranov was eager for news of the world. While O'Cain was still articulate Baranov learned that Napoleon had involved all Europe in war, including Russia. That explained why no ship had come from home for so long. O'Cain's next item disturbed Baranov profoundly. There was a rumor that a Spanish frigate was on its way to attack the Russian holdings. Spain was an ally of France, so Spain and Russia were at war! Baranov drank in all the information he could along with the rum.

When Baranov finally pushed his chair back and stood erect, Hubbel was lying peacefully unconscious under the table, and O'Cain was snoring loudly, his head down on an arm thrown across the table. Payment was to be in foxskins. Baranov had saved his precious sea otter for the Siberian trade.

He returned to his house, his mind busy with plans for hiding his furs against Spanish attack, if one came. The trade goods from the *Enterprise*, he knew, would quell the remnants of the Nektar uprising. When the last debt had been paid off to the Aleuts, the elders would send in their levy lists, quite as if nothing had happened. He could then turn his mind again to such matters as worry about the *Phoenix*, definite confirmation about the loss of which he had never received.

He decided to try a letter to Larionov, who might not have been on the *Phoenix*. ". . . Because the managers told me, in case I wanted to leave, to turn this end over to you, I had greatly hoped to see you here . . . But when I heard criticism and such scoffs as 'Don't rest on your laurels,' I began looking at the matter from a different light and to realize that I had no right to leave this enterprise managed by me so long as my strength holds out. . . ."

He stopped writing, feeling rather than seeing a movement behind him. He turned to face Anna Grigoryevna. She had discarded her shoes and was wearing strips of hide tied to her feet. Her dress was torn and stained. Her body was almost emaciated. Her eyes were brilliant as with fever. "My child?" she asked.

"Antipatr is alive," he assured her. "You are hungry? There is bread and molasses in the kitchen."

She nodded, turned from the room. Baranov continued to write his letter. ". . . for my leaving would be the signal for the immediate outbreak of all sorts of disorders caused by dissatisfied officials and prejudiced monks and missionaries who would at once proceed to carry out their wild fantasies and crackpot ideas."

15

"For Faithful Service in Hardship and Want"

YEAR passed to the spring of 1802, Baranov's most inactive year since coming to America, for he hardly stirred from Kodiak and sent Podgasch to make his inspections at St. Michael, Yakutat, and the other posts. He remained partly because he could not bear to be away in case news came from home, partly to keep a grim eye on St. Paul. The priests had been long since released from the stockade, and Talin still kept to his house and things were peaceful, if a sullen going about his business on everyone's part can be called peaceful; but he knew it would take only his leaving for things to explode violently and dangerously again.

The colony was in despair and want. In four years not one word had come from Russia and no supply ship other than the *Enterprise*. Men whose turn it had been years before to go home watched their children grow up to be eight and ten years of age and cursed. What could be happening at home, that they were all so forgotten? Was Europe being torn asunder?

In Baranov's house the same tension obtained. Anna Grigoryevna had returned to living with him but the conflict between her and the priests was not dead, he saw; she had come to yearn greatly for the color and beauty of the Russian faith. She bore a second child, a healthy, dark, fine-nostriled little girl whom they named Irina Aleksandrovna.

In desperation Baranov finally persuaded two Russian volunteers to try making Unalaska by canoe with his letter to Larionov to ascertain if he was alive. He was overjoyed in receiving an answer by the same route, though the loss of the *Phoenix*, somewhere west of Unalaska, was confirmed. "God sends us punishment in the kind of government officials we have," Larionov wrote in sympathy with Baranov's recital of his troubles. "They consider themselves above us because we are of the merchant class. They have often insulted my partners and me too . . . Do not fear to use harsh measures with them. They won't complain to higher authority. Their own misdeeds might come to light . . . You ask me for tea, sugar, and vodka? My dear friend, I have forgotten the taste of tea!"

By canoe finally came news from home. A ship had touched at Unalaska in so much trouble she could not proceed, but her news was so important that Larionov made the man who bore it go on to Kodiak by the frail craft.

Ivan Banner was a Dane and one of the foreigners who had entered Russian government service for the pay and remained because he liked the life. An honest but easygoing and characterless petty business administrator, he had for years been a provincial inspector at Irkutsk and bore the minor rank in the *tchinn* of titular councilor. When he was fed and rested from the ordeal of his journey, he told his news.

On the accession of Tsar Paul, a capricious and unstable ruler, said Banner, the merchants of Irkutsk had been stricken with panic, for Paul distrusted business combinations, revoked their freedoms, and threatened to have the Navy take over their American holdings. But in Petersburg a brilliant young man of noble blood who had married Shelekhov's youngest daughter rose to political power and by supremely clever handling of the mad tsar secured his signature on the charter of a great firm called the

Russian-American Company. At the merchants' darkest hour everything of which old Shelekhov had dreamed was realized. Every other trading firm in the Pacific was ordered to merge with the new or cease business. The North Pacific was acknowledged as Russian and the new Company would rule it after the manner in which the British East India Company controlled its holdings. The imperial family and other noted people held stock, but direction was to be in the hands of a board which would have headquarters in Petersburg, thenceforth, not Irkutsk, although the real power would remain in the hands of the old crowd—Natalya Shelekhova, Golikov, Rezanov. The charter had been signed three years before, in 1799. Since then Tsar Paul had been assassinated and Alexander I had become tsar, but on his accession Alexander had confirmed the charter in all particulars, and Rezanov was more powerful than ever.

But Baranov was not forgotten; far from it. He had been given a substantial share of stock in the new Company and appointed colonial governor, with jurisdiction as far as Kamchatka. Finally, there was conferred on him the Cross of St. Vladimir; ". . . for faithful services, in hardship and want, and for his unremitting loyalty . . ." read the patent signed by Tsar Alexander.

Finally, there was a message from Larionov. This Banner was an employee of the new Russian-American Company and the original plan was to have him found a post in the Bering; Larionov had sent him on in case Baranov did not wish to assume his honors and would consider turning his authority over to him.

Baranov was stunned. He told Banner he would have to think all this over.

Everyone at St. Paul who could crowded into the bunkhouse. Talin, drunk as usual, sat in the front row with the priests. No one seemed to know why the gathering had been called. Talin alone was confident of his guess. "It is all over now," he told Father Nektar. "Banner brings the news and Baranov knows what's going to happen to him."

But Nektar was very uneasy. The rumor was strong that the *Phoenix* had been lost and Bishop Iosaph with her.

Necks craned as Baranov entered, followed by the Danish official with papers in his hand. Banner faced the audience, raised his arm and cried, "Tsar Paul is dead! Long live His Imperial Majesty, Tsar Alexander Pavlovich!" The crowd reacted with shocked surprise. Outdoors the little cannon boomed, the flag was lowered to half-mast, then raised again. Now Banner unfolded the papers, read aloud the charter and bylaws of the new Company, and then announced Baranov's appointment as governor. Then he lifted the ribbon of the Cross of St. Vladimir and placed it around Baranov's neck, reading at the same time the patent of conferment.

The crowd listened, awed. When Banner at last lowered his papers there was a moment of silence, then the hunters leaped to their feet and cheered—and none cheered more loudly than the old hunters who had first come to America with Baranov and remained now at Kodiak because their hardships bade them rest awhile.

The little fair-haired Russian could not bear it. He lifted his hands to his eyes but could not conceal that he had burst into tears. When he could control his speech, and silence was restored, he said, "I will pray from the bottom of my heart for our great tsar who has rewarded me so well despite the fact that I deserve so little in view of all my sins . . . As a small token of my gratitude to all of you, I would like to give a thousand rubles toward the establishment of a school for the education of the Russian and Aleut children alike here at Kodiak. And"—some of the old quizzical smile returned—"I want you all to be my guests at tonight's *praznik*."

"The Almighty, in His infinite mercy, has overlooked and forgiven our sins," Governor Baranov wrote, when announcing his plans to his friend Larionov, over whom he was now commander. Banner would return to Unalaska by canoe, see to repairing his ship and bringing it back together with what men he had, after which Baranov would make him "northern commander" at Kodiak while he went on to Sitka for an inspection. But there was no hurry. Medvednikov reported the Kolosh at Sitka to be peaceful; Rodionov reported all quiet at Nuchek, and at Yakutat everyone had been faring well since Polomoshnoi's death. Meanwhile he would think about appointing Banner to more authority.

"Truly," he wrote, referring to O'Cain's warning that a Spanish frigate might attack them, "should such a terrible emergency arise it would take more than mortal eyes to find our furs. I have built a battery in a commanding spot, but big guns are scarce with us and we haven't even one of forty pounds caliber."

He signed the letter with a new flourish to his name.

16

The Massacre at Sitka

JUNE 20 at Fort St. Michael. The islands of Sitka Sound lay
like green wool on an indigo sea. Mount Edgecumbe raised
his hoary crest into a sky lazy with sunlit clouds. Two years
of weathering and the huge logs of the two-storied fort would have
seemed almost a part of the forest surrounding but for the large
space of earth packed hard with many feet sloping down to the
beach where lay the unfinished keel of a sloop. The devil's-club
and salmonberry flashed their colors among the hemlock and
spruce, and back of the fort's palisades the ferns grew like a
thicket.

Usually the scene was one of busy men and activity, for Commander Vassili Medvednikov had followed all winter Baranov's
strict injunction to keep his twenty-nine Russians and two hundred Aleuts occupied at hard work. But a few days before, nearly
all his Aleuts had set out in ninety bidarkas under Urbanov to
meet Kuskov, who was coming southward with four hundred and
fifty canoes to meet them for the summer's big drive on furs. Medvednikov had allowed this Sunday as a holiday for the twenty-six
Russians, twenty-odd Aleut men, and the eighteen Aleut women
remaining at Sitka. Gleefully the garrison prepared for a feast and
the best remaining marksmen put out in two baidars to bring in
fresh seal meat and wild geese. Erlevski, Baturin, and Vassili Kochessov, the last the best shot of them all, had already left, and now

the hunters Izokhtin, Kuzmichev, and Tarakanov settled themselves on their knees in their boat and followed them. Lebedev, who had been injured and was therefore on sentry duty, sat smoking his pipe on the second-story parapet, his musket across his knees. Ekaterina, the Chiniak girl who was his wife, and the other Aleut women did small tasks with much high laughter and talking, preparing for the meat the hunters would bring home when they returned some time around noon. Probably because so many men were away, everyone thought, the fort was unusually free of Kolosh women who hung about—notably the insolent one who wore on her ankles the wealth of copper rings Kuzmichev had given her.

Everyone was happy on a holiday. In the big downstairs room of the fort the windows were unbarred and open and there was a little desultory work. Some of the men, including a Boston sailor let out of the guardhouse, shredded rope for oakum. A circle of giggling Aleut girls plaited walrus hide with skillful fingers. On the forest side of the big room a cannon pointed its snout through the gunport. Along the walls hung several baskets in which amiable Russian-Aleut babies contentedly sucked pieces of dried salmon.

Upstairs several more men, including the commander, either slept or did small tasks lazily. Down by the outdoor kitchens a group talked with loud laughter, leaning easily on their muskets. Abrossim Plotnikov wandered toward the sheds where the cows were, banging a bucket on his canvas trousers. In the cove, Rushalov staked out some fish nets, wading over the pebbles with bare feet. In the guardhouse were five Yankee sailors who had deserted from a ship; they had been troublesome and Medvednikov had had to order them confined.

Suddenly everyone dropped what he was doing and listened. The cry came from a distance. "The Kolosh!" An instant of paralysis, then all those outdoors began to run for the fort. On the beach, Rushalov's feet tangled in the nets. A shot rang out and he fell headlong. Someone began pounding the iron ring used as an alarm. Up from the beach, the kitchens, the sheds, all ran for the fort. More shots rang out, more men fell. Plotnikov, running from the cowshed, turned back and plunged into the brush. Inside the fort the men downstairs were struggling to close the windows and bar them or were pulling back the cannon. There was no doubt the Kolosh were coming. They ran like panthers from the forest, shooting as they came, their faces painted in intricate totemic designs, some wearing hideous masks of the raven and wolf—gaping beaks and long teeth—and bore down out of hidden coves as if on signal in their long canoes. Quickly Ska-out-lelt showed himself the commanding officer. He mounted a knoll and directed the attackers as they deployed around the building. The windows dropped into place one by one, quickly, but not quickly enough, for the Kolosh were fast and managed to get their musket barrels into more than one and pull the triggers before they could be closed. More Kolosh came running with brands of burning pitch which they threw into the upper story. The answering fire they received was completely ineffectual; the Russians had been caught off guard.

Inside the upper story the men fought bravely, shooting down on the attackers and trying to throw the burning brands out as fast as they landed inside; but the inflammable material caught and the blaze of the whole upper story was soon such that everyone had to jump to certain death below. Downstairs Tumakayev and others worked like fiends over the cannon and fought hand to hand with the attackers coming through the windows. The trapdoor to the basement had been opened and the women tumbled down inside, but their screams came up nonetheless. The trapdoor to the upper story had long since been slammed shut by someone upstairs; a man ran up the staircase to pound at it with an ax. It opened, suddenly, to let a long tongue of flame down into the lower. The room filled with choking smoke.

On the cool earth in the basement the women lay and moaned or screamed with terror. Most had grabbed their babies when the shooting started and they lay over them, now, in an effort to protect them. Overhead they heard the stamp of running feet on the heavy timbers, shouts, firing, the rumble of the cannon's wheels as it was moved about. The cannon went off—the concussion blew open the door leading from the basement outdoors. The women screamed with terror, jumped up and ran blindly into the hands of painted demons who hustled them, arm to arm, and threw them in a heap with their babies on the sands of the beach. Everything was in flames—the storehouse, kitchens, palisade, the new keel. Smoke billowed from the roof of the fort. To her horror Ekaterina noted that the imprisoned Boston sailors had been liberated by the Kolosh and seemed to have joined in helping set everything afire. One by one the hunters jumped from the fort's upper story. The sentry Lebedev fell squarely on a spear. Old Nakvassim hung from the parapet by his hands, fell, picked himself up, and ran for the woods with four catlike Kolosh after him. He stumbled—immediately the Kolosh were on him and severed his head. Another man, cornered, tried to fight the knives and spears with his bare hands until a spear transfixed his throat and tore out his windpipe. Still another, his belly opened with a cutlass, tried to run holding onto his entrails; with a yell of glee a Kolosh rushed him and cut off his head. Hand-to-hand fighting took place in the lower story —successful, evidently, for the Kolosh began throwing out bales of furs piled there. The Boston sailors ran to help them.

The sound of distant firing reached Tarakanov and his two companions as they stalked a tribe of seal sleeping on a ledge. The fort lay behind them a good twenty minutes' paddling away. Hearing a shout they turned to see Vassili Kochessov, Erlevski, and Baturin paddling toward them like mad and pointing to the sky. In horror Tarakanov saw the column of ascending smoke, gave the order to turn about—but that which he saw made them change their minds and paddle for shore as hard as they could go. Ten long cedar canoes, each manned by half a score of masked and painted Kolosh, bore down on them swiftly, their viking prows cutting the water at many times the speed of the Russians.

Kochessov, Erlevski, and Baturin landed first and sprang nimbly up the rocks and managed to get away; but the Kolosh were on Tarakanov almost the moment he beached. Izokhtin tried to fire but fell with a spear in his ribs and Kuzmichev fell as a musket cracked. In thirty seconds the Kolosh had Tarakanov's hands tied and had thrown him, like a sack of meal, into a canoe and pushed off to join the massacre. By now the shouting and noise had died down and the fort was a roaring mass of flame. Ska-out-lelt directed that the heads of all the dead men be severed from their bodies and impaled on sticks; the bundles of stolen furs were being piled into canoes. A few men had escaped, but not many. The hands of the Aleut women prisoners were tied behind them with leather thongs and they, too, were thrown face down into the canoes. Their babies the Kolosh knocked on the heads with sticks to still their cries and threw them into the water. One by one the canoes began putting out for the north; they meant to surprise the party on Frederick Sound where the bidarka fleet under Urbanov was encamped to wait for Kuskov's fleet.

Night. Urbanov's encampment showed against the forest as a line of small white tents redly lit. Two hundred Aleuts lay sleeping on the sands. The fight was even shorter than at St. Michael. The Kolosh were upon them by the hundreds, devils from the uttermost pit, cutting, slashing, spearing, shooting. The Russians kneeled and fired futilely, the Aleuts with frightened cries ran straight into their enemies' hands. In an hour the beach was slimy with blood and the brotherhood of the totem—Awks and Chilkats, Hootsnahoos and Sitkans—grimly chopped off the heads to impale them on sticks stuck in the sands. Northward the handful of those who escaped paddled frantically to warn Kuskov not to approach.

All night the canoe in which Tarakanov lay face down traveled until before dawn it beached at a remote Kolosh village and he was tied to a tree. The warriors went to a creek to wash their bodies of blood and paint, and then gathered in one of the long houses to eat. A woman, filthy and lackluster of eye, apparently a slave, brought him some fish to eat. "Where are we?" he asked in Aleut and the Sitkan dialect but she only shook her head and shambled away. What would happen to him? Were they going to torture him to death or make him a slave?

Apparently they decided on the latter, for he was cut down and sent dog-trotting after a file of warriors to a distant village where he was put to work cleaning fish with other slaves. Like the old woman they were filthy and spiritless and did not even know where they were. Treatment was brutal in the extreme. Five days passed. Tarakanov saw some of the bundles of furs stolen from St. Michael appear in the village to be divided, and some of the Aleut women were brought in for slave work. One of them said that a Kolosh, more kindly than the rest, had told her that Kuskov's party had escaped.

Suddenly canoes began arriving before the village bringing Chilkats, Awks, and Sitkans, their faces gay with the paints of pleasure, their hair matted with goosedown, and with laughter their women showed the meat they had brought for the feast. And from one of the canoes Vassili Kochessov the twin and Erlevski were taken and tied to trees. Something was about to happen.

Tarakanov was confined in the slave pen until the sun was high in the sky. Then his hands were tied behind him and he was led to a cleared space before some ground marked off for the foundations of a new tribal house. Erlevski and Kochessov were still tied to the trees. The intent manner of the Kolosh crowding around indicated they were about to witness a torture.

The shaman stepped up to Erlevski and began by tearing out his fingernails, one by one, with clamshells. Erlevski, his muscles bulging under the leather thongs that held him, his black beard glistening with the sweat that ran from his face in rivers, cried again and again upon the mercy of Christ; but the Kolosh laughed and cut circles around the skin of his knees until the skin hung, like grotesque bloody stockings, about his ankles. Then they turned to do the same to Vassili Kochessov. Kochessov died, quickly and mercifully, for he was half-Aleut and that blood does not stand torture; but Erlevski lived to endure eight more hours of Kolosh ingenuity before they cut him down too, and threw his body with Kochessov's into the pits intended for the foundations of the new house, as the custom was.

Perhaps the blood lust of the Kolosh was satisfied for the day. Tarakanov was thrown back into the slave pen.

Captain John Ebbets on the *Alert* was rounding Sitka Island when he bespoke the *Unicorn* under British colors, knowing her to belong to the veteran Nor'wester, Captain Henry Barber. A day behind him was the *Caroline* of Boston, Captain William Sturgis. Ebbets knew the passage; he had been here twice before. His astonishment at finding only a blackened, deserted place where St. Michael had stood was exceeded only by Captain Barber's profanity at the evidence that there had been a massacre.

But they anchored, and that night the *Alert's* lookout reported cautious hails from on shore. A heavily armed crew put out in a small-boat and brought back the hunter Plotnikov, an aged Aleut, and an Aleut girl with a half-dead baby, who fell on food like starved animals. By signs, Plotnikov conveyed that it was eight days since they had eaten more than berries. At dawn they saw a figure swimming desperately toward the ship. It was Baturin, who had been among those out hunting. Like Plotnikov, he had lain hidden for a week in the brush. He had seen no other survivors. The Kolosh had captured Kochessov and Erlevski, he said, after a desperate hand-to-hand battle.

That afternoon, Ebbets, Plotnikov, and a fully armed crew rowed ashore. Nothing remained of the building but a mass of ashes, of any property but the half-melted barrel of a small cannon. Everywhere were drying heads impaled on sticks, their white teeth grinning through beards matted with dried blood. The decaying, headless bodies lay stripped of their clothing. They found one fair-skinned body which Plotnikov said was that of the Yankee allowed out of the guardhouse. Some of the sailors recognized him, saying he was off the *Jenny*.

They buried the dead where they lay and returned to the ship. The *Caroline* had come to anchor and now the Kolosh put out in canoes to trade from Sitka village as if nothing had happened.

Captain Ebbets called Barber and Sturgis to a conference, proposing joint action to force the Kolosh to deliver any survivors whom they held captive. Barber, who had reason to fear the Kolosh whom he and his men had robbed and murdered, instantly agreed. For his part, he said, he'd be delighted to see the devils blown to hell.

Captain William Sturgis of the *Caroline*, a tough, beetle-browed son of a Cape Cod shipmaster, had been on the Coast before as a foremast hand on the *Eliza* and cherished a belief that he understood the Red Man. Also he knew on which side his bread was buttered. He refused to have any part of it. The Sitkans, he said, were his customers, and besides he thought it likely that the Russians had got exactly what they deserved. So he was counted out, went back to his ship, and the other two continued their discussion.

The following day, Barber and Ebbets began to put their plan into action. A long canoe came alongside in which sat Ska-out-lelt, his nephew Kot-le-an, and several other natives, including a bold girl wearing many copper rings about her bare ankles whom Plotnikov recognized as the woman who had often come to sleep with Kuzmichev and who probably had told the Kolosh that many of the hunters were away and that the Russians were having a holiday. The moment they stepped aboard Barber's ship they were instantly seized, the chiefs put in irons, and the rest peremptorily ordered to return and tell their people that Ska-out-lelt and Kot-le-an would be hung at dawn if the survivors were not instantly forthcoming.

At dawn the beaches were lined with glowering Kolosh, but no move was made to deliver anyone. At noon Barber ordered Ska-out-lelt brought on deck and put astride the forward gun. A noose was dropped from the rigging around his neck. With yells several warriors ran for their canoes and pushed out to paddle furiously toward the *Unicorn*. A cannon boomed. When the smoke lifted a moment later the canoes were overturned and the men struggled in the water. Barber took the chief off the gun and gave them one more day. The display had its effect. Within several hours all the eighteen Aleut women were aboard the ship, including the wife of the sentry Lebedev. Plotnikov questioned them, then made Barber understand that at least one more Russian was being held. While the bickering went on, the Kolosh insisting they had no more prisoners, one of the subchiefs manacled with Ska-out-lelt succeeded in freeing himself and ran for the taffrail. There was a scuffle and the crew had the man down again. Instantly, Barber ordered him hanged.

He was put astride the forward gun, the noose dropped. When the gun was fired he dangled from the yardarm. Plotnikov then shouted to the Kolosh on shore saying that Ska-out-lelt would be next unless they brought out any surviving prisoners and all the furs they had seized.

That night Tarakanov and forty or fifty bales of skins were delivered to Captain Barber.

Ebbets and Barber prepared to part company. But what was to be done with the three Russians, the two Aleuts, and the eighteen women who had been rescued, and the furs which had been retrieved? When Barber offered to take them back to Kodiak and deliver them to Baranov, Ebbets praised him highly. But the British captain waved his words aside. It was but an act of Christian charity, he said.

17

Captain Barber Trades in Blood

THE somnolent peace of a warm July lay over the Aleutians. Baranov was making a leisurely inspection trip from village to native village in the *Olga*, still waiting for Banner to return from Unalaska, when the message came to him that there had been a terrible massacre at Sitka; a twenty-gun British ship with twenty-three survivors lay before St. Paul. He piled canvas on his sloop fast enough after that and soon scrambled aboard the *Unicorn* to welcome the survivors and hear their story first-hand.

But it was not so simple as that. Captain Barber, who had expressed such lofty human sentiments to Captain Ebbets, demanded fifty thousand rubles' worth of furs as ransom for the people aboard, saying that that must be the price of the time he had wasted at Sitka, and forbade Baranov to talk to the survivors.

Baranov, fighting for time to think, refused. He told Richard to say he had no authority to pay out such a sum, which was true. Barber gave Baranov two days to make up his mind; if he refused after that, he told Richard, he would not only sail away with the Sitka survivors pressed into his crew but he would blow St. Paul off the map. England and Russia were, he said, at war.

Perhaps something warned Baranov that this was a bluff. He believed his country and England at peace but no one ever knew for certain, so far from Europe. He demanded permission to talk to the survivors but this the Englishman continued to refuse. Baranov, shrewd and sharp even in the midst of the most terrible calamity, now felt certain that Barber was bluffing.

But he said nothing for the moment, returning ashore and turning aside from the wails of the village to go to his house and think over what he had been told.

In the morning, haggard and red-eyed from lack of sleep and hot with contempt for the Englishman, he again boarded the *Unicorn*. "Ten thousand rubles' in furs will be given on Mr. Baranov's own responsibility, no more," said Richard. "That is on condition you deliver up the survivors at once and whatever you have rescued in the way of property and get out of here immediately."

Barber laughed but Baranov was not to be beaten down. In fact he was ready to capture this Englishman himself and would have welcomed the slightest excuse to try it. It was Barber more than anyone else who had roused the Kolosh nation against all whites; for ten years he had been known as the most brutal and dishonest trader on the whole Northwest Coast.

"He will accept ten thousand," said Baranov to Richard, "or he will choose to have me make a full report of all this to St. Petersburg and prefer charges of piracy against him. Say I know he lies about war existing between our countries but that if he cares to contest it, I will gladly open fire from my batteries on the hill."

There was answering bluster from Barber but in the end he agreed, as well he might, for Baranov had said no more about the furs aboard saved from Sitka. When the ten thousands' worth was delivered he could indeed count it a profitable summer.

The *Unicorn* having sailed away, the village settled down to a week of sick anxiety, for there was no report as yet of the four hundred and fifty bidarkas under Kuskov and Urbanov, or the *Catherine* under Podgasch, or the garrison at Yakutat. Therefore when the *Catherine* was finally sighted escorting home from Yakutat all but one canoe of Kuskov's fleet, Father Nektar and his priests chanted a *Te Deum* mass at which all the village sang with full hearts the song of thanksgiving. But when the miserable remnant of Urbanov's fleet came in the rejoicing changed again to wailing. All that was left of those attacked at Frederick Bay were ten out of one hundred eighty—seven Aleuts and the three Russians, Urbanov, Karpov, and the Kochessov twin, Afanassii. Of the two hundred and fifty who had that spring been at Sitka, forty-two souls were alive. Dead and gone were the best shots, the bravest hunters, and Baranov's second-best lieutenant.

Kuskov was able to throw light on the events leading up to the massacre. When he left Nuchek with the fleet nothing unusual seemed afoot until he reached Yakutat, where the Kolosh kept a curious watch on his movements. Then an aged Sitkan warned him that the Hootsnahoo Kolosh, who were among the most critical of the Sitkans for tolerating the Russians' presence, had called tribal conferences along five hundred miles of coast. At the meeting the Sitka *kwan* was told that if it did not join in a plot to exterminate the white men along the coast, they, too, would be attacked. Ska-out-lelt, chief of the Sitkans, had therefore been forced to consent to the war, fearing deposition in favor of his nephew Kot-le-an if he did not, and the Kolosh women living with the Russians in the fort were instructed to keep their people informed about those days when the Russians would be most off their guard. Upon hearing this, the cautious Kuskov sent seven canoes on ahead to Sitka to reconnoiter while he held back his main fleet in a place they temporarily fortified. When six of the canoes returned to say the seventh had been captured and Sitka was in ashes, Kuskov had at once ordered the retreat to Yakutat, where he left reinforcements and extra ammunition before coming on back to base. Kuskov concluded his report by saying he believed it was unlikely Yakutat would be overpowered—knowing that what had happened at Sitka because of lax watchfulness had immeasurably strengthened discipline.

It was no use to ask who was to blame. One could go back and place his finger on each small cause, of course. The crimes of the Lebedevski to begin with. The first taste of Russian blood with the unavenged killings of Father Juvenal and Samoilov. The outrages of British traders against the Kolosh and the Kolosh tendency to lump all white men together as enemies to be revenged upon. The powder and shot sold by the Yankees. The Russians' refusal to sell them any powder and shot.

It was not necessary to decide who had begun it. There are two things that may be done when one is faced with a state of war. One is to run away, the other to accept battle. Baranov did not run away.

18

·····································

Honest Joe Gives a Hand

THE reconquest of Sitka became with Baranov an obsession beside which his earlier passion to build the *Phoenix* seemed a passing whim.

On the face of it it was the sheerest nonsense. He had virtually nothing with which to attack an enemy so formidable and so far from his base. His very powder and shot were running low. He had not the ships for transport. The Aleuts turned sullen and listless at his harangues and the Russians fingered their belts with embarrassment. "What's the use?" their shrugs indicated. They built at a cost incalculable in blood and sweat only to have it all swept away. Not a soul in St. Paul village but had lost a close friend or a relative. Why throw more good lives away? Everyone stubbornly settled down to village life with an air of meaning to stay at it. Hunters who in the past had disdained anything less masculine than hunting or getting drunk as a pastime began planting flowers around their cabins, the church services were crowded, and the school, where Father Herman was teaching, was attended as never before.

Baranov stayed closely within his house and drew plans. He made sketches of flotillas of rafts on which cannon were mounted and towed by canoes, then threw them away. He thought of building another *Phoenix* and abandoned that idea.

In September he was heartened by the return of Banner who

brought the news that his old ship would be repaired and sent on, and later by the arrival of the brig *Alexander* from Okhotsk with men, supplies, and a good skipper, Vassili Petrov. Then, on November 13, long after a vessel could with reason be expected, the galiot *Zachary and Elizabeth* cast anchor at St. Paul. Her navigators were First Lieutenant Nikolai Khvostov and Midshipman Gavril Davidov, both of His Imperial Majesty's Navy.

Baranov welcomed them eagerly to a banquet at his house, but had to nurse a disappointment. They could give him no help against Sitka. They had been commissioned by the new Company only to go to Kodiak, get the furs that had not been shipped home in five years, and return with them in spring.

But the officers brought a great deal of news, some of which gave Baranov much hope. The Napoleonic upheaval in Europe had come to an end with the Peace of Amiens. Many of the Russian naval men had seen service with the British, said Khvostov, and the taste of excitement thus given had decided him and Davidov to take the offer of service in the Russian-American Company's colonies for full wartime pay without loss of rank. Probably many others would follow their example.

However, the officers continued, the Russian-American Company seemed about to send more than just officers. When they left St. Petersburg two English frigates of the finest type had just been purchased and were going to make a good-will trip around the world, after which they would be in colonial service. Baranov could expect to see them in a year or two. Definite expansion of the previously nonexistent Russian merchant marine was being planned to carry on the Company's colonial policy.

And gone was the old indifference of Petersburg to what went on in the Pacific. The policy emanating from the Imperial Palace was now one of definite competition with England on the seas. Tsar Alexander I was an enlightened man of democratic leanings, utterly different from any ruler that Russia had ever had. His ministers were young men, trained in the French tradition. The minister of commerce was Count Rumiantsov, who opposed the

English. He had taken the Russian-American Company under his immediate supervision and scanned its plans with great interest.

Throughout this recital the name of Nikolai Rezanov occurred again and again. He it was who had married Shelekhov's youngest daughter. Now he was procurator of the Senate and deep in the affairs of the new Privy Council. It was he who had designed the Company's charter and had maneuvered its signing by mad Tsar Paul. He had continued in power when Alexander had become tsar and had pushed the Company to its present high place in favor.

The documents brought by the officers carried out this impression of circumstance: "The General Administration of the Russian-American Company under Highest Protection: Secret Orders to Aleksandr Baranov, governor in America . . . With regard to the pretensions of England . . . advance . . . so we may force the British Government to some settlement of the international boundary . . . To do this you will be given enough men. Should you, however, encounter trouble, simply insist on Russia's claims, but pretend you have no authority to treat the question and that it must be referred to His Imperial Majesty. . . From the copies of Vancouver's and Puget's *Voyages* we send you you can see they pay you great honor. . . ."

Baranov now abandoned all thought of putting Banner in command. Bluff, good-natured Banner would never recapture Sitka.

Midshipman Davidov has left us an interesting picture of the Baranov of this time:

"He (Baranov) is below average size, flaxen-haired, and thin. His face habitually wears an ingenuous expression which apparently has not been affected by either hardships or age, for he is already in his fifty-sixth year. He is reticent with strangers yet will argue with great warmth when he is interested . . . He has lived for years among savage tribes, surrounded by continual danger, struggling against the innate depravity of the kind of Russian sent to this country, suffering endless privations and hardships—even hunger—unable to depend on a single man for the furtherance of his plans . . . I have the feeling he would, in time, have found some means of establishing this huge enterprise all by himself, if he had been forced to . . . He makes few acquaintances but stands firmly by his friends . . . Complete disinterestedness is probably his chief characteristic. He is not eager to become wealthy and sends his gains to absent acquaintances in want. . . ."

Baranov, on his part, passed the winter impatiently counting the days until spring and drawing his plans, most of which he still threw away. He was strongly advised to wait for the two frigates on the way but that was not in his character. He had lost Sitka himself and wanted to regain it before the gold braid and rank arrived in America.

Spring came at last and he felt he had a plan—a weak one but the best with the materials at hand. It consisted of sending everything he had to Yakutat as a base and operating against Sitka from there.

But he dared say nothing about it. The two naval officers were getting ready to leave with the *Zachary*. Kuskov was heartsick with all the bloodshed and strife of the past few years and disappointed at having received no notification of raise of status or pay from the new Company. He was determined to leave, too, especially as he did not agree with Baranov's determination to attack Sitka with the means at hand and felt it was sending the rest of their brave force to futile death. To make matters worse, Banner also wanted to go back to Russia.

Baranov was frantic. Kuskov and Banner were his only literate lieutenants. He succeeded in persuading them to remain only by giving them some of his own shares in the new firm—to Kuskov he gave one-and-a-half shares, or a tenth of his own salary raise.

Baranov set his plan in motion the moment the *Zachary* was gone, but saying merely that he intended strengthening Yakutat. He dispatched Kuskov with the bidarka fleet, Vassili Petrov in the *Alexander*, and Podgasch in the *Catherine*, then followed himself in the *Olga*, leaving Banner in command at Kodiak.

The garrison at Yakutat fell to its knees when he landed, begging to be allowed to leave and declaring they were unable to endure, day and night, the threat of a fate similar to Sitka's; but he refused to consider abandoning the place. Instead, he set most of the men to work strengthening defenses, put Kuskov out with most of the fleet cautiously to hunt otter, and then set everyone aghast by announcing his intention of going himself in the *Olga* with only Richard to survey the damage at Sitka.

When he arrived there not a living thing moved in the square where Fort St. Michael had once stood. Here and there rotting stakes marked the places where Captain Ebbets had buried the dead, but soon they would be hidden by the lush grasses and ferns that were already overgrowing the charred beams. From a distance only the remains of a keel at water's edge and the half-burned shipway indicated that once a settlement had stood there.

The sight enraged Baranov. Wanting to reconnoiter the stronghold of the Sitkans, he cruised the sloop southward of the island to have a look at the high knoll, the *kekur*, which he had once fancied as the best site for a fort and atop which the Kolosh had their own log bastions. He convinced himself that the place could be rushed by a surprise attack with the men and means at his disposal, and he started back with that determination in mind.

On the way back to Yakutat he encountered part of the bidarka fleet and by it sent orders for all canoes to meet at a certain small inlet. Going on, he sighted the *Catherine* and went aboard to meet Kuskov and give him the same peremptory order.

A violent scene ensued, with Kuskov pointing out the obvious madness of such an expedition and Baranov swearing he would wait no longer. But Kuskov finally won his point by showing that if another failure were sustained, Russian prestige among the natives would sustain a blow from which it might well never recover. Kuskov for the past two years had been closer by far than Baranov to the mainland folk, and his opinion had to be respected.

They simply had not enough ships, and worse, not enough armament for what they had. Baranov had to bridle his impatience and content himself with ordering the whole fleet to remain at Yakutat that winter to build two sloops, under Kuskov's and Petrov's direction.

It was October 26 when the *Olga*, as usual putting in well after the dangerous gales had started, came in to St. Paul Harbor to see at anchor a brand new schooner named *O'Cain* and flying the American flag. It was like Honest Joe to name his first vessel after himself. When Baranov was seated before the tasty meal of bread, beans, and beef, washed down with New England rum, O'Cain regaled him with the saga of his recent deeds. He had made a partnership deal with the Winship family of Brighton, Massachusetts, various sons, uncles, and cousins of which were in the China trade. Old Jonathan Winship, who had made his fortune supplying beef to the American Revolutionary Army, had listened to his plan to load a vessel specifically for Baranov's needs, and here they were, with Jonathan Winship, Jr., himself as first mate under O'Cain. Baranov shook hands with a keen-eyed, intelligent young Yankee who could not have been much more than twenty on his first voyage with authority, and enjoying every minute of it.

Baranov went over the manifests with a sinking heart. For thirteen thousand dollars O'Cain offered not only rum, sugar, tobacco, cloth, knives, bolts, nails, molasses, and many other articles, but a fine collection of good Yankee firearms, powder, shot, and even some pieces of heavier artillery. Here were the means of taking Sitka—but Baranov had not the furs with which to buy them. They had done too little hunting the past two years.

There was nothing to do but tell O'Cain the truth. The Irishman, of course, was taken considerably aback. It appeared that he had come with the intention of selling Baranov far more than one cargo of goods. He had meant to propose nothing less than a trade alliance. The Winships planned an invasion of the Northwest trade and were buying two more vessels to go into it. They meant also to engage in selling sandalwood at Canton for King Kamehameha. O'Cain had always remembered his first meeting with Baranov aboard Hugh Moore's *Phoenix*, when the Russian had told of the necessity of taking their furs halfway across Asia to Irkutsk before they could sell them to the Chinese. If the Winship bottoms would guarantee to bring the Russians supplies, why could not Baranov give them commissions to sell his furs under the American flag directly at Canton? And O'Cain meant in time to tie Baranov in with trade at the Sandwich Islands, too, and with the California missions. The king knew all about the destruction of Sitka, O'Cain told Baranov, and he was greatly concerned; through O'Cain he had sent a message asking if there was any assistance he could give.

To find Baranov unable to pay, however, was a problem which O'Cain had not foreseen. Extending credit was out of the question; the years between voyages were too long and expenses too heavy. But the ever-resourceful Irishman soon saw a way to accomplish both his object and Baranov's. He proposed that Baranov give him fifty or sixty Aleuts in canoes to go along the California coast to hunt sea otter. They would go halves on the catch and Baranov could use his half to purchase the cargo.

At first Baranov refused point-blank. He was not selling his Aleuts to another. But O'Cain warmed to his idea, which was undeniably practical, though hinting at a form of slavery. He promised to see that the Aleuts were cared for and that they were fed. He wanted that agreement with Baranov, he insisted—there was also his brother-in-law, Captain Oliver Kimball, anxious to come in with them on further deals. Baranov, who wanted this cargo more than anything he knew of at the moment, at length consented—on certain conditions. O'Cain could have half the otter catch, the Company must have the rest. The Aleuts had to be paid, two dollars fifty Spanish for each full-grown otterskin. If anyone was hurt, two hundred and fifty dollars must be paid his family. The present cargo must be left at St. Paul as security. A Russian overseer had to go with the Aleuts and alone be allowed to give them orders. That overseer must be allowed to take notes freely and observe everywhere they touched.

So it was agreed, and Baranov, O'Cain, and young Winship shook hands on the deal.

19

Sitka Is Retaken

THE *O'Cain* returned from California on March 12, 1804, with the Aleuts safe and sound and a thousand skins for the Company's share, representing a gross profit of approximately eighty thousand dollars Spanish. Baranov was able to take possession of the supplies he needed so badly, but he was more hesitant about committing himself to any permanent agreement with the Winships. Shvedzov, the overseer sent to guard the Aleuts, had watched the Irishman very closely during all tradings with the missions and he was certain O'Cain had not reported all profits correctly. O'Cain and young Winship took their departures with the promise to send another vessel in not less than a year's time, and O'Cain said he would endeavor to interest capable men to enter Baranov's service.

The schooner left behind most of her armament, which Baranov immediately ordered installed on the *Catherine* and *Alexander*, and thereupon he turned his whole attention to the storming of Sitka. The stern word went out to every Aleut village to levy all the able canoe men, except those absolutely needed at home to provide food, and to send them without delay to St. Paul.

Among other items of news, Shvedzov told him he had heard at San Quintin in California that the Madrid government had written to all provincial authorities instructing them to receive hospitably two Russian frigates on a round-the-world tour if they landed in California. This sounded like confirmation of Khvostov's story and again he was tempted to wait. But he did not.

On April 4, a fortnight before he left for Yakutat with his newly armed vessels and the bidarka fleet, a baidar came sailing in from Unalaska with a story now grown wearisomely familiar and a dispatch case. "Our ship has been wrecked but here are your letters." The letters yielded a paper he had never dreamed he could ever possess.

"Know ye all," said the patent of the Imperial Government, "we do confer upon said Aleksandr Andrevich the rank in Civil Service of Collegiate Councilor. . . ."

Collegiate Councilor! In life, in political preferment, in social standing, he would henceforth be equal in rank to a colonel of the army, a captain-lieutenant in the navy, an abbot in the Church! Worthy of being addressed as "Excellency"—the little man who had never been anything but a merchant of the second grade, not even a member of the Guild of Kargopol except by courtesy! The document was signed by the emperor himself, "Alexander I."

Baranov wrote two letters. Taken together they are a poignant revelation of his character.

To the tsar he wrote: "Born of a humble merchant family and limited to nature alone for my education, without any of the scientific training men of standing and character know, I never flattered myself I would receive the distinction Your Imperial Majesty has bestowed on me. But since that is the pleasure of your powerful right hand, allow me to take the liberty of throwing myself at your feet and thanking you from the bottom of my heart for such condescension. . . ."

To the directors of his company, he wrote: "I am now a nobleman, but Sitka is destroyed. I cannot live under the burden, so I am going forth either to restore the possessions of my august benefactor or to die in the attempt!"

On April 16, Baranov took leave of Anna Grigoryevna, the seven-year-old Antipatr, and the two-year-old Irina, gave Banner his last-minute orders to send the half-legendary frigates to his help if they showed up, and set out with the *Catherine* under Podgasch, the *Alexander* under Petrov, and three hundred bidarkas under Demianenkov for Nuchek, where another bidarka fleet waited for them. Continuing to Yakutat, Baranov found to his great satisfaction that Kuskov had indeed almost finished two crude but serviceable vessels, the *Yermak* and the *Rotislav*. Everyone pitched in to finish them and Baranov calculated he would have their guns installed by about September 1.

So it was still another summer, ax in hand. But at night he tried his hand at composing a song. The martial mood was on him. He called it "The Spirit of Russian Hunters," though his men came to refer to it simply as *"Pyesnya Baranova"*—"Baranov's Song."

By September's beginning he had finished arming the vessels with the cannon that had once done duty against the British in the American Revolution and had also worked out his tactics. The larger vessels would go on ahead to Sitka and the bidarka fleet, convoyed by the two new vessels, would gather at Cross Sound which, because it was usually shrouded by fogs, they thought offered a good rendezvous.

On September 6, he called on the four hundred men gathered at Yakutat to kneel on the beach to pray for their success. The flag was raised and Baranov called for "my song." His hand beat slow time as his little navy sang:

> The will of our hunters, the spirit of trade,
> On these far shores a new Muscovy made,
> In bleakness and hardship finding new wealth
> For Fatherland and Tsardom.

> Sukharev's towers old Moscow adorn,
> The bells ring at evening, the guns boom at morn;
> But far off's this glory of Ivan the Great—
> We have naught but our own bravery.

> Our Father Almighty we pray for thine aid
> That Muscovite arms may here be obeyed,

That we may dwell in amity and peace
Forever in this region. . . .

The *Catherine* and the *Alexander* put out, the *Rotislav* convoyed
out of Yakutat Bay the advance of the bidarka fleet, and Baranov
led the second convoy of canoes on the *Yermak*. A third party of
canoes was to follow under Kuskov, who remained behind to attend to certain details left undone.

Baranov arrived at Cross Sound the following morning, the 7th,
and found that the fogs obscuring the place were the only point in
the place's favor. Through that rocky pass high tide runs like a
millrace and at low the waters fall to within five feet of the jagged
bottom. And, because of the high walls cutting the wind off unless it blows from the sea, little tacking can be done. The *Yermak*
was almost immediately sucked in by the race and the men labored
hours to keep her off the rocky walls. It took a day for Baranov,
his voice hoarse from shouting, to get his brood quietly at anchor;
they had already lost one bidarka.

But the respite was brief. The wind whipped up, the deep water
offered no anchorage. They spent three days trying to get out.
Baranov seemed destined to fail before even reaching Sitka. He
solved the problem by deciding to escape by the intricate interior
waterways, a thing never before attempted by a sailing vessel.

It was a foolhardy decision; the tide rips through most of the
passages of the archipelago as it does through Cross. By some
miracle Baranov got his unwieldy craft through the Lynn Canal
and into Chatham Strait, where he anchored boldly before a native
village he saw and trained his guns on the chief's house. He then
told his Aleuts to gather all the otter they wanted and himself
went ashore with a strong guard. The inhabitants fled, but a
straggler or two was caught and told that Nanuk had come back
and wanted all the Kolosh at Sitka for a talk when he got there.

He reached Sitka Sound without mishap, and there received a
surprise. His *Catherine* was there, the *Alexander*, and the *Rotislav*,
together with the enormous bidarka fleet camped ashore. But that
which made his four vessels look like fishing smacks—and not very

well built ones at that—was the presence in their midst of a magnificent 450-ton frigate flying the Russian flag named the *Neva*.

Baranov at once went aboard to be called "Excellency" for the first time by someone of rank and to meet Captain-Lieutenant Lisianski, a quiet, competent Russian seadog who had been trained in the British Navy.

It was quite true about the two frigates sent carrying the Russian eagles around the world for the first time, Urey Lisianski told him. The *Neva* and her sister frigate had left St. Petersburg the previous year, carrying an ambassadorial suite headed by His High Excellency, Imperial Chamberlain Nikolai Rezanov; the original intention was for the two vessels to go together to Japan, whither Rezanov had been commissioned to treat for the opening of the ports of that hermit kingdom. When they touched at Hawaii, however, and Rezanov heard from King Kamehameha of the destruction of St. Michael, he instructed Lisianski to take the *Neva* at once to Baranov's aid and had gone on in the one ship to Japan. So here they were, ready to give assistance, said Lisianski. Rezanov would probably come to visit Russian America as soon as his Japanese ambassadorial mission was finished.

Formalities finished, Baranov discussed strategy with Lisianski. He wished to try a parley first. Too much blood had been spilled already, he thought. In the meantime, would Lisianski care to inspect his force?

Lisianski was indeed curious to inspect Baranov's force, and the two went ashore. For more than three hundred yards the beach was covered with canoes. Everywhere sentries sat on stumps and fallen trees, scanning the forests and the sea, heavy Moscow muskets in laps. Hundreds of little tents had been pitched, knots of men hung clothes to dry by the fires, or lay in the sands to snatch a few hours sleep, or cut wood or tended the cooking kettles. Always Baranov was greeted familiarly by his first name but there was perfect discipline.

Baranov pointed out to Lisianski the position they had to attack if the parley failed—the Sitkan settlement alongside the high hill, or kekur. Lisianski counseled moving the frigate close to it; accordingly the next morning a hundred bidarkas fastened their seal-gut strings to the frigate's heavy cable and began the all-day job of towing her until by evening she was right under the kekur.

Meanwhile, Honest Joe O'Cain put in with his vessel and opined that because he was Yankee the Kolosh would not hold what was going on against him, that they would trade with him just the same. He had himself rowed ashore but was met with a withering fire which sank his small-boat and narrowly missed killing him. Lisianski had hurriedly to send a launch full of armed sailors to his assistance. A bullet had passed through the collar of Honest Joe's coat; he lost no time in beating out of the neighborhood for less troubled regions.

Chief Kot-le-an, Ska-out-lelt's nephew, came by in a long canoe to demand the reason for the frigate's nearness. Baranov told him he wished to parley but demanded hostages. Kot-le-an said he would give no hostages unless the Russians gave an equal number, which Baranov bluntly refused to do, saying he distrusted Kot-le-an. As the chief, in a rage at this insult, pulled away, one of the *Neva*'s smaller cannon sent a shot whistling above his head.

The Sitkans deserted their settlement and moved further up the Sound to a place at a river's mouth where they had a strong, wooden fort shrewdly placed on a bluff just out of range of white men's cannons.

Baranov went ashore to take command of the abandoned place. He mounted the deserted kekur, planted the flag, and called the place New Archangel.

The rest of the day was spent by sweating men getting timbers to the top of the knoll and a few cannon. As this work went on, Lisianski from the *Neva* saw some Kolosh canoes sneaking along shore. The *Neva*'s guns roared and sent the canoes to the bottom. That evening an envoy came with a proposal for the parley. Baranov consented but stipulated that the chiefs from every village in the archipelago must be present to hear an important announcement.

The parley was held on the slopes of the kekur, under the guns above. Sixty glowering savages faced Baranov. All were ominously silent, unfriendly, every detail of their facial designs, armor, and shields showing their warlike intentions. As what Baranov told them through the interpreter penetrated their understanding their faces grew even darker. He told them that every Aleut slave in their possession must be delivered up, and that every person of Kolosh blood must at once leave Sitka Island and never again set foot upon it except when requested.

Kot-le-an stepped forward. "Since the Kolosh nation first was," he cried, "this has been the home of the Sitka kwan. Our totems are here and our spirits. What you ask is impossible."

"Once we asked only to live at peace with you," answered Baranov. "We lived in one narrow place and asked for no more. We did you no harm. We always paid for what you brought us and we never gave you the firewater that drives men mad, as the British did. But you chose to live in war and I no longer trust you. Those are my terms. Evacuate your fort up the sound and get off the island, or we will blow you all into the sea. Tell Ska-out-lelt to give me his answer not later than tomorrow morning."

"We will deliver up the Aleut slaves and we will let you build a new fort," was the answer. "Many Kolosh disagreed with the policy of warring with you and we all now agree with them. But we will agree to no other condition."

"Then," said Baranov with finality, "we will drive you from this place."

At dawn of October 1 some of the *Neva's* guns were transferred to the *Catherine*, the command of which was taken by Lieutenant Arbusov, and she, with the three other Baranov boats, moved to a point below the Kolosh stronghold. It stood high on the bluff above them, a breastwork six or seven feet high and two logs in thickness with brushwood piled around it. The snouts of two small cannon, probably sold the Kolosh by some trader, thrust out their threats but evidently they could not be lowered to fire down on the attacking flotilla. Lieutenant Arbusov opened his battery's fire, but after a few hours of futile pounding at the logs and brushwood Arbusov told Baranov the place had to be stormed.

So it was agreed that two parties should attack, one on each side of the bluff, each party comprising one hundred and fifty men and a couple of light fieldpieces. Baranov would command one and Arbusov the other.

They got ashore without mishap but the undergrowth was dense and wet, progress up the hillside with the fieldpieces slow, and the two parties lost sight of each other. It was late afternoon when Baranov's men succeeded in getting the cannon even halfway up the hill toward the ominously silent fort.

The order went down the line and at hand's drop everyone began running uphill for the fort. But the enemy's silence had not come from timidity. The Kolosh yells suddenly sounded and a withering fire from a surprising number of guns met them from above. As usual the Aleuts dropped everything and ran back down the hillside to the beach, leaving Baranov with a handful of Russians and the little cannon. "Retreat!" he yelled. The Kolosh saw them scramble down and jumped over the parapets after them. A bullet caught Baranov in the arm. He fell. Someone pulled him to the beach. Arbusov's party, too, came tumbling down in ignominious retreat. Fortunately a fusillade from the ships covered them and they as well as the Kolosh retreated to safety.

As Doctor Nordhorst, the *Neva*'s surgeon, extracted the lead slug from his arm, Baranov acknowledged that his charge, which had cost ten in dead and twenty-six in wounded, had been badly executed, and asked Lisianski to take command.

Lisianski had the *Neva* towed alongside the other ships under the fort and, aiming high, pounded the enemy all morning. In early afternoon a white flag went up and the Kolosh sent a messenger to say that they promised to free all Aleuts and to give nothing but sons and daughters of chiefs as hostages if the Sitka kwan could remain on the island.

When Baranov refused to give in, Lisianski again opened siege and this time the Kolosh promised to leave at high tide, at noon, the following day.

High tide came but no movement. Lisianski mounted some of his guns on a heavy log raft which he moved still nearer the fort and the battering again began. The logs could finally be seen cracking under the terrific pounding. Near nightfall an old man was seen at water's edge with a white flag; in a canoe he brought several Kolosh children as hostages, but Baranov's answer was the same. Evacuate at once or the place would be blown up. The old man promised, if successful in persuading his people to leave, to let the Russians know they were going by a peculiar cry.

About nine that night the cry was heard—three times a high-pitched ululation. The artillery ceased firing.

About midnight there floated down from the fort a strange wailing song. A heavy drum began to beat a slow rhythm and one by one other distant voices took up the song until the Russians felt their scalps prickle with the ominous, unintelligible message being conveyed by the dirgelike hymn. The moment it began, several of the Kolosh children on deck fell into attitudes of prayer. The song would rise and fall, mounting to a queer crescendo of sorrow then falling again almost to silence when it would once more be lifted by the voice of the shaman who phrased it. "They express their relief they are no longer in danger," was all the explanation the hostages would give.

The song continued all night, not ceasing until an hour before dawn. When the sun lit the summits of Mount Verstovia and Mount Edgecumbe, no living thing could be seen ashore but a few vultures wheeling in the sky. The Russians hailed the fort but got no answer. Cautiously a boatload of fully armed men went to investigate. An hour later they returned with a story so incredibly horrible that few believed it until they saw the inside of the former Kolosh stronghold for themselves.

Within the fortress lay the murdered bodies of many children of Sitka kwan. The weird chant of the night before had apparently attended some gruesome ceremony of defeat and surrender no Russian or Aleut knew of or could explain. Perhaps the children had been killed to aid their elders' flight. In any event the elders were nowhere to be seen. They had taken their canoes in the night and fled, no one knew whither.

Having buried the bodies, Baranov took possession of Sitka Island.

20

Eyes on Hawaii

THAT winter following the recapture of Sitka was perhaps
the worst in the history of Baranov's stay in America. The
Sitka kwan had been driven from its home but remained far
from cowed; the whole Kolosh confederation from Yakutat to the
Queen Charlottes beat the council drums and planned revenge.
Only because Captain Lisianski kept the *Neva* at anchor in the
neighborhood and her guns constantly ready were they able to
survive at all. Kolosh always lurked in the woods, picking off the
Russians and Aleuts whenever they stirred out after fish or game.
More than half the garrison had to be always on guard. Baranov at
all times wore a shirt of chain mail under his regular clothing, but
that did not prevent his getting shot in the hand. They could build
no adequate shelter and he lived in a temporary hut through the
bark roof of which the rain sluiced down on his bed and aroused
his long latent arthritis. Supplies from Kodiak were so meager,
hunting so difficult, that scurvy and even starvation faced them.
They took a desperate chance and sent the sloop *Yermak* to King
Kamehameha at Hawaii to beg for food; they hardly expected the
unwieldy, home-built craft to make such a voyage at that season
but she did, and returned with the king's gifts of preserved pork
and taro which saved their lives.

Spring relieved them of their discomforts and brought the presence of trading shipmasters, which helped keep the Kolosh away,

so they were able to build better shelters and a fort; and in August, 1805, Nikolai Rezanov arrived with his manservant, his personal physician, and two naval officers in attendance.

Rezanov was at first irritable and critical. His diplomatic mission to open Japan's long-closed ports had ended in complete failure; so had another mission to open China to Russian ships, not conducted by him but nevertheless his plan. He had seen the colonies as he traveled the length of the Aleutians from Siberia; he had visited Unalaska and listened to the priests at Kodiak.

Baranov knew perfectly well that this man who had designed the Russian-American Company had come to America to reform the administration and in all probability to replace him. He awaited the man's coming with impatience; he would be glad to go, as he had told Kuskov. He was finished. Jonathan Winship had told him he would take him wherever he wished and had invited him to visit Boston. He burned with curiosity to see it. And he was glad of Rezanov's coming at this precise time, for a perverse reason; if the tsar's own inspector could not see things at their best, he might as well see them at their worst. And so it was with grim satisfaction that he welcomed the man who had been one of Shelekhov's sons-in-law but now was chamberlain to the Court, and conducted him to a hut with a leaky roof—the best dwelling, he explained, they could offer.

Rezanov was tall, handsome, of commanding military presence, of noble blood and exceptional intelligence. Ordinarily he was disposed to be agreeable and charming but the failure of his Japanese mission and his long months at sea had almost ruined his health. Then, as he inspected Russian America, shock and disillusionment were added to his unease of body. He had always thought of the country in the light of what Shelekhov had told him. He left at Kodiak the fine books and paintings he had brought to found his academy of learning in America, and came on to Sitka prepared to dismiss Baranov summarily.

But Baranov neither quailed nor stood cap in hand before Rezanov's titles, power, and ignorance of Russian America. The day when that would have been his attitude had long since passed—not because he at last had a measure of rank, however low compared to Rezanov's, but because there comes a time when suffering and hardships lend a man a dignity that no social or political distinctions can affront.

Fortunately, Rezanov was a just man. It was almost enough to affect a complete revulsion of feeling within him to see the people who should have been Baranov's able assistants, but were not. Already, on Kodiak, far from sympathizing with the priests' stories to him, he had upbraided them for their disinclination to understand, their failure in many cases even to learn the native languages, and compared them bitterly to the more efficient Jesuit missionaries. Now he perceived the utter fecklessness of four new naval cadets ostensibly under Baranov's orders; one of them had drunk himself so far into debt that he could not be discharged. He saw them insult Baranov and heard their threats to have Kuskov beaten because he did not issue supplies in the manner they wished. Rezanov had greatly loved the daughter of Shelekhov, his wife who had died before he set out on this journey, but now, when Baranov told him the truth of everything, he cursed the memory of the old merchant for the lying intriguer he had been. And Rezanov was able to fit the last pieces into many a puzzle in Baranov's mind —the full story, for instance, behind sending the priests and serfs to America, eleven years before.

"We all live poorly at New Archangel, but worst of all lives the founder of the colony," Rezanov wrote the directors in a letter for transmittal by the *Neva*, which was leaving for Petersburg with furs. ". . . I tell you, gentlemen, he is truly an extraordinary person and a most original character. His name is famed the length of the Pacific. The Bostonians esteem and respect him, and savage tribes, in dread of him, offer him friendship from the most distant places . . . Had Baranov given up New Archangel as lost after its destruction and not returned here, the value of the Company's stock would not be where it is, but down to two hundred and eighty rubles. The employees who received a half share, or one hundred and forty rubles, would thus have had nothing, as their expenses for food and drink now exceed one hundred and forty rubles yearly. . . .

"While he is overwhelmed with praise by foreign nations he has to drink the bitter cup of disappointment at home . . . The directors should, in a body, approach the Throne and ask for new honors for him, or at least protect him from further slander . . . (For Kuskov) I ask at least the rank of Collegiate Assessor, to protect him, if not from insult, at least from beatings with which he has often been threatened. . . ."

But Baranov was indifferent, now, to the reports going out about him. Rezanov begged him to stay, perceiving he was the only man capable of bringing the colonies out of their pioneer stage, but Baranov refused; he was too old, he said, too worn with hardships.

Rezanov stayed with Baranov that winter. Things were even worse than the previous year. It seemed as if weather, sea, and Kolosh united their forces to show Rezanov what it meant to advance the tsar's cause on the Northwest Coast. When it did not snow it rained. The gales howled for days. They had the saddest marine disaster since the *Phoenix*'s loss; the *Zachary*, commanded by one of the indifferent cadets, went down with all hands. They lost a whole bidarka fleet at sea. At the end of February, 1806, of the one hundred and ninety-two Russians at Sitka sixty were down with scurvy and eight had died. The garrison might have been weakened to the point of disaster had it not been for the appearance of the schooner *Juno*, Captain John D'Wolf of Bristol, Rhode Island, which Rezanov bought with all her cargo of supplies. Five of her discharged crew took service with the Company but the remainder, rather than remain in such a place, sailed for Canton in the ungainly *Yermak*.

"Our cannon are always loaded," wrote Rezanov, "and not only are sentries with loaded guns placed everywhere but arms are our chief ornaments. After sundown, all night long, signals are given every few minutes from the parapets and the watchword passed until daybreak. Baranov maintains strict military discipline and we are always ready to repulse another savage attack."

He had good reason. The Kolosh, infuriated by their failure to oust the Russians the previous year, planned complete extermination. They approached northern tribes, with whom they had always been at war, with proposals to affect a union and succeeded in stirring up Cook's Inlet and Prince William Sound to the point where Molokhov had to send a frantic request for reinforcements. Baranov sent ten men, all he could spare. Fortunately, his wife's people remained staunchly loyal and by their help and the most extreme vigilance at Fort Constantine that outpost escaped destruction.

Yakutat was less fortunate; an end was finally written to the sorry history of that establishment. Only eight men, two women, and three children escaped death, and they were captured. Witnesses who saw the remains testified that nothing was left but a mass of ashes, and the heads of the poor serfs who had once screamed with terror at seeing the American wilderness had all been cut from their bodies and impaled on sticks along the length of Yakutat beach to advertise the savage triumph. Then the Kolosh converged on Sitka, a thousand of them, pretending to mass in order to scoop up the spring herring running in the sound; but they wore their war paint and totemic symbols of hostility.

The appearance of Captain Jonathan Winship, now commanding the O'Cain with his brother Nathan as mate, saved the situation. Winship brought the Russians the first supplies agreed on with Joseph O'Cain; he unlimbered his schooner's guns and told the Kolosh he would not trade until they removed the threat of their presence to his friends. Naturally, Baranov was touched deeply; he let young Jonathan go to Kodiak and pick up four Russians, one hundred Aleuts, and fifty bidarkas to hunt the California coast for sea otter, as he had done with O'Cain two years before. Winship eventually returned with thirty thousand dollars' worth of skins as the Company's share—and thus Baranov kept business going in the midst of disaster.

Not far behind Winship, Captain Oliver Kimball, O'Cain's brother-in-law, appeared with the brig *Peacock* and several men willing to enter Company service—O'Cain had kept his promise to find good men. So the shipbuilder, Lincoln, came to New Archangel, and the educated Abram Jones and one Benzemann, a very fine navigator of Prussian birth.

During all of these hardships, Baranov and Rezanov never stopped planning the extension of Russian-American enterprises. Two small vessels were built. Rezanov held many a council to explain his plans. He took a liking to Kuskov and insisted upon having him present at all conferences.

"Although he has not Baranov's humility of soul," as Rezanov wrote, and was relatively far from being as good an administrator, Kuskov was the best appointment as chief at New Archangel when Baranov left. At those councils Rezanov discussed establishing funds for aged hunters and training Company clerks, for the education of half-castes and for medical attention. There had never been a surgeon in the colony. He arranged for the Governor to sign bills of exchange on banking firms in Europe with which to make independent purchases of ships and supplies when needed. He told of his ideas for Russian domination of the Pacific, putting consuls in the Company's name at the Philippines, Burma, and elsewhere. He talked of gaining footholds on the Columbia, designating that as their next objective—they had Vancouver's books and charts open before them—in California, the Sandwich Islands. He urged in strongest terms abandoning the exclusive preoccupation with the fur trade and engaging in a general merchandise business as well. There could be no delay, he insisted; the time was almost at hand when the Peace of Amiens established by Napoleon would be shattered again. It was inconceivable that Europe would long tolerate the Corsican; his presence meant war inevitably and the longer it was delayed the worse it would be. But it would be their opportunity; Europe's attention would be distracted from the Pacific and they would have a free hand. He, Rezanov, had seen the Pacific. He had seen the Sandwich Islands, Japan, Kamchatka, the ports of South America. He was a military man, trained in artillery. He knew how to measure strategic values. The Russians had a perfect springboard for their plans in the north. Rezanov was first in the world to recognize fully that he who controls Alaska may control the Pacific.

Nor did Rezanov only talk. In spring he himself set out in the newly bought *Juno* with his manservant, physician, and two attendant officers to investigate the mouth of the Columbia as the site of their next outpost and from there proceed perhaps to Manila. But the most scurvy-ridden and otherwise unfit had been given him for a crew, they were unable to negotiate the Columbia River bar, and so they kept on to San Francisco Bay despite the Spanish restrictions against visiting ships.

While Rezanov was in California, Honest Joe O'Cain visited New Archangel in the *Eclipse*, proposing to take Russian furs to Canton. Since his last visit to Baranov his plans had grown even more grandiose. He had some Japanese aboard, rescued from a wreck, and he planned, after visiting Canton, to use their return home as a pretext to start accomplishing what many a diplomat had failed to do—open Japan's closed ports. He was jubilant about the idea and proposed that, having accomplished his object, he would come back to Kodiak, pick up Baranov, and take him with him for a visit to Boston.

Baranov accepted eagerly, planning to give Rezanov his definite resignation when he returned.

That summer Rezanov came back from California with a fat and healthy crew, a hold full of corn, salt, meat, tallow, and hides, and an astonishing change in plans.

At San Francisco Presidio he had fallen in love with the Spanish commander's daughter. The forty-two-year-old plenipotentiary of the tsar and one of the wealthiest men of Russia had betrothed himself to a girl half his age, and he saw in the union a powerful force for the uniting of power on the American West Coast.

He was full of enthusiasm for what he had seen—the soil, the water, the grazing lands, the harbors—and of contempt for the policy of Spain which kept the wondrous place closed to the world. He had found the governor, old Arillaga, secretly full of the same contempt. He foresaw great ranchos there under Russian control and worked by coolie labor brought from China. He saw a Russian-American alliance directed from the New World and virtually independent of Europe. He still perceived the necessity of gaining a foothold on the Sandwich Islands as a means of controlling the "general business" of the Company, but he now visualized that business as having a firm basis in California agriculture and cattle raising as well as fur trading.

But he had to have the permission of Petersburg for his extraordinary marriage, and of Rome as well and Madrid, and he wished to leave at once to began the long overland journey across Siberia to Russia. He listened with dismay to Baranov's request for immediate relief, and finally became convinced the little man meant what he said. "He insists he will not stay longer than May of next year," Rezanov faithfully wrote to the directors, "and implores me to make the fact very clear. I am sorry we must lose such an excellent man. On his departure the best men will go with him . . ." That fall of 1806, Rezanov took his departure in the expectation of returning in two years to marry his Spanish betrothed.

Baranov, worn out with strain and hardships, left Kuskov in command at Sitka and retired to Kodiak to wait for O'Cain, meanwhile withdrawing from all but the most formal tasks of his office. May of 1807 came, but no O'Cain.

He heard that his Russian wife, whom he had not seen in twenty-five years, had passed away. It was a tremendous relief to him, for now he could take his children to Russia. He wrote to Mikhail Buldakov, chairman of the Company's board, to intercede with the tsar for a special decree legitimatizing Antipatr and Irina, and was happy when the ukase was issued in his favor. That document, incidentally, recognized Anna Grigoryevna as "The Princess of Kenai," following the old Russian custom of confirming the titles of conquered peoples, which meant that his son and daughter could enter nobles' schools.

Then, in swift succession, came two shattering blows. O'Cain
and Rezanov had both died! O'Cain's vessel went down off the
Aleutians on the return voyage from Japan. Rezanov, though convoyed by six Cossacks across Siberia, had fallen from his horse and
died at Krasnoyarsk of brain-concussion. He never reached St.
Petersburg.

It seemed Fate, surely! Each time someone set about arranging
to relieve him, that person died—old Shelekhov, Father Iosaph,
O'Cain—and now Rezanov!

The directors wrote that because of the violent war raging in
Europe a successor would not immediately be arranged for and
they urged him to carry on, and specifically to put into operation
without delay the great plans of which Rezanov had written—
advancing to the Columbia, to California, and to the Sandwich
Islands—for the time was ripe. Europe's attention was altogether
occupied by Napoleon.

Baranov had no belief in his ability to push these gigantic plans.
There is abundant evidence for this. Quite aside from his wish to
leave with his family, he felt he did not have the necessary background. The host of diplomatic questions which penetration in
California alone was certain to raise needed more than skill with
an ax. But, like an old general on war's declaration, Baranov put
aside his plans and returned to New Archangel.

He hardly knew the place. Kuskov had built mightily; Baranov
was proud of the onetime bookkeeper he had trained in the art of
empire building. New Archangel was a veritable Kremlin. The
governor's residence, two stories high, crowned with a beacon
tower to guide ships entering the sound, stood riveted to the old
Kolosh rock with long metal bolts. Upstairs were fine sleeping
apartments and downstairs an office overlooking Sitka Sound,
reception rooms, kitchens, and a large banquet hall with an enormous fireplace and a dais at one end for musicians. Steps from
broad veranda led down to a bastion commanding the harbor
with a force of sixty guns. The settlement below, surrounded by a
high, strong palisade, comprised bakeries, kitchens, storehouses,

a commissary, and the homes and gardens of almost a thousand people. Military discipline prevailed; the guard, which saluted smartly and was changed at stated times, was composed no longer of the sick and infirm but of men specially assigned to that duty, some of whom had seen military service at home. Poles, some of them, and a few Finns. No Kolosh had lived on Sitka Island since Baranov had banished them, but New Archangel still sat on a powder keg, for the Kolosh nation had not forgotten. Periodically councils were still called on exterminating the Russians and all knew the attempt might come again at any time.

Baranov brought his family from Kodiak and the Rezanov collection of books and paintings, which he installed in a room he called his "library" and which he further adorned with some good furniture—including a pianoforte—that he ordered through Yankee friends.

Evidently he prepared grimly for a possibly protracted stay. He lost no time pushing the advance on three fronts. Kuskov would go to California to seek a site and make estimates of the men and supplies needed. To look at the Columbia he planned an expedition headed by Captain Bulygin and Tarakanov. To King Kamehameha of the Sandwich Islands he planned to send Captain-Lieutenant Leontii Hagemeister, a naval officer who had seen service with the British and had just brought the *Neva* back to the Pacific.

None of the three expeditions were to force anything, but only to survey and reconnoiter. Baranov seems to have hesitated longest about choosing his man for the Sandwich Islands. Diplomatically it was the most delicate mission. King Kamehameha was his friend. The king had sent him food when he was in want and by almost every ship sent messages as from one allied ruler to another. One of Baranov's men had been given a great fan of exotic feathers to take as a mark of special favor from the king, and His Majesty had even talked of coming to New Archangel to visit Baranov.

Baranov wanted to gain the king's permission for what he had to do. He wanted a trading station on the islands, possibly a place where Russian ships could put in for repairs, perhaps a plantation under Russian-American Company management, from which Russian influence could spread and supplant the king's present British advisers. The delicacy in the matter came from the fact that the king, despite his interest in foreigners and shipping, had always refused to allow permanent stations of any kind on his islands.

Baranov needed an able man to present his case, and one able to estimate commercial possibilities. Hagemeister was easily the most literate man in the colony, he spoke English and was an excellent navigator, yet Baranov hesitated, as well he might. Hagemeister had the arrogance of his rank and made no secret of the fact that he was in America because of the money. But—nobody was in America because he loved it.

Baranov gave his orders to Hagemeister with great care, trying to win the man to the Company's point of view. Whoever controlled those islands controlled Pacific trade. Russia could not neglect this one opportunity when England was busier with her own affairs than for a hundred years. The islands were rich in food and fortunate in sandalwood. The king owned a lake of salt large enough to supply their fur-curing needs for generations. To all appearances Hagemeister understood the objectives. Baranov watched the *Neva* depart and settled down to the business of governing the colony, transacting the trade of New Archangel, and enjoying family life in his "castle," as the place became known throughout the Pacific.

His children loved the place. Antipatr was fascinated by ships and his father indulgently let him take trips with friends among the shipmasters. Irina already showed signs of becoming some day a rare beauty. Both had until now gone to school to Father Herman at Kodiak, who carried on there as virtual patriarch of the colony aided by Father Gideon and others who had come since the old days; now, at New Archangel, they were tutored by Abram Jones, the young Yankee sailor O'Cain had sent.

New Archangel had become a busy port. Lincoln, foreman of his shipyard, had already built the brig *Sitka*, rebuilt the old

Alexander, and recently launched the *Discovery.* For the shipmasters it was a way station second in importance only to Honolulu, for the Spaniards still kept San Francisco a closed port. Furs had become a prime item of trade; Europe and Asia both demanded them as a major article of clothing. But the skippers no longer traded as indiscriminately with native villages as before; now they saw Baranov first. He gave or withheld permission to trade or took goods off their hands himself and paid in furs. It was all much faster than in the old days. And there was no nonsense; Baranov was shrewd and knew textiles. No skipper *had* to see him, of course, for the coast was still an enormous stretch of strand and the Russian patrol ineffectual, but if old Baranov ever heard of a shipmaster selling natives guns and powder, he was never again granted favors at New Archangel.

And that loss of trust could be costly. Baranov, because the old treaty between China and Russia after all these years was still unchanged, could not send a ship of his own to Canton; he had to commission others to do his business there. But most skippers cultivated Baranov because they hoped to be trusted enough to get in on the most lucrative commission of all—to hunt the California coast for sea otter with bidarkas and Aleuts leased on shares from Baranov. The two Winship brothers had a solid claim on it, of course, and a priority, but as time went on Baranov allowed others to try it, such as Captain Oliver Kimball of the *Peacock,* Swift of the *Derby,* and the famed George Washington Ayers of the *Mercury.*

So, many visitors came to New Archangel, to be entertained in a manner becoming legendary even in distant places. These days Baranov affected clothes he considered more fitting to his dignity —black silk waistcoat, worn slippers with silver buckles and, if he thought the visitor important enough, a black dress-wig that never fitted too well. He liked to have pinned to his lapels the insignia of his rank in the tchinn and of his two orders, the Cross of St. Vladimir and a second distinction, received after the regaining of Sitka, the Order of St. Anne of the Second Class. He had become quite bald and his face had grown pinched, accentuating his shrewd air, but it still bore its old alert look.

He loved to show off his residence to his visitors. When he moved he gave the impression of doing so in pain. He limped a little, some days a great deal, and his fingers often swelled with arthritis—the result of too many years of sleeping in wet forests or standing at the tiller of his sloop in wind and snow. He put on square-lensed spectacles if he had to look at a document, but more often he handed it to his secretary—his nephew, Ivan Kuglinov, filled that office now—to read. If his visitor had business it was transacted in the office with the wide view of the sound. He sat much at the desk in that room, these days; he had had to abandon his former kind of activity.

Before his guests were taken in to dinner in the famed banquet hall, they were always shown his "library." There were twelve hundred volumes, some handsomely bound, on theology, Church history, metallurgy, navigation, astronomy, mathematics, grammar, and a few works of literature. Half were in Russian, three hundred in French, one hundred and thirty in German, thirty in Latin, and the rest in Spanish and Italian. There were framed letters from well-wishers, too, on the walls, and on the bookcases stood interesting ship models, sent to the colony by Admiral Chichagov.

Dinner was served in style and rough abundance—roast wild geese, wild duck, venison, salmon, or halibut, Russian bread, pickles, and cakes. The servants were Aleuts and always made a great flourish of bringing in the famous bowl of hot punch to set in the center of the table.

Baranov no longer had Richard as interpreter; around 1806, Richard had at last asked to be allowed to go home to Calcutta by a passing ship. The old man really understood more English than he pretended to and knew well enough what was being said if it was to his liking, but he always talked through his nephew, Ivan Kuglinov, who fancied himself quite a linguist, or Abram Jones or Kyrill Khlebnikov, the chief accountant at Sitka after

1810, a fair-haired, bespectacled, very correct young man from Riga.

If there were several guests, things were likely to become very convivial. And when a Russian man-of-war happened to be in port, Baranov really put on a display, meeting the officers he invited ashore with a guard of honor, firing off guns, having musicians on the dais at the end of the banquet hall and singing the "Pyesnya Baranova."

Washington Irving, who obtained his information second-hand, wrote: "He is continually giving entertainments by way of parade, and if you do not drink raw rum and boiling punch as strong as sulphur he will insult you as soon as he gets drunk, which will be very shortly after sitting down to table."

That picture Irving got from a man whom Baranov deliberately tried to insult, but the general connotation is accurate. Baranov liked to drink freely and could get offended when guests refused. Some of the shipmasters, probably those bested by Baranov at business, complained this practice was part of the Sitka governor's technique in trading with them, but the majority liked the robust hospitality and they admired him. Captain John Ebbets wrote ruefully to John Jacob Astor: "They all drink an astonishing quantity, Governor Baranov not excepted. I assure you it is no small tax on the health of a person trying to do business with him."

21

•••

An Assassination Is Thwarted

Pᴀssɪɴɢ the winter of 1808–09 in domestic tranquillity and the cares of his office, Baranov did not dream that the garrison below him were plotting nothing less than his assassination. Like all men who have brought peace from chaos and have guaranteed prosperity, however rough, he imagined he was beloved by all. Actually he was blindly revered by the majority. The Aleuts underwent their privations on the California expeditions not because they needed the money the Yankees paid for their services but because he told them to. The older hunters, those who remembered past history, the men who now commanded the northern outposts or who lived at Kodiak and went on the long California trips with Aleuts as overseers, the Shvedzovs, Tarakanovs, and Slobodchikovs, looked on him with a peculiar mixture of respect and intense affection. He had always been generous with them when he had anything to share; when misfortune struck he had carried their families on the commissary's books, and in a few cases he had sent at his own expense the more promising of their sons to Russia to be educated as navigators.

But as always the Russian population was essentially an impermanent thing; new men came nearly every year. Fewer of the old ones returned to Russia than in the past, but they usually did retire from active duty after their terms had expired. And with the new men came the ferment of a strange new unrest in Europe, an unrest formless as yet and without the ideologies and literature to come in later years, but already active and born of a desire for release from the world's despotisms.

The ferment seethed hottest in Poland, where it flourished as hatred for Russia. Secret societies formed there, undercover confederations, to form and re-form again with more and more definite ideas and increasing hatreds as fast as the Russian secret police could send their members to remote Siberia, whence a few of them found their way into service with the Russian-American Company.

Baranov had always asked for "men of good caliber," meaning by that, men who could read and write. He attached great importance to that accomplishment. When he began getting these men with a literate air and some with military backgrounds he abolished the old hit-or-miss method of sentry duty by the sick and unfit and organized a permanent garrison for New Archangel which he hoped would some day form the nucleus of a coast guard. He appointed captains and corporals. He had them stand at attention, drill with guns on the bastions, and change watches with regularity. He was proud of the air they gave the port of New Archangel.

He would have sensed a tension at once among the old sort of men, but these successfully hid the fact that for more than a year a secret society had existed among them. Its name was something like the Order of Yermak, after the legendary Cossack who had led his people to freedom from the wrath of Ivan the Terrible and began the conquest of Siberia. The nucleus was made up of nine men headed by a Polish corporal of the night guard named Naplavkov, seconded by a Russian whose name was Popov. Twenty to thirty more were in on a plan to leave the Northwest Coast, but only these nine were parties to the inmost secrets, which called for the assassination of Baranov and all his family, the seizure of the ship *Discovery* in the harbor, the forcing of all the women in the settlement aboard, and sailing to Easter Island where they planned to set up a republic. At one of the sessions of the nine, Baranov was tried *in absentia* for the crimes of murder, oppression, and brutal treatment, and condemned to death. His condemnation was written on paper and signed.

The revolt was planned for the late summer of 1809, as soon as the harbor was clear of vessels that might render Baranov assistance.

Some of this leaked out, of course, but Baranov waved it away impatiently. These were educated men, not stupid, plotting peasants. He had other worries to occupy his mind.

Summer came but, surprisingly, no foreign shipmasters and none from Russia. Supplies were running low. There seemed no explanation until, in July, Jonathan Winship arrived again with the *O'Cain*. The Jefferson administration had forbidden all foreign commerce as a protest against Napoleon's blockade of Europe and Britain's impressment of seamen on the open ocean. Winship had managed to run out of Boston only with difficulty. He had other news for Baranov which he gave during the round of dinners at the castle while the cargo was being priced, and he waited for the hunting masters to levy the Aleuts for whom Winship had just contracted under a new agreement to hunt the California coast.

Winship, naturally, had touched at Hawaii. Hagemeister's mission to the old king was worse than a failure, he reported; far from improving relations it had ruptured them. Winship knew what he was saying; his firm had been very close to the king in several important deals over sandalwood. Apparently Hagemeister, although received with the utmost friendliness and courtesy, had been arrogant and rude to various native princes and stupid enough to say that Russia intended to take the islands by force, if necessary. The most significant result of Hagemeister's visit was that he had caused the king to seek stronger ties with Britain.

"When I left the islands," continued Winship, "Hagemeister had taken the *Neva* to Oahu so I did not see him myself. He may not know there is a state of war between Russia and England."

Winship told of the new and startling coalition in Europe—to the consternation of the world no less than to Baranov: Tsar Alexander had joined with Napoleon against Sweden, Austria, and England.

While Winship was still in port a member of the Order of Yermak, a Pole named Lezchinski, confessed the plot against Baranov. He said the assassination and revolt were planned to follow immediately on the departure of the *O'Cain* and as soon as certain members were back from duty elsewhere.

Naturally, Baranov was incredulous. Why should anyone wish to kill him? The Kolosh would be on them within a week, if he were killed. But when another Pole, Berezhovski, and a Russian, Sidorov, separately asked permission to see the governor on a matter of the utmost importance and each told the same story he listened.

Meetings, presided over by Naplavkov or Popov, were taking place at the various cabins of the nine highest members almost every night to perfect their plans. The men who were to murder him, to take possession of the bastions and turn the guns against those not in the plot, and those who were to rifle the commissary and take the ship, had all been designated. They awaited only the *O'Cain*'s departure.

His three informers agreed to co-operate. On nights when he entertained guests it had always been his custom to distribute free drinks to all the garrison who were off duty. On a night when he would be entertaining Winship he would give Lezchinski and Berezhovski, who occupied the same cabin, a *vedro* of brandy to get the conspirators drunk. They would hear the sounds of revelry from the castle and feel free to unbend. At the right moment for the attack Lezchinski would give the signal by bursting into a certain song. A number of trusted old hunters placed at strategic places would then converge on the cabin and arrest everyone.

The Winship banquet was given the night of August 7. The young shipmaster and his mates sat down to a table loaded with roast meats and pastries and the famed bowl of hot punch in the middle. The musicians sat on the dais as usual and played. The "Pyesnya Baranova" was sung.

But their host did not as usual remain until the last mate had slid under the table or had been helped, singing, upstairs to bed. Instead, when a whispered message came, he rose somewhat hurriedly, excused himself, and went to his office.

Kuglinov reported everything had been done as ordered. The trusted men had taken their positions. Upstairs his family slept under heavy guard. The meeting in Lezchinski's cabin was fast growing audibly drunken.

Baranov put a loaded pistol in his belt and with Kuglinov's help walked cautiously down the steps to the dark bastions. Behind them the Yankees were singing at the tops of their voices. Overhead glowed the summer skies of Sitka at night. Below them lights showed in a few cabins. "It is that one," whispered Kuglinov, indicating a shaded window. A guard came pacing down the bastion, his tread slow on the heavy timbers, his pipe a red glow against his beard. It was Sidorov. "Corporal Naplavkov slipped away from duty an hour ago," he whispered. "He is with them now."

Baranov nodded, grimly. They waited.

The signal came at last. Someone threw open the shaded window and began to sing. Immediately several cabin doors opened and men ran out to take their appointed positions on the docks and bastions. Sidorov shrank into the shadows; he did not want to be shot by his fellows as a traitor. There came the dull sound of shoulders against a door and finally the splintering of wood. Running feet thundered on the bastions.

It was all over by the time Baranov reached the cabin. A dozen men stood against the wall, their hands high in the air, as they faced the muskets of Baranov's old hunters. Popov lay on the floor unconscious from a blow on the head and Naplavkov stood whitefaced at the head of the table and held his arm in which a saber had cut a deep gash. A stove in the corner glowed red, for its door was open. From it had been snatched the half-burned but still legible papers hastily consigned to the flames at the attack, which told a clear story of the treasonable plot.

22

John Jacob Astor Proposes Alliance

IMPERIAL Russia forever lost her opportunity in the Pacific afforded by the Napoleonic wars, that night of August 7. What Baranov read about himself in those papers taken from the conspirators and about their intention to murder him and his family, robbed him of vanity, deeply injured his pride, and paralyzed his initiative. He suddenly knew fear for almost the first time in his life—fear for the lives of his children, who were dearer by far to him than his own life. As quickly as he could he got his family out of New Archangel and sent them with Abram Jones to Kodiak, putting them under Banner's protection, though thereby he lost his only joy and interest in daily living. He could not comprehend why anyone should want to kill Antipatr and little Irina; he was savage toward the six men who were finally determined on as the ringleaders and intended sending them to Siberia charged with attempted murder and treason to the state. In the half-burned papers he read charges that he had been found guilty of the crimes of inhuman feeling, of capricious and arbitrary exercise of power, of lack of regard for all that makes exile in strange lands bearable, and of the sale into slavery of unfortunate native peoples. ". . . For these things the said Aleksandr Baranov is condemned to death, and that his breed may perish, his children and all his family here present shall die with him . . ." He read the plans for running the republic on Easter Island in accordance with the democratic principles of Yermak's time, the plan for escape from Sitka, the names of those involved, the "declaration of independence" setting forth their reasons for revolting, and a list of grievances against Russia, Baranov, the Company, and the Northwest Coast. It all passed his comprehension. He could not know that such documents were the fashion of the times, that since Thomas Jefferson's Declaration had so forcibly given form to the ideas of the United States, and the American Revolution hope to Europe, every conspirator from Warsaw to Madrid wrote such manifestoes and changed the name of the condemned ruler with every shift in the political wind. All he knew was that he had lost his trust in his men.

He had immediately written hotly and bitterly to the directors, upbraiding their inaction, demanding that they cease wrangling forthwith and appoint his successor, reminding them that he had been ready to leave since 1806 and had remained only because he felt it his duty. Now he could no longer be responsible.

That, however, was but a starter to the writing he did that night. Baranov had never been superstitious but it takes a severe shock to make his kind write their wills. He wrote his that night. It is a curious document.

"Since my life is in constant danger not only from the hostility of wild tribes but from men often unwilling to submit to discipline," it began, "since my strength is exhausted and my health dissipated battling the hardships I have had to endure, I feel that that natural time, the hour of my death, is for me more uncertain than for most men, and therefore I make my will."

The bulk of his estate he left to his son Antipatr, except that Irina and her mother were to receive half the property at Kodiak and New Archangel, that Irina receive further five thousand rubles when she came of age to marry, that his daughter Afanassya by his Russian wife, married to Vassili Belyaev, be given ten shares and five thousand rubles, with lesser bequests to his sister Avdotya, who had never married, to his other sister Vassilissa and her son Ivan, his secretary. He closed by stating that, since he had always done so much for his brother Pyotr, who still operated a fur station at Ishiginsk, he felt sure he would not wish to share under the will, and begged Company chairman Mikhail Buldakov at Petersburg and Father Herman at Kodiak to be guardians of his children at his death.

He then proceeded to spend the winter in solitary, lonely drinking, indifferent to the success of the southward push or much else but what the directors would reply.

Hagemeister had gone to Russia and had taken the dispatches with him. The lieutenant had returned from the Sandwich Islands with the news of war between Russia and England and asked to be released from Company service so that he could go home and engage in the business of war. Baranov indifferently let him take the *Neva* to Okhotsk, though it meant depriving himself of his best vessel and only frigate. Baranov knew, from gossip and from the way Hagemeister had reported everything, that relations were indeed strained with King Kamehameha, but despite the enormous importance of getting matters straightened out he sent not even an apology to the old king. Baranov heard that the expedition sent to the Columbia had been lost somewhere off the coast, but though he also heard that the Winships had stolen a march on him and put a trading post on the Columbia he did nothing about that either. Finally, when Kuskov returned from California enthusiastic about founding a colony there and with all his plans drawn, he scarcely listened. No one was with him in the castle but Ivan Kuglinov. The old man could be cheered only by hearing from his children. Kuskov, disgusted, proceeded with his plans on his own—and Kuskov's colony was the only one that was ever established.

The letter from the directors received that spring of 1810 could not have been sent more promptly or contained better news if Baranov had written it himself.

A successor had been chosen, he was leaving for Kamchatka at once rather than by sea because of the war dangers, with his son and two daughters—and it was none other than Baranov's old friend Ivan Koch, onetime commander of Okhotsk.

General Ivan Koch now, for since his Okhotsk days Koch had served on the imperial army's general staff and retired in 1802 with the rank of quartermaster general. He had accepted the urgent offer of the Russian-American Company to serve as governor at New Archangel, and if all went well he should be arriving some time the following year.

Baranov was excessively delighted. He could think of no one he would love to see more in his place than the man who first persuaded him to come to America. He immediately began planning the reception he would give Ivan Gavrilovich when he arrived. On that day there would be a praznik such as had never been seen, or would ever be seen again, in America.

Summer brought the greatest number of visitors so far received at New Archangel; the Jefferson embargo had been lifted in the United States. George Washington Ayers came in the *Mercury*, William Heath Davis in the *Isabella*, and Nathan Winship in the *Albatross*. The first two brought goods which Baranov thriftily bought against the morrow; Nathan Winship confessed failure to maintain a trade station on the Columbia. Yet Baranov still did nothing further about settling there—this time his excuse was that all that was up to his successor.

All three shipmasters, however, contracted for about fifty bidarkas and twice that many Aleuts to hunt the California coast. While they waited, guests at New Archangel, for the Russians at Kodiak to levy the bidarkas, Captain Brown of the brig *Lydia* came into harbor with the rescued survivors of the lost Columbia River expedition. Brown had discovered their presence while off Juan de Fuca Straits by Tarakanov's clever trick of flying a kite that could be seen far out to sea. There was celebration over these returns—and mourning for lost lives. Captain Jonathan Winship returned with more than five thousand otterskins, a good catch. Captain Vassili Golovnin came in with the Russian sloop-of-war *Diana*, which called for salutes to the imperial emblem by all the visitors, and for more entertaining. Also came Captain John Ebbets, savior of the Sitka Massacre survivors.

Ebbets brought the *Enterprise* (not O'Cain's old ship, but another) with a large cargo and important business proposals for the Russian-American Company from John Jacob Astor at New York. Astor was sending two expeditions by land and sea to found an important settlement on the Columbia River to hold that frontier for the American flag, and he desired close ties with New Archangel. He guaranteed whatever number of ships of supplies Baranov would need each year and promised to exclude firearms and munitions from all native trade if Baranov would make an exclusive contract with him. He would also execute all Baranov's commissions with Canton, where Astor already had reputable agents and banking connections. Astor had conceived these schemes after talking to Andrei Dashkov, newly appointed Russian consul general at Philadelphia, among whose instructions were those to bring pressure to bear on Washington to stop traders from taking firearms to the Northwest Coast. As earnest of his intentions, and samples of his goods, Astor sent by his agent John Ebbets the *Enterprise* loaded with sugar, rice, jackknives, and a thousand other articles including, as the invoices put it, "61 Roram hatts." The letters were in both French and English, from both Astor and Dashkov, who urged Baranov to accept the contract.

Baranov was embarrassed. He owed Ebbets a debt but he owed debts to the Winships, too, and to many others, and this contract called for freezing them out. It probably would not stop the firearms traffic but only drive it from the governor's control. Moreover, in all this fine scheming of Astor's for monopoly of trade, the founding of a colony on the Columbia to hold his country's frontiers, and general patriotic talk about enhancing international feeling by suppressing the trade in firearms, there was a great deal strongly reminiscent of Shelekhov at his best.

Besides, this too seemed a matter for Koch to decide when he should come. Baranov took refuge in his well-known inability to understand when he did not want to. Ebbets had confidently looked forward to the success of his mission; he was anxious to secure his position as agent to America's richest man. He found himself royally entertained, but to his consternation Baranov could not seem to grasp what he was saying, and as for his French and English letters, Kuglinov, who was usually eager enough to show off his knowledge, only followed his uncle's example, looked at them helplessly, and shrugged.

Ebbets might have left New Archangel baffled, mystified, and chagrined had not the *Diana's* officers interfered. Lieutenant Rikord understood French very well and Baranov could no longer pretend he had no interpreter. He therefore put the best face on the matter he could, bought Ebbets' cargo for twenty-seven thousand rubles though his warehouses were bursting, and commissioned him to go to Canton to sell a huge cargo of furs and ivory; but as for an exclusive contract, he left that to Koch.

Winter came and he spent it in the pleasant expectation of General Koch, and when spring of 1811 brought its meed of news and trade he wore the most genial air in years.

Trade was excellent, news bad. The fragments of the war picture in Europe were in fact deeply disturbing. A man of military experience and worldly background was indeed urgently needed. The alliance between Tsar Alexander and Napoleon seemed to be cooling, there was talk of Russia's alignment with England against France, and relations were straining between England and the United States. That might make the Yankees technically his enemies.

Early in spring Kuskov left for Bodega Bay in California, which he had picked as the port of his projected settlement. But that was Kuskov's own enthusiasm; Baranov made no further moves in the two other directions he had once planned, though the opportunity was still at hand. Shipmasters later reported that Kuskov was building a fine settlement which he intended to name Fort Ross. A revolution had taken place in Mexico; the California Spanish, lacking sympathy with it and seeing no source of supply but Kuskov, made him as welcome as they could without openly flouting the laws. California's Governor Arillaga had sent him—off the record, of course—a gift of several head of horses and cattle to start his herds. So, everything considered, the California settlement seemed off to a good beginning. John Ebbets returned from Canton with an excellent record of trade in the form of a cargo representing a profit of more than 100 per cent on the furs and ivory. The *Isabella, Mercury, O'Cain,* and *Albatross* returned with their Aleuts and furs from California where they had first gone to hunt with Drake Bay as their base; and then, because of the rumors of the English war, they had gone on to the Sandwich Islands. But Captain Thomas Meek in the *Amethyst* came with cargo and to contract for fifty-two bidarkas and their hunters, and William Blanchard of the brig *Catherine* took fifty bidarkas. There had been a few accidents, of course, and some losses, but as a whole the Russian-American Company had never been so prosperous. Baranov began sending goods to Siberia, reversing the old balance. General Koch would find the material part of his job made easy.

All summer and well into the fall, Baranov kept looking for the ship that was to bring Koch. It was therefore a blow of the utmost cruelty when in October the brig *Maria* put in with the news that Koch had fallen ill crossing Siberia, had lain sick at Kamchatka for weeks, and had there died. His son and two daughters waited there for word from Baranov as to what to do.

The gods dispose, mortals suffer; the drama begins to assume the structure of a Greek tragedy. As a disappointment it was staggering. There seemed small solace in hearing, by the same messenger, that the directors knew of the occurrence and had immediately picked another, one Bornovolokov, who would arrive the following year. Koch had been the man he wanted, for sentimental as well as practical reasons. There seemed nothing to do but send a sum of money for the relief of the son and daughters of Koch who were stranded at Kamchatka, and then get very drunk—which he proceeded to do with thoroughness.

He became very cantankerous that winter. The best way to approach him was to bring some item of news from his children at Kodiak. He beamed to hear that Antipatr was doing well in his navigation studies or that Irina wished for lessons in music; but to suggestions that he act in important matters he answered irritably that action was beyond his powers and as for delegating authority there was no one he could trust.

Discipline in the garrison had always been strict since Naplavkov's day, but now the slightest infraction of the rules set off within him explosions of rage, as a result of which he ordered punishments out of all proportion to the offense. But he was also likely, after cooling off, to stop the punishment and beg forgiveness for his injustice by some small gift. All over the coast the Kolosh pricked up their ears at the rumor that Baranov was becoming feeble.

The summer of 1812 brought confirmation of the war between the United States and England. It was unfortunate, for visitors might have roused him from his bitter mood and now he would have few. The Yankees everywhere scuttled to safety in friendly ports, mostly at Honolulu, out of reach of the British raiders. Only Captain Whittemore of the *Charon* dared to come to contract for Aleuts for California—only to be captured by the English months later when laden with furs off the Farallones; and except for the hurried return of Meek and Blanchard from California with about seven hundred skins each for the Company, his only other recorded visitor was Wilson Price Hunt, manager and founder of the Astoria colony on the Columbia, in the *Beaver* with another cargo Astor wished Baranov to buy.

Astor had wanted Hunt and Baranov to be friends, to form an alliance, so that, if his property were ever threatened, it could be taken to New Archangel for safety. Baranov had a universal reputation for integrity, and Astor had not been rebuffed by his first answer. But Hunt and the Russian did not like each other, as Washington Irving makes clear in *Astoria*.

Baranov certainly received the man with the utmost hospitality, eager to talk, exchange news, and get acquainted. But Hunt was probably not eager to be entertained; he was worried about the preponderance of men of British allegiance at his colony and was in a hurry to be gone. He disliked excessive drinking and hated to have it forced on him. He did not have a seaman's tolerance gained by wide contacts with the world but was an inland American businessman with a typical confidence in his ability to "handle any foreigner." He was not a trusting man and was inclined to haggle.

Perhaps Baranov was annoyed, perhaps amused. At any rate he made Hunt dally before New Archangel for two months and beat him to his knees at trading. The cargo included corn meal, rice, sugar, tobacco, tar, handkerchiefs, 733 pairs of shoes—hundreds of articles over which any experienced trader could waste time for days. And finally Baranov allowed him to go into the Bering Sea to collect his own sealskins at the Pribylov Islands in October, which was certainly no courtesy, for at that season the Bering is scarcely a playground for ships.

Hunt arrived at the lonely, fog-draped, rocky sealing station on October 31, landed with the greatest difficulty in the violent surf just before a gale blew up to drive the *Beaver* scudding out of sight beyond the horizon. For days he lived with the seven resident Russian sealers and the hundred natives in their malodorous huts made of whalebone covered with old sealskins and earth before the *Beaver* again reappeared. When he finally left Russian America it was with a fervent prayer never to have to do business with Baranov again.

Late in the fall of 1812, word came to Baranov that Bornovolokov was on his way and that indeed he might arrive before winter was over.

It was now safe to take the *Neva* out of Okhotsk and the naval officers with the new governor would navigate her. For confirmation had come of the startling change in the Napoleonic coalitions. England was now Russia's ally and it was Russia against Napoleon again, or rather Napoleon against Russia, for he had set foot on Russian soil with almost seven hundred thousand men of twenty different nations to begin an invasion which all the world watched in the barely suppressed hope that the conqueror would now meet his match.

In January, the gales blew up bitterly, the rains turned to blizzards, and the garrisons shivered in the unaccustomed freeze. And day by day the foul weather got worse until by the third week the enormous seas pounding the mainland coast washed hill-high into the fiords of Sitka Archipelago.

Suddenly New Archangel rang with hoarse shouts, banged doors, and the thunder of running feet on the bastions. Down on the surf-drenched beach a dozen half-dead sailors were being helped out of a crowded sailing launch, and on the boards lay others unable to move, their lips black gashes in burning faces. Quickly they were carried into shelter, wrapped in blankets, and given rum. Down the staircase came Baranov, hobbling as fast as he could on Kuglinov's arm.

Lieutenant Podushkin, exhausted, his clothing caked with salt, his eyes red and almost blinded from flying ice particles, gave his report in jerky sentences. The Neva had made it safely across the Pacific but had been caught in the Gulf of Alaska storms; they had put in at Resurrection Bay, where they picked up a pilot named Kalinin. He had tried to take them to Sitka but they had been driven against Edgecumbe promontory, where the frigate foundered with the loss of thirty-three lives and a fortune in art treasures being brought to found a cathedral at Sitka.

One of the lives lost was that of Bornovolokov, on the way to take charge of Russian America. Baranov's fate was still pursuing him relentlessly.

23

Baranov Accepts the Will of God

DESPITE the contradictory nature of the data that exist on Baranov, from his life and deeds the picture emerges clearly of a man of action with a strong stubborn streak, an independent spirit, high honesty, and genuine pride in legitimate achievement. But the precise motives that moved his being remain obscure. They could remain obscure with a mountain of letters from which to draw, for no character is more baffling than one that seems to have nothing to gain by the course of action which he chooses.

His chief motivation had never been the desire for money. Despite his great satisfaction in making the Russian-American Company pay big dividends, his own large profits he gave away. This was attested by all who knew him and proved after his death when his books were audited. He paid part of Kuskov's and Banner's salaries himself, supported several families at Kodiak, and paid for the education of their sons.

Nor was he driven by a desire to remain in power; his requests that he be relieved are too obviously genuine to admit of that decision.

Once it was clearly his duty to stay but he had long since fulfilled his duty. Why did he stay? For almost four years he had been of little real use, having taken no action, and he knew it. He could long since have put Banner, who had remained as chief at Kodiak, in charge. The Dane would have done no less than he. It was not that he felt himself indispensable; Kuskov in the two years he had ruled New Archangel had done a very good job. He yearned to travel and visit his friends in foreign places; yet he watched the years slip by into futility; honors and rest awaited him in Russia but he remained under circumstances and in a climate that gave him no ease.

The conclusion seems inescapable that he remained at New Archangel for the same reason that he had built the *Phoenix* when it meant nothing but trouble, and had driven on Sitka when he was ill prepared for victory. It seems plain stubbornness. He was in the habit of visualizing things in a certain way and never giving up until they were that way. He had imagined the ceremony of handing over his command to another, going over his books, and explaining with loving care the details of what he had built, and he was not going to budge until it happened that way.

But on the death of Bornovolokov everything became simpler. He seemed now to have been convinced it was the will of God that he remain in Russian America. They had all died, all who had sworn to replace him or had come themselves to do so: Shelekhov had died, leaving the Company in a bad way, Bishop Iosaph had gone down with the *Phoenix*, Rezanov had fallen from his horse in Siberia, Koch had been stricken at Kamchatka before he could even take ship, O'Cain had been drowned. And now this one!

He now felt himself obliged to reconsider his lifelong scorn of superstition; a man far more literate and free of thought than he could have been forgiven for seeing in all of it the hand of God— in whom, incidentally, he had never disbelieved. The pattern of his life emerged at last before him. He was fated. There was no use railing longer against the circumstances or the directors; indeed it might be sin to do so longer. All that his requests for relief accomplished was to send men to their deaths. The Sitka accountant, Kyrill Khlebnikov, who had begun gathering notes for a biography of Baranov, wrote, "Providence had always interfered with his wishes; now he bowed before the will of the Almighty. From this time on he petitioned no more for relief but resumed the discharge of his duty as cheerfully and efficiently as in former days."

He made preparations to remain for good. He sent for his family. He advertised, probably by writing to Russia, for a governess for his daughter. Antipatr and Irina returned, aged sixteen and eleven, but Anna Grigoryevna seems to have desired to remain at Kodiak, where she had become very pious and now lived in the daily exercise of the Orthodox faith, and Baranov did not press her to return.

He also wrote to Russia for a white priest who could perform the sacred liturgy in New Archangel; the old fathers now labored quietly in parishes from Unalaska to Cook's Inlet and he was not going to disturb them. And although he was sixty-six and old for his years because of the rigors of his life, he drew upon some inner reserve of strength and reassumed the leadership of the push toward the south.

It may seem strange that the Russians had little turned to explore the interior of the land they owned. With Baranov's old interest in metallurgy some surprising discoveries might have been made. There is an old legend that he had a man whipped for spreading the rumor that there was gold in the interior, for fear his fur trade would be ruined. It is of course absurd as a fact but true in implication; the Company policy had not changed since Rezanov had laid down his plan, which was essentially a St. Petersburg creation calling for a constant imperialist push to new lands, and Baranov was following orders.

The problem of extending his operations was more difficult by far than it had been four years before. He could count on no help from Russia. The fragmentary news of Napoleon's invasion and the burning of Moscow told him that. The value of the ruble had declined to the point where it was worthless effort to send furs to Siberia to be traded at Irkutsk; to make any profit he had to trade directly with Canton. But his friends the Yankees who did his trading were in hiding from the British. The Winships were bottled up at Honolulu, Wilson Hunt and the *Beaver* were interned at

Canton, Astor's other vessels were unable to leave New York. British warships had taken possession of Astoria. Russia was still allied, the last he had heard, with England, which made awkward any advance on either the Columbia or the Sandwich Islands. The one good thing about the situation was that he did not have to wait for approval for all his actions from Petersburg; he was on his own responsibility. He acted with a rapidity reminiscent of his earlier years. The change in him must have been very noticeable, for the Kolosh, who had been gathering for an attack on New Archangel, abandoned their attempt.

It has always been hard to understand how word could traverse so swiftly the length and breadth of the Pacific in those days. When it was understood that Baranov would buy ships and put them in active duty under the protection of his flag, several men quickly ran the gauntlet of the British across the Pacific to New Archangel and begged him to save them from bankruptcy by taking their vessels. A Captain Bennet came with the *Atahualpa*, once considered the finest in the China trade, and a teakwood three-masted schooner, the *Lady;* Baranov bought them and renamed them *Bering* and *Ilmen*. When William Heath Davis leased his *Isabella* to Baranov, seven bottoms capable of long-distance voyaging were in the Russian-American fleet in addition to four for coastwise sailing. To his staff of resident masters Baranov added an Englishman, Young, and the Yankees Bennet, Davis, and Wadsworth. At the same time he hired a very valuable man whom he counted on to patch up the harm Hagemeister had done with Kamehameha.

Don Juan Eliot y Castro is a figure unaccountably overlooked in histories of the Pacific. An amiable surgeon of questionable skill with a roving disposition and mixed blood from Rio, he had somehow become personal physician to Kamehameha, who looked on him with great effection and bestowed on him the royal nickname of *Naya*. In some ways Don Eliot had more influence with the old king than John Young, the king's longtime prime minister. How he came into Baranov's employ this summer of 1813 is a mystery;

he traded wisely and may have been on one of the vessels that put into New Archangel, or, which is very possible, he may have engineered their sale. In any event Baranov pounced on him to do several jobs.

He put all of his new staff members to work without delay, sending Davis in the *Isabella* to the Philippines for a report on trade conditions and markets there, Bennet first to the Pribylovs, then to Okhotsk with Fort Ross grain, and finally down to Hawaii in the *Bering*, and Wadsworth in the *Ilmen* to poach for otter along the California coast with Aleuts under the often-captured Vassili Tarakanov as hunting master. From there the *Ilmen* was to go to Hawaii to meet Bennet, carrying Don Eliot who would take orders from the missions they passed. Eliot had had much experience with the Franciscans, and Baranov could not have found a better agent to take over the smuggling of goods into California, which the Yankees had been forced temporarily to abandon. He was trustworthy and spoke the fathers' language. At Mission San Francisco alone, his first port of call, he closed a ten-thousand ruble deal in trade goods to be delivered at a future date for furs and grain. If he could have gone on as successfully and have reached Hawaii to lay Baranov's proposals before Kamehameha, in one year enough would have been done to make the Yankees, when they returned to active duty, find that the Russians were not so much allies as competitors.

But Baranov made a serious error of judgment in sending Eliot to cultivate trade relations with the Spanish in the same vessels with hunters who poached for furs along their coast. They needed goods but the poaching never failed to irritate them. Soldiers captured Eliot and Tarakanov off San Luis Obispo, put the first in jail at Monterey and the second into his third captivity at Santa Barbara Mission, and the *Ilmen* had to go on to Hawaii without them.

So, when Bennet in the *Bering* arrived at Hawaii after delivering the Fort Ross grain at Okhotsk, he had to negotiate for his cargo of sandalwood himself. The king, however, seemed agreeable to the contract and sent him to Kauai Island to get the wood. Unfortunately Kauai was the one island not fully controlled by Kamehameha; a secondary king ruled there, a shifty character called in his native tongue Kaumualii but known to foreigners as Tamori. While Bennet was ashore dickering with him a squall blew up that made the *Bering* drag her anchors and by morning she was on the beach. Tamori offered the services of his people to help bring the cargo ashore and when it had all been rescued, he treacherously claimed ship and cargo as salvage. Nor was there any way to make him disgorge. There seemed nothing to do but return to New Archangel and report.

Baranov was having another busy season when the *Ilmen* returned. The two British warships that had taken possession of Astoria had made a brief call, and two more vessels had placed themselves at his service, the brig *Pedler* and a fast, low-slung vessel of eighteen guns, a former French sloop-of-war called the *Forester*, which flew the British flag.

Actually they were both Astor boats. Wilson Hunt had freed himself from internment at Canton by buying the *Pedler* and had come, on Astor's instructions, to leave with Baranov the papers relative to the colony's affairs and the few men who remained loyal to the merchant when the colony was taken by the British. The other flew British colors falsely; Astor had so sent her to determine the fate of his colony. Her captain, Pigot, having on hand a valuable cargo, decided to go to "Sheetka," as he recorded it in his log, to dispose of it "to that most noble scoundrel, Governor Branoff" in "the pleasing anticipation of making the fortune of myself and friends."

It was always the wrong attitude to take with Baranov and that most noble scoundrel gave Pigot a drubbing at bargaining—Pigot recorded that "he would give no more than two dollars a gallon for the rum and fifteen dollars a box for fine Irish shirtings." But he did extend both Pigot and Hunt his protection and sent them to trade along California in his name.

Meanwhile he wrote to Kuskov empowering him to negotiate

with the Spaniards and offer to pay whatever fines they might ask
for Eliot's release, but he had small hope; they seldom released
prisoners caught poaching except under great pressure. The
thought of sending the Davises, Wadsworths, or Bennets to Kamehameha he dismissed at once; they were not trustworthy enough
for his purpose. He could only wait to see if the necessity would
bring forth the man who would lead the Russian advance on to
their next important foothold in the Pacific—the Sandwich Islands.

24

Conflict with Lozarev

As the year 1814 drew to its close Baranov could with reason
look back on the twenty months which had passed since
the *Neva* had been wrecked and Bornovolokov drowned as
his most successful as a business administrator. In 1813, despite the
loss of the *Neva* and the heaviest buying of ships in Company history and the need to pay hired foreign shipmasters high wages, the
dividend to the stockholders was close to half a million rubles;
and this year, despite the loss of the *Bering* and other losses including a million sealskins at the Pribylovs and a cargo of furs worth
eight hundred thousand rubles off Okhotsk, the returns would be
707,670 rubles—good sums for those days.

Some of it, of course, was due to Kuskov, who ran Fort Ross on
a pleasantly profitable basis and kept the old balance of trade re-
versed with grain, beef, and hides to Siberia. Yet the problem of
shipping it was vital too, and all traffic was directed from the little
kremlin at New Archangel.

In November, the *Suvarov* cast anchor before New Archangel.
The guns boomed, the standards dipped, the garrison danced and
huzzahed on the bastions, not only because she was the first vessel
in four years to come directly from Petersburg but principally
because she brought the good news of Napoleon's failure to conquer Russia and his utter rout from its soil.

She was one of two fine vessels of frigate proportions just bought by the Company from the French; like her sister ship, the *Kutusov*, which also would soon make her appearance in the new world, she was named after a general who had fought against the French and was manned by the flower of the Russian Navy. From her commander, Lozarev, to her surgeon, Scheffer, every man aboard her had taken part in the gigantic effort to expel the Corsican from Europe and crush him; they had fought long, bravely, and desperately alongside the men of other nations; they had tasted victory against the French nation whose culture they had always envied and which had kept St. Petersburg half ashamed of being Russian. For the first time, therefore, since Peter the Great decreed there be a Russian Navy its officers and men were filled with national pride.

New Archangel turned itself inside out to stage a praznik for such heroes, and Baranov put on his black wig and badly fitting waistcoat and pinned to his lapels the insignia of his rank and orders, delighted at the prospect of banqueting the commander and his officers and welcoming them into Company service.

The guns boomed more salutes as the brilliant uniforms were ferried ashore and the garrison stood at what they thought was smart attention to receive them. Upstairs in the castle the Aleut servants stood ready with trays of *zakuska* and glasses of chilled vodka, and in the banquet room they ran to load the table with roast meat and pastries around the hot punch bowl.

But pride ran headlong into pride before the reception was over. Lozarev and his officers laughed at New Archangel. None of them had yet awakened from the exciting dream of the past few years; all the way around the Cape every mess had fought and refought each battle and each skirmish and toasted the heroes thereof. They had battled the brilliant French; they had helped reduce the strongest forts to rubble; they had not flinched from the fire of frigates; to see the backwoods now was to laugh. They saw the wooden bastions as crude; the garrison as a joke, the kremlin atop the rock as primitive as a *voyevode's* stronghold. They saw Baranov as an aged trader with ridiculous affectations—admirable in many ways, perhaps, for there were remarkable stories told about him, but to be removed as soon as the Admiralty got around to peacetime pursuits again and took control of the Pacific. They had a hilarious time at the banquet. The food was good, the Yankee rum unfamiliar but potent, they made the musicians sing the songs they wanted, they patronized Baranov and thought they were being pleasant. Lozarev lightly chose the room he would occupy and observed that since they would not leave until spring Baranov had best arrange to get him a native girl for the winter.

Immediately there began a bitter conflict between Baranov and Lozarev which was to last many months. Baranov told the commander of the *Suvarov* that, far from settling down for the winter, he must leave in his ship immediately to go to the Pribylovs and collect all of the sealskins there. Lozarev was incredulous, but Baranov made it clear that it was he who issued the orders in Russian America, and two days later the frigate put to sea.

But in five days she was back, Lozarev announcing that she had sprung a leak. Guessing that this was a subterfuge, Baranov asked to see the leak, and pointed out that he had an excellent shipyard. Lozarev countered by showing Baranov the ship's articles which provided that the commander alone was authorized to arrange for repairs to his vessel, and announcing that he intended to repair the *Suvarov* the following spring. Baranov had no recourse. Week after week he watched, trembling with rage, while the *Suvarov* rode at anchor.

Meanwhile Lozarev baited him, flouting his authority as even Talin never had. Ostentatiously he sent men ashore to buy a native girl "for the winter" and made preparations for a long stay.

The old rule barring Kolosh from Sitka Island had of late relaxed somewhat and at the gates of the settlement a small native camp had sprung up; whenever a ship was in the harbor its people paddled out in canoes and offered to sell trinkets or smuggle prostitutes aboard.

The sailors came off the big ship every night, now, and raised havoc in that quarter. When Baranov protested at their disorder

Lozarev coolly answered with a threat to investigate Baranov's own administration of public morals. This seemed to give Lozarev a new idea and he began inviting aboard Aleuts, hunters, and garrison men to ask them detailed questions about conditions at Kodiak and elsewhere, their trips with the Yankee captains, how long they remained on such trips, how many died, and whether they believed Baranov derived personal profit from such transactions.

As with Talin's similar acts sixteen years before, the rumor suddenly spread that Company rule was about to be abolished and the navy would take over. People counted up on their fingers and realized the Company's charter would, in five years more, have run its first twenty-year franchise. Would a renewal be granted? Old hunters came to ask Baranov whether it might not be best for their families to retire now from hunting and start farming somewhere.

But not all the officers aboard were amused by their commander's baiting of New Archangel's governor. Their criticism flared into open quarrel and some moved ashore, among them the ship's surgeon, Doctor Scheffer.

Baranov welcomed the doctor. The colony had never had a resident physician or even an apothecary. "We doctor ourselves as best we can," Baranov once remarked. "If a man is so badly wounded as to need surgery, he must die." Scheffer was made at home at the castle.

Sometime that winter the thought of sending Scheffer as his representative to the Sandwich Islands occurred to Baranov. Perhaps he thought that, because the man was a physician, it might be a pleasing gesture to send him to Kamehameha to replace the still-imprisoned Don Juan Eliot.

Scheffer was of German-Russian parentage and spoke several languages with facility. He had been surgeon to the police garrison of Moscow. He was an inventive genius of sorts; when Napoleon had marched on Moscow he had been one of the builders of the famous balloon planned to watch the invader's movements from the skies—a plan which had fizzled out in the attempt. He dabbled in many enthusiasms, among them botany and agriculture, and talked learnedly of them all but, as events proved, he had not a particle of loyalty in his make-up. However, he was plausible and just the sort to make Baranov think he was a supremely clever and intelligent man.

In the spring, Baranov put an order in writing for Lozarev to go to the Pribylovs for sealskins, which he would need for his summer's trade. To his surprise the frigate weighed anchor and went on her errand.

A few days later the foreign shipmasters began to arrive. First came Wilson Hunt in the *Pedler*, returned from her errand to California. The fact that Hunt had been arrested by the Spanish for smuggling and almost interned for good in one of their jails did not increase the total of his affection for Baranov. But the Yankee War of 1812 was still in progress, by all reports; for safety's sake he had no choice but to remain in Russian service and wait before New Archangel for orders. Then Astor's other vessel, the *Forester*, under Captain Pigot, was warped to her anchorage, with some shipwrecked Japanese aboard he had picked up. Captain Pigot had been luckier than Hunt in that he had got into no trouble, but he was worried as to how long his luck would hold out. Thanks to his own loose tongue everyone knew his British colors were fictitious; he constantly risked capture by the Yankees because he was ostensibly British and by the British because he was really Yankee. He therefore offered the *Forester* for sale to Baranov, skins aboard, cargo collected and all, just as she lay.

But he wanted cash—bills of exchange on Petersburg. One reason Baranov had always shown a profit was that he always paid in furs when he could. This was a first-rate vessel, a former French man-of-war and fast, but he refused cash and they were deadlocked. Pigot, who already would have to face Astor and admit his voyage had not been too profitable, now seemed to take Baranov's refusal as a personal affront and sulked, seeking in his mind for ways to get the best of the Russian.

Other vessels now arrived in rapid succession—the Company's own brig *Maria*, the *Isabella* with Captain Davis and the *Albatross* and the *O'Cain*, which the Winships had sent to Baranov with cargo past the Honolulu blockade under Captains Smith and Maclean. Then the *Suvarov* returned with sealskins, much to Baranov's relief, for he needed his currency; but her return proved not to be to his relief for long.

For Lozarev did not deliver the skins to the warehouses ashore but himself proceeded to talk to the visitors about their business. This, as ranking naval commander in his own waters in time of war he had a right to do, and to look at their papers, but he did it in such a way as to confuse the visitors as to who was in real command. He entertained them, and when Pigot poured out his tale of Baranov's unwillingness to take the short end of his proffered bargain, Lozarev outlined a way to outwit him. This was not the Russian-American Company's only office, Pigot heard; there were others, at Kamchatka and Okhotsk, both out of Baranov's jurisdiction. Indeed, Lozarev offered to give him a letter to the commander of Kamchatka, where he might sell his vessel. From there he might enter Siberia with his furs and sell them to private traders in Irkutsk at much higher prices than the Company would offer.

Pigot went immediately to Wilson Hunt. Had Hunt checked the story with Baranov he would have learned that Lozarev was not only being disloyal to his employers but also mistaken. Foreigners were forbidden to sell furs in Siberia; anyone trying it ran the risk of great trouble and probable heavy fines. But Hunt was ready to approve anything that would work counter to Baranov's purposes. Without telling the reason, he took out of Baranov's keeping the precious papers representing all that Astor would realize from his unfortunate colonial venture and gave them to one of his men, Russell Farnham, who would sail with Pigot and cross overland to Siberia with them.

It was about July 1 when the *Forester* quietly took her departure without so much as a farewell ashore, leaving the other shipmasters uncertain as to just where authority rested now. Hunt was jubilant at what he thought was an outwitting of the old Russian governor he so cordially disliked. Baranov was given to understand that Pigot was sailing toward Asia to take the shipwrecked Japanese home.

When Baranov understood the truth he naturally was furious at Lozarev and Hunt for undermining his prestige and for sending Astor's agent on what at best would prove to be a futile errand. He demanded the *Suvarov* deliver her skins forthwith into the shore warehouses and cease communicating with the visitors. Lozarev replied that he intended weighing anchor for Petersburg very soon, and would take the skins there; Baranov's trading could somehow take care of itself. Each time Lozarev sent his replies in the form of neat notes couched in elegant but barbed official language. Baranov sent word that if the frigate so much as moved without his permission he would report the whole affair to the directors; but Lozarev retorted that *he* intended to do the reporting, and that when he did he would reveal enough to hang Baranov.

Meanwhile Lozarev continued coolly to deal with the visitors. Some of them had been at anchor for weeks, waiting for the quarreling to subside, and amusing themselves by calling on each other back and forth or trading with the Kolosh who came to the ships in canoes begging for small articles. Always these Kolosh asked for guns and powder, but no one in his right mind ever sold them any, at least not in plain view of New Archangel. Baranov's violent prejudice was too well known.

Disregarding this, Wilson Hunt sold them a few cans of powder. Hunt, above all people, should have known better. Not only had Astoria lost a ship to savages who possessed guns and powder but Astor's original agreement called for prohibiting the trade. The incident was of course immediately reported to Baranov. On July 29, he unhesitantly sent orders to Lozarev to seize the *Pedler*.

He sent his order as a matter of form; the *Suvarov* was the ranking vessel. When he received Lozarev's contemptuous refusal Baranov at once gave orders to load the fort's guns and train them full on the *Suvarov* as if to sink her where she lay.

The garrison, which to a man hated the frigate's sailors, enthusiastically did as they were told. There was a moment of surprised confusion aboard the *Suvarov*, Lozarev came furiously out on deck and ordered his crew to train their guns on the fort; a few minutes later the frigate's gunports opened and a broadside threatened to answer New Archangel's first fire.

But Baranov was not checkmated. His intention was only to immobilize the shipping where it lay. Broadcasting the message that he would open fire on the vessel that so much as sent a small-boat to anyone's help he ordered thirty men to arm, go aboard the *Pedler*, seize her powder, and arrest Hunt.

The skiffs quickly pulled away from shore and a few minutes later the men swarmed up the brig's ladders. Her deck could plainly be observed from the bastions. Hunt was seen to order the Russians off but they backed him and his navigator, Captain Northrup, against the rails and went below from where they soon emerged rolling kegs of powder across the deck. But Hunt and others suddenly made a dash for the ladders and slid down to fall into the skiffs and began pulling hard for the *O'Cain*.

The *Suvarov's* officers crowded the rails with their telescopes and the rigging of other vessels was thronged with seamen, but under the bastion's ominous loaded guns no one moved. Baranov had himself taken aboard the *Pedler* with sixty men. It was five o'clock in the afternoon when they helped him up the ladder and he stepped on deck to order Captain Northrup to haul down his flag and consider his ship seized on the grounds that her owner had committed an act unfriendly to the Russian government.

Northrup, who had had little experience with the Russians and could not understand how a can or two of powder could call forth such drastic action, protested the legality of the seizure; what Baranov answered is not in the log of any of the ships but he could have said that his government was still technically an ally of Britain, which was at war with the United States. He ordered Northrup not to leave his vessel, had the flag taken down, the crew disarmed, the guns spiked, the powder taken ashore. Then, after detailing a guard to remain aboard the brig, he had himself rowed to the *O'Cain*.

After the astonishing sequences of the afternoon, when the *O'Cain's* Captain Maclean (the Winships were in Honolulu) and her crew saw Baranov approaching they naturally did not know whether they, too, were to be arrested, for harboring Hunt. The old governor was evidently in a towering rage. Maclean was no coward; when Baranov stepped aboard his crew was armed and deployed for trouble, in the rigging and against the rails. Hunt stood white-faced beside Maclean, who replied, in answer to Baranov's order to arrest Hunt, that Hunt had sought his protection and could not be taken from the vessel. Baranov replied that he therefore held Maclean responsible for Hunt; Hunt must remain aboard and the *O'Cain* neither stir from her anchorage or attempt to communicate with anyone until otherwise instructed. He then took his departure to return to the fort.

Back once more in his office he dictated an order to Lozarev to send the supercargo ashore to start arranging for the discharge of the sealskins and to stand ready to receive other merchandise and dispatches for transmittal to Petersburg.

To his satisfaction he saw the supercargo come ashore with the invoices and when there was activity that looked as if the discharge of cargo would start, he relieved the tension by untraining the guns.

But before dawn August 8, he was excitedly awakened with the news the *Suvarov* during the night had silently raised anchors and was drifting out with the tide. The supercargo was still ashore, no skins had been discharged, no letters were aboard.

He ran out of the castle and down the stairs, the accumulated angers of the year at last boiling over into uncontrollable rage. He ordered launches, skiffs, bidarkas—whatever floated—out to chase the frigate and fire on her. The ridiculousness of it shows the extent of his exasperation. The order went from mouth to mouth down the settlement. New Archangel always obeyed Baranov to the letter. Aleuts and Russians piled down to the beach, pushed out and began to paddle, push, or row toward the *Suvarov*, which could have sent them all to the bottom with one volley. But their chase was futile; she now had her canvas up and soon was out of musket-shot.

On the wharves stood the marooned supercargo and Doctor Scheffer.

More inclined, these latter days, to accept omens, Baranov may well have taken the fact that Scheffer had been left behind as another sign that here was his man for the delicate task that needing doing at the Sandwich Islands.

Scheffer was more than willing to be the man. The record of the precise instructions he received is conflicting, but what Baranov hoped for is well known; the establishment of a station on the islands at which Russian ships could stop for exchange of cargo or repairs, and including a land grant the size of a plantation where foodstuffs could be extensively cultivated and shipped to New Archangel as Kuskov did from Fort Ross. He hoped for some hold on the sandalwood business and a supplanting of British influence on the King. Scheffer's first act must be to get back the *Bering* and her cargo from King Tamori.

It is certain Baranov wished to do Kamehameha no harm but it is also certain he meant to proceed gingerly no longer. Scheffer was to go with only a small retinue of men at first, but in spring the *Ilmen* and *Kodiak* would be sent with at least sixty men which he could use for building his station or on his plantation, if by that time he were successful, or as a threat if he were not. As to the exact manner of accomplishing everything, Baranov seems to have trusted Scheffer's discretion; he provided him with virtually unlimited credit on the Russian-American Company and gave him gifts to take to Kamehameha.

From the circumstances we know that Baranov finally decided to choose Scheffer shortly after Lozarev left. Meanwhile most of the vessels remained in the harbor for five weeks more, perhaps waiting for more sealskins to come from the Pribylovs, the *Pedler* still under seizure and the *O'Cain* still under orders not to move. On September 15, the *Ilmen* returned from Canton with a cargo and the glad news that the War of 1812 had ended nine months before. The Yankees rejoiced at their deliverance from the past long months of fear and poor business, and Hunt demanded the return of the *Pedler* on the grounds that she had been seized after peace was declared.

Baranov consented to release the brig but refused to release Hunt unless he made a certain bargain. He must agree to transport Scheffer and his retinue to the Sandwich Islands. Hunt, of course, had no alternative but to agree.

25

•••

Mission to Honolulu

I F genuine concern for the happiness of his people is the measure of a ruler's worth, then King Kamehameha deserves to
rank with the world's greatest. He had one invariable question he asked of every measure proposed for his approval: Would
it make his "children" happy?

When a young man, before the coming of the whites in force,
he had sickened of the strife among the petty chieftains on the
various islands and brought all but the Island of Kauai under his
hegemony; after which he proceeded to rule with great firmness
and sagacity. As he told the Russian explorer von Kotzebue, "Since
Kamehameha became king of these islands, no European has had
cause to complain of injustice. I have made my islands an asylum
for all men and have honestly supplied with provisions every ship
that desired them."

There is abundant evidence of his real admiration for Baranov,
on whom he looked as a brother king in the Pacific. Through the
shipmasters he kept himself informed of every detail of Baranov's
life and often expressed his amazement that one man could endure
so much. When Sitka was destroyed he was ready to send armed
assistance. He told Rezanov in 1804, when the Chamberlain
touched Hawaii, that he would make a trade treaty with no one
but Baranov. In 1806, he thought of visiting Sitka in person. So it
had been a great shock when Hagemeister let drop his unfortunate

remark that Russia meant to take his islands. His ministers had never shared his trust in the Russians and this confirmed in their minds what they had always suspected. Kamehameha believed them at last and with characteristic royal abruptness altered his attitude. It changed back to good feeling again only slowly, and because nothing happened for a long time.

There is little historical doubt that if Baranov could have visited the islands in person and the two of them have talked matters over the palm wine the king loved, the Russian-American Company might have secured everything it desired. There was a strong inner resemblance between those two; they could have understood each other.

When the *Pedler* dropped Scheffer and his retinue on Hawaii Island on December 11, 1815, he was warmly received at the royal straw greeting-palace on Kailua Bay. The hair of John Young, the king's prime minister who interpreted, was graying now, showing his twenty years of service to the king, whose own hands trembled with the years as he poured the wine of welcome for his guest. The king expressed his gratitude for Baranov's gifts, especially the one of a physician to replace Don Juan Eliot, still in a California prison, and said he would return gifts of his own by the very next vessel. "His Majesty is especially grateful that someone has come to explain to us that Hagemeister could not have meant what he said," said Young. "We could never understand why he threatened our people on Oahu Island and said your country meant to take our islands. Naturally His Majesty was upset at the time and re-affirmed the protection of Great Britain."

Scheffer said that he was a scientist going about the world under the auspices of the Russian emperor to study soils and plants for a book on the resources of the Pacific. In the course of his travels he had met Baranov at New Archangel, had become very much impressed with the man, and so had consented to come to Hawaii on his urgent request to visit King Kamehameha, for whom Baranov entertained the highest esteem and affection. If it met with the king's approval he would like to investigate the islands as a scientist and possibly remain as a sort of resident Russian consul.

It was exactly the right approach to Kamehameha, who was excited on hearing that Scheffer was a scientist as well as a physician. He immediately granted him permission to go wherever he pleased and placed at his disposal a residence at Honolulu on Oahu Island, a pretty place planted to citrus and pineapple. As for the *Bering* and the cargo, the king regretted his inability to discipline the chief on Kauai Island. Scheffer would have to go there himself but he was welcome to use what force he needed. "But His Majesty adds one warning," concluded Young; "there must be no thought of establishing a settlement. He has never permitted one and will never do so."

Scheffer expressed his deep gratitude for all the royal favors, as well he might, and they drank the healths of Tsar Alexander I and King George III in the palm wine of the region.

It took very little investigating on Scheffer's part to convince him that the Russian-American Company was entirely right in believing that a foothold on these islands would be desirable. In addition to their enormous strategic importance as a shipping center, he could see the soil and climate growing fortunes in sugar alone. He set his own men and the Kanakas kindly placed at his disposal to readying his residence among the pleasant fruit trees at Honolulu, and then went on to Kauai Island.

He found that island not as perfect for agriculture as Oahu but still rich enough in that respect and richer still in sandalwood, the article as dear to the Chinese as furs. Tamori received him like Kamehameha, in a straw greeting-hut, and Scheffer found himself in luck; Tamori was shaking with fever and his wife was heavy with dropsy. A few grains of quinine to one and a surgical trocar to the other quickly brought relief to both and made Tamori his friend.

When eventually he returned to Honolulu it was in a very

thoughtful frame of mind. He had not pressed the return of the *Bering* or cargo. Tamori might be too valuable a friend to risk his displeasure immediately. He had discovered how much Tamori hated Kamehameha and seemed disposed to listen to any scheme against his old rival, with whom in youth he had waged bitter war. The fact might be turned to account, if Kamehameha went no further than Young indicated in the way of concessions.

He first ran afoul of the Hawaiians when building a wall around his place at Honolulu. Inadvertently, he included the *morai*, the temple sacred to Kalanimoku's family at harbor's edge; though told that he trespassed on sacred ground he ordered the morai destroyed. A riot almost ensued. The Hawaiians seized spears, arrows, and their few guns and forced his men off. His next mistake was to raise the Russian flag. He could not understand when he suddenly got an order from the king ordering him to take his men and get off the islands at once.

He did not know that the lie about his being a scientist had been exposed. The *Forester* had meanwhile touched at Hawaii from Siberia, where Captain Pigot had remained to get into a great deal of trouble, as Baranov had predicted; Richard Ebbets, who brought the vessel to the king to offer for sale, knew all about Scheffer and could tell His Majesty that, far from being a scientist-at-large under tsarist auspices, he was just a lowly ship's sawbones. Kamehameha was thoroughly disgusted. When he heard Scheffer had raised the Russian flag he sent the order to get out.

Instead of hastening to apologize and trying to preserve his really extraordinary success, Scheffer abandoned Honolulu and moved to Kauai, where he laid an interesting proposal before Tamori. In return for protection from the Russian Imperial Government and five hundred men to help Tamori overthrow Kamehameha and make him ruler over all the islands, Tamori must turn over all rights in the island's sandalwood to Scheffer personally, deed a huge acreage for the setting up of taro and fruit plantations, and allow forts to be built. Furthermore he stipulated that, in the event that the conquest of the islands proved successful, Honolulu must belong exclusively to Russia. And, incidentally, the *Bering's* cargo was to be restored.

Naturally, Tamori was delighted and agreed. Scheffer hastened to send to St. Petersburg by a passing shipmaster a report on his "conquest" and Tamori's pleas for a formal protectorate. He also reported to Baranov, although he could hardly have expected approval from that quarter.

In early spring of 1816, well over a year after coming to the islands, Scheffer should have been able to count his work a success. The *Kodiak* and *Ilmen* had come bringing sixty men from the north, as promised, and he had been able to build in the beautiful valley of Hanalei, which Tamori had deeded for a plantation, a residence for himself and a fort of lava blocks, and he could survey his taro pools and his field of sugar cane backed by the cabins for his workmen. He had also built a fort at Waimea four hundred feet square with lava-block walls fourteen to thirty feet thick and twenty feet high on the leeward side. Tamori had turned over all his rights in sandalwood and the Yankee skippers came no more. Yet Scheffer was in trouble.

Baranov had sent him a peremptory order to close everything, but this he had ignored. Much more serious was the complete silence from St. Petersburg. Tamori grew restless, frightened, despite Scheffer's reassurances, by the storm of resentment stirred up all over the Pacific. At first the rumors of old Kamehameha's rage at the news of what had happened gave him cause for dancing with glee; but when he also heard that the shipmasters were conferring with John Young about driving him and Scheffer off his island he was less pleased and demanded those five hundred men.

Also he discovered he had not been too intelligent in turning over all the sandalwood to Scheffer in quite so sudden a manner. Scheffer had kept the *Kodiak* and *Ilmen*—they were still commanded by Captain Young and Wadsworth—at hand but he feared to let them go to Canton. To keep Tamori quiet he had had to spend twenty-one thousand rubles of Company funds for supplies of various kinds. Then he made the mistake of paying him in advance, to quiet him further, the enormous price of two hundred thousand rubles for a year's cut of wood.

At this juncture the answer seems to have come from Petersburg. The emperor sent to his friend King Tamori, said the embossed letter, the gift of a beautifully mounted cutlass with gold tassels and conferred on him the Order of St. Anne, but as for imperial protection His Imperial Majesty did not think it expedient at this time to grant it and begged to refuse the honor.

Tamori ordered Scheffer from his island. Scheffer refused, although his situation was rendered desperate by the desertion from his service of Captain Wadsworth, which left him only Captain Young and the *Kodiak*.

But he does not seem to have realized just how desperate his situation really was. Some months before, Vassili Tarakanov had been released after three years' imprisonment at Santa Barbara Mission, had been dropped at Hawaii, and had come to Scheffer offering his services; but Scheffer had contemptuously put him to work cultivating taro with his workmen at Hanalei.

Tarakanov, who knew natives, immediately sensed that trouble of a serious kind was brewing. For one thing the women who had attached themselves to the workmen, both Russian and Aleut, were deserting—always an ominous sign, whether in the South Seas or in the North.

Years later, when he dictated his reminiscences, Tarakanov testified that Scheffer brushed all warnings aside and seemed determined to stand off the whole world at Hanalei. Yet he was totally unprepared when the attack came. Everybody had barely time to drop tools and run from field or house to the fort for protection before the sudden onslaught of the natives armed with bows, arrows, and a few guns. Scheffer tried to offer resistance but it was worse than useless. He had not known how to build a fort and he and his men were greatly outnumbered. It was only a question of time before they had to make a break for the beach and try to get out to the *Kodiak*. Captain Young stayed with them. Fortunately the attackers seemingly only wanted to get them off the island or they would all have been certainly killed when they dashed for the surf. By the time they were aboard their fort had been taken and their own guns sent shots whistling through their rigging as a final warning to leave.

But there had been mischief aboard the *Kodiak*, too; the moment Captain Young tried to move her, leaks developed; no one could explain them and they could not investigate for the bilge came up too fast. They were between the devil and the deep sea in a literal sense. There was no alternative but to keep her afloat with the pumps and try to make Honolulu with as little sail as possible, trusting to the mercy of the natives there. Setting out to sea was impossible.

For forty-eight hours every man of the sixty aboard kept the logy old *Kodiak*—she had been Captain Barber's *Myrtle*, once—afloat by incessant work at the pumps while they crept at snail's pace down to Oahu. They were too exhausted to care that a delegation of four hundred armed, glowering natives awaited them on the beach when they entered Honolulu harbor. Like the rest, Tarakanov fell to the deck in sleep the moment they felt the vessel's bottom touch sand.

When he awoke it was to be told that he had the responsibility of what was left of the Scheffer expedition. John Young, despite the howls of the Hawaiians, had allowed Scheffer to escape with his life aboard a Yankee vessel leaving for Canton. There he disappeared, never to be heard from again.

There remains but one more thing to be said of the last colonial venture beyond the seas in Russian history.

The sixty Russians and Aleuts remained eight months longer, living and working about the islands, before arrangements could be made to take them all home. In those eight months under the discipline of Tarakanov, who was devoted to Baranov and kind to natives, their behavior was such that the island women who gradually attached themselves anew to them wept when the time came for their departure; and the old king, though the whole affair had aged him and shaken his trust in foreign friends, was almost won to let them stay when the women entreated him, for he refused to let the women go with them—"My children die in foreign lands. They are not happy among strangers." But Tarakanov knew the cause was irretrievably lost, for his government had had to make apologies and complete withdrawal was necessary as a gesture; besides, he sickened for the North after five years' absence in his fourth captivity and for a sight of his wife and children at Kodiak Island. So he arranged with Captain John Ebbets, the same who had rescued him after the Sitka Massacre, to take them all away at last on the promise to hunt otter for him on the way to pay their passage.

The illiterate promyshleniki, faithful to their duty, might have done what the St. Petersburg Russians had consistently misunderstood and failed to accomplish.

26

A Life's Work Rewarded

A T daybreak on a morning in November of 1817, the frigate
Suvarov entered Sitka Sound for the second time after
rounding half the world from Petersburg, fired a gun for
a pilot, and soon was being warped to anchorage before New Archangel. Her commander was Captain Leontii Andreanovich Hagemeister, the same who had alienated Kamehameha, on his first visit
in nine years, and her chief officer was Lieutenant Simeon Yanovski, who had also been here before as an officer under Lozarev.

In the lifting mists they discerned another frigate flying the
Russian-American Company flag, the fine *Kutusov*, of 525 tons
burden. They had left Petersburg together but the *Kutusov* had
arrived four months ahead, in July, because Hagemeister had been
delayed on the way, at Peru, San Francisco, and elsewhere.

Hagemeister stared grimly at the looming mass of Baranov's
castle. He came with orders to replace the old man, if his investigation found him unfit to continue, or to appoint another. The
Baranov-Lozarev dispute had rocked official circles at home. The
Company's board, on receiving Baranov's charges, had brought
them at once to the Admiralty. Lozarev defended himself with
countercharges against both Baranov and the board. The navy
aligned solidly to protect a brother officer, and the affair reacted
seriously against the prestige of the board with the government;
the board was already in serious embarrassment trying to get the

Scheffer matter explained to the minister of foreign affairs, who in turn had had to explain to Great Britain. Moreover, the Scheffer business had been ruinously expensive, costing well over a quarter-million dollars; Baranov's lack of wisdom in giving Scheffer unlimited credit would cost the Company an entire year's profit. That was the first time any action of Baranov's had depleted profits, but it was enough to make certain board members, heavy Petersburg businessmen for the most part, demand his removal. Fortunately for those who insisted that Baranov could not be dismissed summarily, complaints came from Callao, Peru, and other ports that in stopping at those places Lozarev had behaved arrogantly. This silenced the Admiralty but the government nevertheless sent orders to Commander Vassili Golovnin, chief of Asiatic coast defenses, to prepare a report recommending or advising against renewing the Company's charter, when it ran out in 1821. The Company, of course, wished to renew.

The board decided on an investigation of its own and deemed it expedient to choose a naval man. Why they chose Hagemeister is no longer known and the correspondence on the subject has been destroyed. Hagemeister was esteemed among his own class as a man of discretion; stupid men with little to say often give that impression. He had been suggested as a possible successor to Baranov as far back as 1814. He had found, at Callao, that Lozarev had indeed behaved badly, yet from the first he was determined to depose Baranov. But he meant to reveal nothing of his real errand until he ascertained where Baranov had hidden all his money —the rumor was current that Baranov had a private fortune deposited by his foreign cronies in American banks.

Actually, Hagemeister's chief officer and assistant was a far better diplomat. Lieutenant Simeon Ivanich Yanovski is described as having a pleasing smile, an attractive expression, and gray-blue eyes. He came of an excellent Ukrainian family of Polish extraction. He was looked on as one of the best-educated and most intelligent young men in the service. Having freely read the French liberal writers of the day, he was deeply imbued with "Peters-

burg Russianism" and cherished with his kind an amused tolerance for the art and native literature of his country, looked with
unconcealed contempt on "Holy Moscow," and thought himself
emancipated from religion.

Shortly after they cast anchor, Lieutenant Zakhar Ponifidine,
commander of the *Kutusov*, came aboard to pay his respects and
present his report. It was rumored all over Siberia and here, he
said, that the board had appointed Hagemeister to be governor and
Baranov was aware of it. Hagemeister cursed. How could the story
have traveled here so quickly? Ponifidine could not answer; it
was a mystery to him how news could be carried from Okhotsk
to Sitka in this country without a scrap of paper to bear it. Ponifidine swore he had told no one what he, Hagemeister, and Yanovski alone were supposed to know.

Ponifidine confirmed Hagemeister's findings about the Scheffer
expedition. It had indeed left a bad taste in everyone's mouth.
The long-kept secret of the Company's real policy was out at last
and all, Yankee traders, the Spanish in California, the British, were
on their guard. There would be no more peaceful advances. The
march of the promyshleniki, begun in the sixteenth century, was
over at last unless they cared to do open battle for new ground.

But, Ponifidine added, the episode had affected no one so much
as Baranov. He cursed the day he had ever hired the traitor
Scheffer and moaned because his record of always showing a profit,
despite all calamities, was broken at last. "He grows childish," said
Ponifidine. "He has turned very religious for the first time in his
life."

And he described how, when the previous year the white priest
Father Sokolov had come from Russia to officiate at New Archangel, Baranov set about transforming an old ship into a church
building which was soon dedicated to St. Michael Archangel, the
patron of the settlement whose great shining ikon Father Sokolov
brought with him. From other treasures salvaged from the wrecked
Neva they had built a gorgeous *ikonostas*, or gate to the altar. A
bell cast in the settlement's own foundry rang in the steeple and

the eucharistic vessels had been made of Spanish silver by the local blacksmiths. Baranov had supervised every detail with care and interest. For the vestments he gave some rich cloth of gold and Chinese silks, and himself instructed the Aleut women how to do the beadwork. When they had finished all agreed that never before had Aleut craftsmanship been so beautiful or delicate—a few feet off, the intricate mosaic of thousands of tiny beads looked like heavy painting on the gorgeous cloth. And when the building was finished and dedicated, the old man declared it the happiest day of his life.

Ponifidine also reported that Baranov was now much under the influence of his daughter who could manage him when no one else could, and that his son was advancing creditably as a sailor.

With these bits of information, for whatever they were worth, Hagemeister and Yanovski went ashore for the initial interview, which must have seemed none too pleasant in prospect.

Baranov waited for them with Kuglinov at the head of the staircase, dressed as usual in his badly fitting waistcoat, but he had otherwise changed. He had been an old man when last they saw him but his expression had been alert as always. Now, at seventy-one, his face had fattened and his expression had dulled.

He moved even more slowly than before and had to have much more help from his nephew. His greeting to them was formal and he led them at once to his office where he bade them sit down, while he put on his spectacles with his shaking, crooked fingers and took the letters from the envelope Hagemeister handed him.

He read them over carefully and in silence, and then, ignoring their diplomatically phrased contents, bluntly asked Hagemeister whether he had not come to replace him. Hagemeister denied it, said that he had come simply to make a survey for the Russian-American Company in order to form an opinion as to whether they ought to apply for a renewal of their charter, and asked Baranov for permission to examine his books. Baranov refused this, saying that he would show his books only to the man who came with proper authority to take charge. Hagemeister, still unwilling to divulge the fact that he had such authority, left in a quandary.

Hagemeister must surely have realized that the cat was out of the bag, that the only decent thing to do was to admit immediately his real reason for being at New Archangel, yet he stubbornly refused. He was so sure Baranov had never told, and would never tell, the full truth about his complicated dealings with Boston, Hawaii, California, and Canton, and he was also so sure about Baranov's embezzled wealth. Hagemeister seemingly believed in the old proverb, "He who has not enriched himself in office is a fool or a liar." It would seem that Yanovski was not in accord with his chief's strategy of investigating Baranov secretly but all he could do was follow orders.

Having accepted Baranov's invitation to dinner, they returned ashore with all the officers from both frigates about two o'clock in full uniform. The guns boomed a salute from the bastions, they ascended the staircase and were led to the library for chilled vodka and zakuska. Baranov received them seated in a chair. Several others were present dressed in smallclothes, Ivan Kuglinov, Khlebnikov the accountant, and Baranov's son, a dark youth who smiled with shy pleasure as Hagemeister shook his hand and called him Antipatr Aleksandrovich. But the center of attention was Irina Baranova.

Her native blood showed darkly in the warm tint of her skin but she was inordinately beautiful. She carried herself like a queen, had flashing vivacious eyes and an alert, friendly expression, and acknowledged the introductions with simple, unaffected grace. All of this was not lost on Yanovski even at that first meeting.

The old man's pride in his children was apparent. He asked Irina to sit at the piano and play for his guests, which she did with enough talent to make them all applaud heartily. His son was obviously interested in naval officers and listened eagerly to their talk.

When the Aleut servant appeared at the door to announce dinner Irina excused herself with a smile. The officers chorused their protests but Baranov silenced them with an amiable gesture. "We are an old-fashioned family," he observed. "The banqueting is for the men."

After that evening, Yanovski was not loathe to move ashore when his superior thought they could better conduct their investigations from there. The vivacity and brilliant eyes of Irina Baranova had affected him profoundly. Both Irina and Antipatr were pleased to have him and he discovered that places far from the world's centers need not be dull. He found himself enjoying with zest simple things at which he would have laughed in Petersburg. When the weather was bad they played games and when it was fair they went up Mount Verstovia for a picnic with wine or to the hot springs on the island, where Ozerskoye Redoubt had been built. They went hunting or fishing and even when it rained it was warm in the dark forests and fun to tramp the trails.

Irina was loved throughout the settlement. She took Yanovski to visit in the various cabins where grave old Russian hunters told with simple words the sagas of their journeys with the Yankees to California and their imprisonments by the Spanish or the Indians. With everyone she talked his native language. The Aleuts, who stood like dumb sticks before the questionings of strangers, brightened when she appeared and with many gestures told of their successes at the hunt. Always she was careful to ask about the health of wives and children on faraway Unalaska, Atkha Island, at Kodiak or Cook's Inlet. She even moved freely through the Kolosh village at the gates, greeting the old crones who sat in their doorways repairing fish nets and the men returning from hunting or fishing. Irina knew everything that went on in the Pacific. She could tell the duty a skipper must pay at Canton, the time of sailing from the Horn to the Sandwiches, and estimate at a glance the tonnage of a Yankee brig.

And she was intensely religious with a faith that was as real to her as her raven hair. Doubt and lack of faith to her were things impossible to comprehend. Yanovski found himself closing his teeth on his opinions for the sake of a girl's trust and standing with folded hands and a wooden face when Father Sokolov said mass.

Meanwhile Hagemeister was getting nowhere with his investigations. Baranov might have commanded the entire garrison to keep its mouth closed for all the secrets Hagemeister unraveled.

New Archangel had had its fill of talking with Lozarev three years before; anyway it distrusted naval officers. It was easy to find out what expeditions had gone to California and what foreign ships had called, but nobody could remember just how many skins were brought back or sold. When it came to Baranov's money all only chorused that he was most generous at all times. Even Hagemeister's attempts to inveigle Khlebnikov into revealing secrets failed. That correct young man could only spread his hands helplessly and proclaim his ignorance. Nobody but Baranov himself knew the whole truth about the value and assets of Russian America.

Christmas came and went with a fine service in the little church attended by all the visiting officers and their crews, and afterwards there was a great praznik for everybody. And not long after Yanovski searched his heart and decided that he could not live without Baranov's daughter.

He had known her only six weeks but seeing her almost daily had convinced him that her beauty, kindness of heart, and goodness of soul outweighed all the social shortcomings of her mixed blood, curious legitimatization, patchwork education, and deep piety. Besides, he had little time to waste. He was sure Irina loved him in return but he was not at all sure her father did. She was seventeen, but marrying without his consent was unthinkable; the political situation at New Archangel would shortly be complicated enough without that in addition.

Then there was the matter of obtaining the consent of his own superior officer. Yanovski simply had to bring the farce of their investigation to a quick conclusion and make Hagemeister tell the old man the truth. The more he saw of Baranov the more he was certain they had been wrong in approaching him from the first without complete honesty. Now there was the matter of being further a party to the deception which might anger the old man, when he was finally told the truth, enough to deny him forever the happiness he sought.

Hagemeister undoubtedly expected to hear what Yanovski asked. Everyone at New Archangel had been watching with deep interest the growing ardor between the officer and Irina Aleksandrovna. The commander was willing to consent to Yanovski asking for Irina's hand but loathe to come out with the truth. He was still stubbornly of the opinion that he could find out certain things more effectually if Baranov did not know the real reason for his presence. And now he was beginning to think it might never do to reveal his real orders and step into Baranov's shoes. It had become increasingly clearer each day that a large number of people, perhaps as many as a third, would leave the company service, returning to Russia or retiring somewhere, or if they were of native blood returning to their villages, if a naval officer took command.

He was in a difficult dilemma. It was also clear that the relief of Baranov could not much longer be delayed. The old man had been ill and abed some of the time. The work of actual administration was in great part being carried on by Khlebnikov and others. However, he consented to let Yanovski ask Irina what should be done.

She was shocked to hear the truth from her lover.

"There is but one way to make my father tell his secrets," she instantly replied. "He is frank and open only when others are too. If he refuses to talk it is because he knows Commander Hagemeister also conceals something. Father will hide nothing from you when he knows what you want. Stop playing a game with him!"

Hagemeister listened to Yanovski's report with thoughtful attention. But the problem of how best to honor Baranov did not interest him. That he brushed aside brusquely in his mind. A plan had occurred to him and the more he thought it over the more it seemed the only feasible way to displace Baranov without wrecking the personnel of the colonies, yet at the same time to put the navy in power. The plan was to appoint Yanovski governor after he was accepted as Baranov's son-in-law.

Yanovski was shocked by the suggestion but after thinking it over he saw that it might indeed be the best way to get themselves out of the difficulties in which they had become involved by their first lack of frankness. And when Hagemeister promised to reveal everything to the old man without further delay he consented.

The problem was to get Baranov to accept him first. He carefully put on his full-dress uniform and then, gloves in hand and sword by his side, he called at the castle and found the old man at his desk where, although he spent more and more time in bed, he liked to put in a short while each day to receive the reports of Kuglinov and Khlebnikov.

When the young man haltingly told of his love for and desire to marry Irina, Baranov nodded. He was prepared. His daughter had told him she loved this man. He was relieved to see him approach him in this honorable and traditional manner. He had been greatly worried about Irina's marrying; he had prayed it would be with a Russian of kind heart and good station. So many of the creoles, even after a completely Russian upbringing, preferred marriages with their mother's people. Now he could see her married in his lifetime and the man was all he wished. Characteristically, he forgot that Yanovski had been identified with Lozarev or wore the uniform of the class that had hated him. The man who wanted to be Irina's husband was intelligent, educated, of good family, and well-disposed; that was all that mattered. "God bless you, Simeon Ivanich," he said. "I am very happy."

The happy news ran through the garrison like wildfire and spread from village to Kolosh village until it reached Prince William Sound, whence it was eventually transmitted to the lonely station at Unalaska and even to the Pribylovs. Nanuk's daughter was to be married! New Archangel celebrated the event with a high praznik and Irina and Yanovski had to appear together to acknowledge with laughs and drinks the cheers and good wishes for their happiness.

But Hagemeister wasted no time with festivities. He ordered Ponifidine to take all furs out of the warehouses onto the *Suvarov* and ready her for sailing in three days time to Petersburg with his report that he meant to appoint Yanovski.

He must have revealed his orders at least to Khlebnikov to get those furs out of the warehouses, for there were over two hundred thousand rubles' worth, but with unpardonable cruelty he did not bother to tell Baranov until the old man demanded to know why so important an event as the making ready of a frigate for sailing had not been reported to him. Then Hagemeister called on him, accompanied by Lieutenant Ponifidine. And with the same lack of consideration for personal feelings that had ruined relations with King Kamehameha he informed Baranov that he was no longer governor and placed before him his written authority to appoint himself or anyone else he thought fit. He then demanded that Baranov deliver all books and funds within twelve hours.

Baranov at first seemed not to understand fully. Twelve hours? He had always planned to spend weeks, even months, with his successor to explain everything. Twelve hours was impossible. And as for Company funds—

He suddenly understood. He understood everything. Why they already had loaded furs on the *Suvarov*, why these men had not told them all their powers in the first place, why they had lulled him into believing his successor could not come in reason before spring. Now this Hagemeister laid this paper under his nose and told him to give up the money immediately, to this other man who waited. He was suspected of being a thief!

He fell back in his chair and covered his face. The tears came, the hot, bitter, impotent tears of a man once strong who fumbles vainly for his lost strength to meet the supreme disillusionment of his life.

Even Hagemeister was at last frightened by his own blundering stupidity. They called the servants. Baranov had to be put to bed. Irina wept when they took him upstairs. They took his clothing off and covered him with sheets, and after a time the hard, wracking sobs that shook his frame stopped but he did not seem to hear when anyone spoke to him. He could only stare at the ceiling. It was hours before he at last dropped off to exhausted sleep.

On the morning of January 26, the day the *Suvarov* had been scheduled to sail, as if by the ringing of a bell in his brain that had always roused him to see personally to so important an event as a ship departure, Baranov called for his clothes. But he was very weak and had to be carried downstairs. Khlebnikov was there, with Ponifidine. Without formality, with none of the ceremonial pomp which for twenty years he had planned to mark this occasion, Baranov turned his keys over to the accountant, apologizing for the state in which he would find the books of accounts. Many of them were on scraps of paper, for a better medium was often not available. The financial history of twenty-eight years in Russian America was there, but could anyone save Baranov decipher it? As for money there was little in cash, for his medium of exchange had always been furs. He assured Khlebnikov that he would be of assistance in every way possible.

There remained now that which was perhaps of greater importance even than the transfer of his authority.

Irina Aleksandrovna knelt at her father's feet, as the old custom was, and implored his forgiveness of all her sins. It was the ceremony at the bride's home before the wedding. Downstairs on the bastions the whole garrison of New Archangel stood ready to watch them march down and across the little square to the church where Father Sokolov waited in his vestments surrounded by his native acolytes. Baranov gave his daughter a piece of bread and a grain of salt in token that her father would never let her go hungry even though she left his house for another's. Then the bridegroom kneeled beside her and received from her a little whip braided from her own hair in token of her complete submission to his will, as Baranov put on his spectacles and with shaken voice read the ordained prayers. Then, as Yanovski and his daughter walked out of the castle together, the father left open the door in token that his home would ever be open to receive her if her husband was not kind.

And long was the service in the Church of St. Michael Archangel and the men who surrounded the bride during the March of the Three Crowns had much candle grease on their clothes before they could at last snuff out the tapers in their hands.

The guns of the little battery boomed with an extra flourish as the sloop moved out of Sitka Sound bearing Irina Yanovska and her husband on their wedding journey. They went northward to see Prince William Sound—land of her mother's people—Cook's Inlet, the Pribylovs, and Kodiak where Anna Grigoryevna could see for herself this new son who came from the same land as had her husband.

Who could have probed Baranov's thoughts as he was helped back up the steps to his familiar office after having waved them out of sight? Kodiak, Prince William Sound, Cook's Inlet! Once the Kenaitze people had become an ally of his only because he had married a woman of their people. Now his people, his faithful employees and friends, would give their confidence to their new master because he had signified his willingness to take a bride from among them. At worst it was no different from what he himself had done. He knew very well that Yanovski's marriage guaranteed there would be fewer leaves when he officially let go the reins. Already many an old hunter, who had often said that if the naval men took over he would leave, grudgingly consented to remain because he said he felt Baranov's daughter would never let them be imposed upon.

He began the task of computing funds on hand and deciphering the old ledgers for Khlebnikov's benefit.

It became a passion with him, this delving into the past; before many days he decided to enlarge the task he had set himself on the company's old books and make an estimate of the total value of Russian America. As always when he greatly wished to do a thing he found a hidden source within to give him strength and he sat in his office hours longer daily than he had for years, and went over the old records, until Khlebnikov found spring was passing them by, then summer, and still the task was not finished. But he did not try to hurry Baranov, for almost every item recalled men and circumstances which Khlebnikov took down to put in the biography he intended to write.

Some deep though scarcely perceptible change seems to have been wrought in Baranov by this going over the steps of his life. Memories, like huge waves, rose and in their intensity he was swept from his present life into the past. As usual that summer the shipmasters visited, including the first Frenchman in thirty years; Hagemeister left to visit Fort Ross to remain until late fall and his daughter returned from her wedding trip, radiantly happy with her husband. But Baranov seemed scarcely to notice. There came moments when, lost in his memories, he seemed hardly to realize where he was or why he was there. His mind seemed to be searching for the details of his childhood and youth, facts which might have been lost in the vast anonymity of Russian common life had he not told them to Khlebnikov. As is but natural he dwelt on his times of happiness and slurred over those in which he had been unhappy. He had little to recall of his first marriage, for instance.

Some things he naturally exaggerated; he said he had been made a member of the Imperial Free Economics Society at Irkutsk, whereas all he had done was to read a paper. But after his mind left Okhotsk to come to America for the first time his memory sharpened and was aided by the records at hand.

He seemed to feel no rancor and give no bad opinion of anyone dead or alive, which made the biography that Khlebnikov subsequently wrote often "colorless." Not being analytical by nature, too, he was not preoccupied with seeking the meaning of his life or deeds but only with establishing facts and places. With the details of his crowded life parading thus before him, and living again with much of the old excitement all his battles and accomplishments, the enormity of it all was born in upon him and he seemed to sense that such a life was filled beyond its share.

The first signs of his disintegration began. He began forgetting the use of things. He would stop to stare at a cup in his hand, or at papers before him, as if to ask himself, *What have I to do with this cup*, or *What are these papers to me?* He began to ask Father Sokolov often to visit him.

In September, however, after more than seven months, he finished with the last of the ledgers and Khlebnikov was able to add up the last column of figures, after which Baranov delivered the report of his administration to his son-in-law, concluding the document with these words: "I recommend to your special care the people who have learned to love me and who, under judicious treatment, will be as well-disposed toward those who watch over them in the future."

A few details from the report may serve to show the extent of Baranov's material accomplishments.

The beginnings of 1790 had expanded to twenty-four establishments ranging in size from simple hunting stations to New Archangel, whose worth alone was estimated at two million, five hundred thousand rubles. The north island establishments were: St. Paul village and four stations on Kodiak, the sealing station on the Pribylovs and others on Okamuk, Atkha, Bering, and Unalaska Islands. The north mainland stations were: Katmai, the three old forts on Cook's Inlet, Resurrection Harbor, and Fort Constantine and Fort St. Helens on Prince William Sound. On the south mainland were: two small forts near St. Elias, New Archangel with Ozerskoye Redoubt at the hot springs near by, and Fort Ross in California.

The census showed 391 men and 13 women of pure Russian blood and 244 creole men and 111 women; 8,384 male natives were available for command. One hundred and ninety-eight of the Russians were at New Archangel, twenty-seven at Fort Ross with about sixty natives, and twenty-seven on the Pribylovs. Some stations had but two or three.

The financial worth of the Company in America was estimated

at seven million hard, nineteenth-century gold rubles, an increase of five and a half millions in twenty-one years. Nine vessels had been built in America, five bought from foreigners, and four frigates purchased in Europe.

In those twenty-one years, Baranov had received shipments worth 2,800,000 rubles but had sold at Canton 3,648,002 rubles' worth in trade and through Irkutsk 16,376,696 rubles' worth—an impressive tribute to his ability as a businessman. Net earnings had been seven and a half millions, of which four and a quarter were distributed to stockholders as dividends. The net profit for the year 1816–17 alone was close to a million and a quarter. Russian-American Company shares were quoted at 592.53, with a par value of 100.

"In the cash accounts, involving millions," wrote Khlebnikov, "I found not one single discrepancy." The valuation of raw furs on hand showed two hundred thousand rubles, and total supplies and materials on hand stood at more than a million and a half. Of all the supply accounts the only one showing a discrepancy was the item of liquor.

Of Baranov's reputed wealth in foreign banks there was not a trace. And the amount of money he owned was very small—he had given away, to Kuskov, Banner, the school at Kodiak, and to other charities more than he suspected. His precise earnings are difficult to estimate now; he had thirteen shares, which in 1817 earned two thousand six hundred rubles, but he was also on salary as governor and as commander at New Archangel. In all it probably amounted to about eight thousand rubles yearly. But he had hung onto none of it.

His son-in-law accepted the report with a solemn promise to observe the injunction to rule tenderly and with justice—Hagemeister was still absent in California; then for days Baranov wandered about New Archangel in confusion of spirit, his mind like an old ram that has walked a treadmill too long and cannot understand firm ground. But he had perforce to bring himself back to the present. His daughter and son-in-law understood and by gentle urgings helped recall important, immediate questions. What was he going to do with himself now?

Part of the unwillingness of his mind to return to the present was also due to his shock on appraising his own worth in material terms. He had not realized he was so poor a man. He had always given money away to others without much thought and even now, when virtually all the old colonials were coming to ask him what he thought they should do with their futures, he was forever canceling their commissary accounts from his own funds, without thinking of his own problem. It was hard to give up the old grandiose habits of thought, that he could be generous when it suited him and that when he would be free of his duties he would travel or do anything else he pleased.

Now he had to put his old dream of traveling resolutely from him. What he had left would, with the greatest care, barely support him in comfort the rest of his life; his generosities had gravely endangered even the funds for Antipatr's education. He could not help feeling bitterness toward the directors for having sent him no offer to be useful to the Company in any further capacity. Delarov had been asked to sit on the board of directors when the Company was formed, and sat in their meetings until 1807. Why had not the same been suggested to him? But after the events of the past months he was too proud to ask for any such honor, let alone the pension everyone with reason felt he should have been offered.

They still show, at Sitka, a large flat rock in a nook sheltered with ferns and trees and overlooking Sitka Sound where Baranov is said to have sat often, these last days, thinking out his personal problems. He thought of returning to Kargopol, to the scenes of his youth, but the prospect was like the taste of stale beer. It would be inexpensive, but no one would know him, no one remember. He was strongly attracted to the thought of living in Petersburg but it was beyond his means. He considered retiring to Kodiak, then thought of Ozerskoe Redoubt, on Sitka Island, where he could build himself a little house and live with a servant or two and be near the center of things, on hand to help with his advice and counsel. He talked over each thought with Irina, who seems to have tried to make him think favorably of rejoining his brother, Pyotr, who still lived and ran a trading station at Ishiginsk, in Siberia.

He mulled over the advantages of this course, then decided on it; he would go after visiting a month or two with old friends at Kodiak and seeing Anna Grigoryevna. Then he veered back to the thought of Ozerskoe Redoubt—his desire to be yet useful was the motivating force—and there his mind stubbornly stuck until John Ebbets and the *Enterprise* brought back Tarakanov and the other Scheffer expedition survivors from the Sandwich Islands.

Tarakanov told how he and Don Juan Eliot had been captured off San Luis Obispo by soldiers and how, because of the Aleut clothing he wore and his darkness of skin engendered by much exposure to wind and weather, he was at first unable to convince the Spanish authorities he was not an Indian. They had therefore put him with the natives being christianized by the Franciscans at Santa Barbara.

"They are not true Christians," he said, shaking his head. "They say they alone preach the true Gospel but they make the sign of the cross from left to right instead of in the proper manner, from right to left."

Eventually his skill with tools was discovered by the Franciscans and they made him the mission carpenter with a shop of his own. They called him "*El Russo*" and realized he was not an Indian; but still they would not let him go until the explorer von Kotzebue, happening to touch at California, persuaded the governor to release him and Don Juan Eliot and took them to Hawaii, where they arrived in the thick of the Scheffer troubles. He told all that had happened and described the taro pools, the sunshine, the broad trees, the blue waters. He went on to say that Don Juan Eliot had spoken well of him to the king and that when, after Scheffer had left and the Russians behaved so well that everyone came to love them, the old king became convinced that Baranov had had nothing to do with Scheffer and sent, by Tarakanov, his good wishes and royal blessing to Baranov.

This decided Baranov. He would go to Hawaii and spend his declining years with the king, who was also growing old. He would undo the harm that Scheffer had done. It was the ideal solution. He would live in comfort yet still be useful. He was irritable to find he was opposed. He brushed all objections aside and began making noisy preparations to go, after spending his month or so at Kodiak.

Yanovski was horror-stricken. The best thing to be done with the Sandwich Islands now was to let them strictly alone; for Baranov to go there might provoke nothing less than an international situation. But he had no success dissuading the old man.

Yanovski was in a difficult position. He knew Baranov could be persuaded to stay in America, yet it had been evident from the day he issued the orders for some long overdue reforms that Baranov must be removed from America, and quickly, if he, Yanovski, were to have any authority. Everyone treated him with respect but it was to Baranov that everyone went from habit and the old man, forgetting he had long since been displaced, issued orders and gave advice as always.

Among the needed reforms was the change in the basis of employee pay from the old on-shares basis, na paik, to straight salary —a necessary change if the policy of developing the interior of the country were ever to be started. Old Russians are creatures of habit. From Kodiak came a growl of discontent. The suggestion had been made by the company before, but the men had always refused to accept it. Baranov could be counted on to wreak havoc with the reform, if he got to Kodiak where he could hear the lamentations of the men whose allegiances were still firmly attached to his person.

At this time, Commander Vassili Golovnin arrived on the sloop-of-war *Kamchatka*. His purpose was to make an investigation for the Russian government regarding the advisability of renewing the Russian-American Company charter; his intention to recommend that private control in Russian America be abolished. A bluff, positive old sea dog trained by the British, he had patrolled the Siberian coast for years and knew more about the Pacific than any other Russian officer. To him Yanovski confided his difficulty. How could he get Baranov out of Russian America, yet keep him from going to the Sandwich Islands? Golovnin took the matter in hand.

"Don't you realize," he said to Baranov, "that no one in Petersburg knows the situation here as you do? Why, how can you think of depriving the Company of your advice and counsel by going elsewhere?"

Baranov listened eagerly, but after some thought, shook his head sadly. "Thank you, Vassili Mikhailovich, but they have sent no word and I shall not force myself on them."

Golovnin brushed this aside. "I am the government inspector and make the recommendations. It is unthinkable you have not been put in the post of adviser to the board on American affairs and I shall write and tell them so."

This put the matter in a different light and Baranov's face regained its eagerness as Golovnin expatiated on the good he could render them all by his advice in Petersburg. At length Baranov was convinced. As abruptly as he had switched to the Sandwich Islands he now changed to the new plan and announced with great satisfaction that he would leave for Russia as soon as he had paid that visit to Kodiak.

It is difficult to believe that all of them, Irina and Yanovski and all, would conspire to prevent him from taking that last journey to familiar scenes, to see Anna Grigoryevna, but it must have been impossible to let him go. The *Kutusov* would sail in a month, or shortly after Hagemeister's return.

Again it was Golovnin who saved the situation. He told Baranov it was imperative he sit for his portrait to the painter Tikhanov, who was part of the personnel aboard the *Kamchatka*. Since there was no existing likeness of Baranov, Golovnin pointed out, it was not fair to posterity to overlook this opportunity. So Baranov amiably again put off his trip north and sat at his desk, pen in hand, in his favorite position as Tikhanov set up his easel.

Hagemeister returned, during the process, with a load of goods bought in California. Baranov paid little attention to him. The news had leaked out that he was going to Petersburg as adviser to the board and he had many callers, among them two powerful Kolosh leaders, the chief of the Awks and Kot-le-an, the instigator of the Sitka Massacre and successor to Ska-out-lelt as chief of the Sitkans. There was much ceremony as the two venerable natives who had once helped kill everyone in the place entered the gates and mounted the bastions. They were observed to be hiding with the utmost difficulty their astonishment at what the Russians had built on the onetime site of the home of Sitka kwan.

Their faces were painted in the totemic symbols of their septs, woolen togas edged with ermine were flung Roman-fashion over their powerful shoulders, their thick black hair was combed in long strands and matted with goosedown, and they bore the willow wands indicating a wish for peace. Baranov invited them gravely into the library, seated them on the floor, served them food, then waited in silence until they were ready to speak. Finally, Kot-le-an opened his mouth.

"They tell me you are going to see the emperor."

Baranov nodded. There was another long silence.

"We have hated you," Kot-le-an said. "You drove our kwan from its home. You chastised our people. You kept the foreign shipmasters from selling us guns and powder. You took away our trade. Fourteen years we have planned revenge." There was another silence. "Now, however, we are all old men together and are about to die. Let us be brothers." The Awk chief grunted his agreement.

"Once I came here to Sitka in peace, as I came to Yakutat," Baranov answered, "and offered to pay for a small piece of land on which to dwell. You saw fit to go back on your word and kill my people. But, as you say, we are old men together now. We will soon die. The young should not remember why we have hated. My son-in-law remains here as Nanuk. Send him the copper shields of friendship and amity and I will have nothing but good to say of you to the emperor."

This was considered in silence, then agreed to.

"Now I have a present for you," concluded Baranov. And to the aged savages he gave a suit of chain mail sent to the colonies many years before. "You have often wondered why your arrows never killed Nanuk. This was his invulnerability."

When the chiefs had departed, Baranov grew impatient of Tikhanov's deliberate slowness, and said he was going to Kodiak, portrait or no portrait, but he fell ill and had to take to his bed. He fretted a great deal over the fact but knew he was too ill to go.

One day Antipatr came to see him, sat on the edge of his bed, and took his hands in his own. The boy announced that Commander Golovnin had offered to take him on the *Kamchatka* and sponsor him for the cadet school in Petersburg. It was good news to Baranov. Now his son would have the advantages which his own lack of money made it impossible to secure otherwise.

They came and told him that the *Kutusov* would be sailing on December 1. That was a week off. He called for his clothes, and again began sitting for his portrait.

He seemed to realize at last he was not to go to Kodiak, for during these days he arranged a pension in order that Anna Grigoryevna would never be in want.

December 1, he rose before dawn and tried to be hearty, but it was impossible. All the ships he had seen go, all the farewells he had said to returning hunters, must have risen in his memory, and his eyes filled with tears. Irina kissed him tenderly as did Antipatr, and Yanovski embraced him as a son but he hardly saw them. He seemed but dimly conscious of the fact that several people helped him down the stairs to the bastions, then onto the wharf. He managed to pull himself together, shake off the hands supporting his arms as he wiped his eyes to take his last look standing on Russian American soil. The garrison lined the bastions in silence and the shoreline was covered with canoes and silent, watching Indians. The Kolosh had come, the Chilkats, the Sitkans, the Awks, and Hootsnahoos, in their long canoes to see him go away. He waved and tried to smile but the tears came again with a rush and he was quite unable to see as they helped him into the *Kutusov's* small-boat.

Aboard ship he would not go to his cabin as Hagemeister and Kuglinov urged him to do but stubbornly insisted on watching the raising of the anchor. He remained there, at the rail, watching New Archangel recede and the dark shoreline of Sitka Sound pass until the fogs and the early darkness of winter obscured everything.

27

Death in the Pacific

In the old Grand Hotel at Batavia, on Java Island, the ceilings were all very high and decorated red and gold or blue and gold. At dinner an orchestra of a dozen Negroes played and everywhere uniformed flunkeys stood at attention. But it was all hollow pretense. The old opulent days of the Dutch East India Company, which had called this stuffy magnificence into being for the pleasure of its merchants, had long since ended. The gilt was peeling from the ceilings, the red and blue paint was stained and soiled, and the flunkeys stood rigidly against the walls to hide the patches in their uniforms.

Here, while Hagemeister dickered with Dutch merchants over trade relations and bought one hundred thousand rubles' worth of merchandise, Baranov spent thirty-six days after a stormy ten-week passage unbroken by any stop, even at Honolulu. Hagemeister had not wished to risk even tempting the old man to land there.

Baranov had said nothing to that at the time. He said even less about this delay at Batavia, although he seemed to sense that if he were to see Russia again they had best hurry. He realized now he could never say anything to move Hagemeister. They were all alike. He had learned many things on the voyage. He had learned that Hagemeister had taken from Sitka all the files of records and correspondence and had been spending his time going over them.

Was he determined to find something against him? Why should he take them to Petersburg? Was the navy bound to besmirch his character in order to insure its continued command over what he had built?

It made him sad, reserved, and silent. They wanted him to remain aboard while in port but he insisted on going ashore even though all told him it was healthier on board. He was tired in body of the frigate's buffetings and in his cabin this damp heat suffocated him and the rain annoyed him as it had never done in Sitka.

Installed at the old Grand Hotel he passed most of his time in the ornate, deserted bar or sitting on the veranda gazing at the neat rows of Dutch brick houses with diamond-shaped windows, or staring out across the bay with its multitude of pretty islands into which emptied the Chiliwong River and all the sewage from the motley population that lined its banks.

He was puzzled to account for the speed with which he got drunk in this country. Perhaps it was the arrack they served, he decided; he insisted, therefore, on his familiar rum, but for some reason the rum was worse, so he switched back to arrack.

"Try your drinks cold," someone in the bar managed to convey with many gestures. So he tried his drinks cold, but they made him drunk just as fast as the lukewarm ones.

There were things to see in Java, they told him, curious native dances and barbaric music made by beating sonorous gongs, but he wanted neither to hear nor see anything in this land. "Show me Russia and let me hear Russian singing again," he said. "That is all I wish."

One day as he sat on the veranda, thinking his thoughts, Ivan Kuglinov brought him the news that Kamehameha was dying at the Sandwich Islands.

Baranov looked down at his glass in silence. Now they would never see one another. Hagemeister had passed by, hustling him away from all he had promised himself he would enjoy when he was free.

But it mattered little now. All his hopes, even life itself, had become for him an elusive, empty, half-remembered dream.

On April 13, 1819, by Russian reckoning, the *Kutusov* lay under idle canvas in the Straits of Sunda, which separate Java and Sumatra. The officers and crew stood at attention facing the stern where, on a board level with the taffrail, lay a long, canvas-covered bundle, to the bottom end of which was attached a cannon ball.

Ivan Kuglinov and the two Aleuts who had been Baranov's servants wept unashamedly. Captain-Lieutenant Leontii Hagemeister stepped forward, opened the official naval prayer book, and cleared his throat. "I am the resurrection and the life," he read aloud. "He that believeth in me, though he were dead, yet shall he have everlasting life. . . ."

At the proper signal two members of the crew stepped forward, lifted the board on which the canvas bundle lay, and raised one end. . . . All that was mortal of Aleksandr Andrevich Baranov slid slowly down the board and was received into the depths of the placid, blue tropical waters.

Envoy

EW histories have so definite an end, or one so quickly told. Simeon Yanovski left for Russia in 1821, after less than three years as governor, eager to show his lovely, exotic wife to his family and his friends. He went back a changed man, belief in his people and his people's faith reanimated in his heart. Father Herman converted him, the old monk who lived to become the patriarch of Russian America and who had learned wisdom and tolerance working among Kodiak's Aleuts. "He talked with such force," Yanovski wrote, "he argued so sensibly and convincingly that it seemed that no earthly knowledge or wisdom could contradict his words."

Father Herman warned Yanovski that because Irina had never known cities she would sicken and die young in them, as indeed she did, to Yanovski's great grief, leaving one son and one or two daughters—the record is not clear. The son, christened Aleksandr after his famous grandfather, became the Archmonk Christopher, of exemplary life and now of blessed memory.

Nor did Antipatr long survive cities; he achieved his ambition to attend the imperial cadet school at Petersburg but he died in early manhood without leaving recorded progeny. Baranov had had no son by his first wife. A curious habit, this tendency of the self-made great in history to die out in their issue. There are no male descendants of Aleksandr Baranov.

Ivan Kuskov lost little time resigning at Fort Ross and returning to Russia on the death of Baranov and the coming of the navy, and he died not long after, in 1823. Kamehameha died a month after Baranov's body slid silently into the waters of the Straits of Sunda.

Apparently Anna Grigoryevna, the Kenaitze woman, outlived all the other personae of this drama. She continued for many years on Kodiak Island on her pension as Baranov's widow until, a feeble, wrinkled, pious old woman, she passed away, happy in the certitude she was going to the heaven of the Russians.

Now the country is Yankee; on Cook's Inlet, Prince William Sound, and the mainland southward are towns busy with fishing, canning, and shipping, and up the Inland Passage to Sitka come the boatloads of tourists to be awed and silenced by the stupendous grandeur of what they see. But if you will take ship off the tourist track, farther to the north, retracing the steps of the Russians, one striking difference from the rest of America will occur to you; it is the completeness with which the natives have absorbed the Christian faith. In most white men's colonies Christ came first and trade second, only to have that balance suffer a bad reversal as civilization hardened; but here, where Christianity came ineptly, Russian trade and influence have vanished and the faith remains. From the Cathedral of St. Michael at Sitka to the end of the Aleutians the bulbed domes of Russian Orthodoxy stand. Here the fathers learned at long last, and for many years after the country became Yankee they continued, on funds from home, to care with tenderness and affection for orphans and to face the rigors of their huge and dangerous parishes with courage. When the fall of the tsars crippled their work with dire poverty they kept on nonetheless, living on the country's resources. There finally had come to Russian America a priest who was to faith what Baranov had been to trade: Bishop Veniaminov, great of mind and heart, energetic of body and clever of hand, who sent forth his monks with a new concept of their duty and soon had his faith firmly established in the hearts of all the people.

In the measure in which the spirit of the missionaries strengthened, that of the merchants withered. The Russian-American Company saw two renewals of its charter after 1821 and it existed for forty more years, but it became increasingly apparent that something was missing after the death of Baranov. After Yanovski came a long line of administrators, usually from the navy, each seeming a bit more decorative than the last, each bringing more brilliance

to life at the old castle, until the castle burned and they built another. The greatest brilliance of all was achieved under Prince
Maksoutov, last of the Russian governors of Alaska. But it was all
hollow pretense.

The profits from Russian America went down and down progressively. The importance of New Archangel as a port waned.
The Hudson's Bay Company, which encroached steadily on the
Russians, managed to show a profit from its furs, but the Russian-
American Company complained that the fur animals had decreased
to the point of no profit. California became known as a great agricultural country, but Fort Ross grew progressively less able to
pay its way until it was closed by selling it to John Sutter. It has
been said that the company was unaware of the gold on America's
west coast but this is untrue; the archives of the Department of
Manufactures and Internal Commerce show that in 1848 mining
experts employed by the company to investigate recommended
strongly that the company engage in gold mining in California.
The report moved no one in Petersburg because Petersburg took
no interest.

Petersburg was saying that the whole business had been a mistake and was costing more than it was worth, that the coast was
impossible to defend, and that it had better be sold to the Yankees
than let it fall into the hands of the British, as seemed inevitable.
The Russians were inept as colonists, was another charge; they
could not solve their transportation problems.

Others said that it was all because there was never another at
Sitka as capable as Baranov. But that is wrong. There was another
at Sitka after Baranov who was as energetic and far better qualified
by education and training for the task. Baron Ferdinand Petrovich
von Wrangell loved and understood the north; at the age of
twenty-five he had headed a four-year expedition to explore polar
regions. Appointed, at thirty-six, governor at Sitka ten years after
Baranov, he rediscovered Rezanov's dream and perceived that they
who control Alaska can control the Pacific. He grasped at the last

chance of the Russians to acquire California—Mexico made tentative offers to trade the region to them in return for recognition by the tsar of her independence from Spain. Von Wrangell traveled to Mexico City, then to Petersburg, but in vain. Petersburg would not move, and the merchants could not. The Russian-American Company's once-vast powers to make such treaties as affected its welfare had in effect been completely nullified by the government and the board was helpless.

There lay the real trouble. Rough, crude merchants of Siberia had started the whole enterprise because their initiative had been made free by Catherine the Great. As long as they were free the movement had vitality and force, it was vitiated when Petersburg reassumed control. The conclusion seems inescapable; the acts were simultaneous. Actually Petersburg reassumed control before Baranov was out of office. Rezanov had dreamed of a firm like the British East India Company when many Russians like him thought their country was well out of tsardom's dark days; but those days came back, and in 1863 when the Russian-American Company passed out of existence it was but a faint suggestion of its English prototype.

Von Wrangell in 1840 joined the board of directors and tried to reanimate it with an awareness of what it was losing, but it was already too late; the cold hand of the tsars once more lay heavy on the merchants. Fourteen years later the Russian ambassador leaving for Washington was instructed to awaken the cupidity of the Yankees by offering the whole country to them for as little as five million dollars.

In 1867 he sold Alaska for seven million two hundred thousand—a territory the size of Texas, comprising an immense variety of soils, a stand of merchantable timber fourth in rank in North America, a potential waterpower exceeding that of any state, fishery resources greater than those of any country in the world, and a ring of islands commanding the Pacific Ocean. On October 18, 1867, the Russian flag was hauled down at Sitka for the last time and the American standard raised in its place. Russia withdrew from the world's race for maritime colonies. The despairing cry of Peter the Great that his people would never be a nation of sailors seemed justified at long last.

Sources

Alexander I, Tsar, *Decrees*, in *Arkhiv Pravityelistvuishchavo Senata* ("Archive of the Ruling Senate"), St. Petersburg, 1872.

Alexander, W. D., *Proceedings of the Russians on Kaui*, Proceedings of the Hawaiian Historical Society.

Andrews, Clarence, *The Story of Alaska*, Caldwell, Idaho, 1938.

—— *The Story of Sitka*, Seattle, 1922.

—— "The Wreck of the St. Nicholas," *Washington Historical Quarterly*, January, 1922.

—— "Alaska under the Russians," *Washington Historical Quarterly*, October, 1916.

—— "The Historical Russian Library of Alaska," *Pacific Northwest Quarterly*, April, 1938.

—— "The Song of Baranov," in *Nuggets of Northland Verse*, Seattle, 1935.

Atahualpa, The Log of the, Mss., Massachusetts Historical Society *Collection*.

Bancroft, Hubert Howe, *History of Alaska*, San Francisco, 1886.

—— *History of the Northwest Coast*, San Francisco, 1884.

—— *History of California*, San Francisco, 1884.

Baranov, Aleks. A., Misc. papers relating to, in National Archives, Washington, D.C.; Correspondence with Astor, in K. W. Porter, *John Jacob Astor*; Correspondence, general, in Tikhmenyev's *Istoricheskoye*, and in Kodiak Mission, *Istorya*.

Baranov, Antipatr Aleksandrovich, Petition relating to his mother, Mss. in National Archives, Washington, D.C.

Berkh, Vassili N., *Khronologiskaya istorya otkrytya Aleutskikh ostrovov ili podvigi Rossiiskavo kupechestva* ("Chronological history of the discovery of the Aleutian Islands, or the exploits of the Russian commercial companies"), St. Petersburg, 1823.

—— *Opisanye nestchastnavo korablekrushenya frigata Nevi* ("An account of the disastrous wreck of the Neva"), St. Petersburg, 1817.

Bolotov, Archimandrite Iosaph, *Kratkoye opisanye ob Amerikanskom ostrovye Kadiakye . . ."* ("Short Account of the American island of Kodiak . . ."), Moscow, 1805.

—— *Correspondence*, in Tikhmenyev, *Istor*.

Bone, J. H. A., "Russian America," *Atlantic Monthly*, June, 1867.

Buldakov, Mikhail Matvyevich, Correspondence, in National Archives, Washington, D.C.

Campbell, Archibald, *A Voyage around the world, from 1806 to 1812, in which Japan, Kamchatka, the Aleutian Islands and the Sandwich Islands were visited*, Roxbury, 1825.

Catherine II, Empress, *Decrees*, in *Arkhiv Pravityelistvuishchavo Senata*, St. Petersburg, 1872.

Cleveland, Richard J., *Narrative of Voyages*, Cambridge, 1842.

Cochrane, John Dundas, R.N., *Narrative of a Pedestrian Journey through Russia and Siberian Tartary from the frontiers of China to the Frozen Sea and Kamchatka during 1820–1823*, London, 1825.

Cook, James, *Voyages to the Pacific Ocean*, London, 1784.

Corney, Peter, *Voyages to the North Pacific . . . with a description of the Russian establishments on the Northwest Coast*, Honolulu, 1896.

Coxe, Rev. William, *Account of the Russian Discoveries between Asia and America, to which are added the conquest of Siberia and the transactions between Russia and China*, London, 1787.

Czartoriski, Prince Adama, *Mémoires*.

Davidov, Gavril, *Dvukratnoye Puteshestvye iv Ameriku Morskikh Ofitserov Khvostova i Davidova* ("Two Voyages of the Naval Officers Khvostov and Davidov to America"), St. Petersburg, 1810.

Dashkevich, the Archmonk Anthony, *Arkhangelo-Mikhailovski Pravoslavnyi Sobor iv Sitkhye* ("The Russian Orthodox Cathedral of St. Michael at Sitka"), New York, 1899.

Elliott, Henry W., *Our Arctic Province*, New York, 1887.

Doklad Komiteta ob Ustroistvye Russkikh Amerikanskikh Kolonii ("Report of the Committee on the Retention of the Russian-American Colonies"), St. Petersburg, 1863. Mss. trans. by Petrov, Bancroft Collection, Berkeley.

D'Wolf, John, *Voyage to the North Pacific and a journey through Siberia*, Cambridge, 1861.

Golder, Frank, *Guide to Materials for American History in Russian Archives*, Washington, D.C., 1917.

—— *Russian Expansion in the Pacific*, Cleveland, 1914.

—— *The Pacific Ocean in History*, New York, 1917.

—— "Tales from Kodiak Island," *Journal of American Folklore*, April–June, 1903.

Golovin, P. N., *Obsor Russkikh Kolonii iv Severnoi Amerikye* ("Report on the Colonies in North America"), Mss. trans. H.P., 40th Congress, 2nd session.

Golovnin, Vassili M., *Obsor Russkikh Kolonii iv Severnoi Amerikye* ("Report on the Colonies in North America"), in Tikhmenyev *Materialui*.

—— *Memories of a Captivity in Japan*, 1812–13, London, 1824.

—— *Puteshetvye Ross. Imp. shlyupa Diani iz Kronshtata iv Kamchatku, 1807–08*, St. Petersburg, 1819.

Irving, Washington, *Astoria*.

Izmailov, Stepan, *Zhurnal*, Mss. in National Archives, Washington, D.C.

Judson, Katharine B., *Subject Index to the History of the Pacific Northwest and of Alaska as found in U.S. government documents and in other documents, 1789–1881*, Olympia, 1913.

Juvenal, the Archmonk, *Diary*, mss. of doubtful authenticity trans. by Petrov, Bancroft Collection, Berkeley.

Kaidanov, N., *Sistematicheskii Katalog Dielam Gosudarstnavo Kommertz-Kollegii* ("Systematic Catalogue of the affairs of the Imperial College of Commerce"), St. Petersburg, 1884.

Kashevarov, Father Andrew P., brochure, *St. Michael's Cathedral, Sitka*, Juneau, date not given.

Kashevarov, Father Andrew P., *Herman of Valaam*, brochure from "The Ascetics of Valaam Monastery," Sitka, 1916.

—— Descriptive booklet on *The Alaska Historical Museum*, Juneau, date not given.

Khlebnikov, Kyrill T., *Zhizneopisanye Aleksandra Andrevicha Baranova, glavnavo pravitelya Russkikh kolonii iv Amerikye* ("Biography of Aleksandr Andrevich Baranov, chief manager of the Russian colonies in America"), St. Petersburg, 1835.

—— *Journal*, in Tikhemneyv, *Materialui*.

—— *Zapiski o Amerikye* ("Letters about America"), Morskoi Sbornik Supplements, St. Petersburg, 1861. Mss. trans., Bancroft Collection, Berkeley.

Kluchevski, V. O., *History of Russia*, New York, 1913.

Koch, Gen. Ivan G., *Orders*, in Tikhmenyev, *Istor*.

Kodiak Mission, *Istorya* (Volume on the centenary of the bringing of the Russian Orthodox faith to America), St. Petersburg, 1894.

Kolomin, Pyotr, *Depositions on the Atrocities of the Lebedev-Lastotchkin Company*, in Tikhmenyev, *Istor*.

Kostromitin, Pyotr, *Early Times in the Aleutian Islands*, Mss., Bancroft Collection, Berkeley.

Kotzebue, Otto von, *Voyage of Discovery into the South Sea and Bering's Straits*, London, 1821.

—— *New Voyage around the World*, London, 1830.

Kramer, Benedict Bendictovich, *Correspondence of the Russian-American Company's directors*, in National Archives, Washington, D.C.

Krashennikov, S. P., *The History of Kamchatka and the Kurilski islands, published by order of Her Imp. Majesty and trans. into English by James Grieve, M.D.*, London, 1764.

Krusenstern, Adam J., *Voyage autour du monde*, Paris, 1821.

Kulikalov, Demid, *Reports*, in Tikhmenyev, *Istor*.

Langsdorff, Dr. Georg-Heinrich von, *Bemerkungen auf eine Reise um die Welt*, Frankfort, 1812.

Larionov, Emilian, Correspondence with Baranov, in Tikhmenyev, *Istor*.

Lebedyev-Lastotchkin, Pavel, Correspondence, in Tikhmenyev, *Istor*.

La Pérouse, J. F. G. de, *The Voyage of La Pérouse around the world, in the years 1785 (to) 1788*, London, 1798.

Lewis and Dryden, *Marine History of the Pacific Northwest*, Portland, 1895.

Leymel, Zygmunt S., *The Growth of Russian Interests in the Pacific*, Mss., University of California.

Lisianski, Urey, *Voyage around the world*, London, 1814.

Markov, Alexei, *Russkii na vostotchnam okeanye* ("The Russians on the Eastern Ocean"), Moscow, 1849.

Marchand, Etienne, *A Voyage around the world during the years 1790, 1791 and 1792*, London, 1801.

Morison, Samuel E., *Maritime History of Massachusetts*, Boston, 1921.

Nicholas, Grand Duke, *Peterburg Nekropolis*, St. Petersburg, 1912.

Paul I, Tsar, *Decrees*, in *Arkhiv Pravityelistvuishchavo Senata*, St. Petersburg, 1872.

Petrov, Ivan, *The Management of the Russian-American Company*, Mss., Bancroft Collection, Berkeley.

Politovski, N., *Kratkoye Istoricheskoye Obozrenye Obrazovanya i deistvya Rossiisko-Amerikansko Kompani* ("Short Historical review of the formation and proceedings of the Russian-American Company"), St. Petersburg, 1861.

Ponifidine, Zakhar, *Puteshestvye iz Kallao do Sitkhi* ("Voyage from Callao to Sitka"), in Zapiski Gidrograficheskavo Departamenta, Vol. vii, St. Petersburg, 1849.

Porter, Kenneth Wiggins, *John Jacob Astor*, Cambridge, 1931.

—— "The Cruise of the Forester, *Washington Historical Quarterly*, October, 1932.

—— "The Cruise of Astor's brig Pedler," *Oregon Historical Quarterly*, September, 1930.

—— "More about the brig Pedler," *Oregon Historical Quarterly*, December, 1932.

Pugatchevshchina, Moscow, 1921.

Rambaud, Alfred, *History of Russia*, New York, 18——.

Rezanov, Nikolai P., Correspondence, in Tikhmenyev, *Istor,* and his report to Rumiantsov on his visit to California in "*The Rezanov Voyage to Nueva California*" by T. C. Russell, San Francisco, 1926.

Roquefeuille, Camille, *Journal d'un voyage autour du monde*, Paris, 1823.

St. Michael's Cathedral at Sitka, vital records of.

Sauer, Martin, *An Account of a geographical and Astronomical expedition . . . stretching to the American coast. Performed by Commodore Joseph Billings in the years 1785-94*, London, 1802.

Schafer, Joseph, *The Pacific Coast and Alaska*, Philadelphia, 1905.

Scheffer, Doctor, Data relating to, Hawaiian Historical Society Publications, 1909.

Shemelin, Fyodor, *Zhurnal Pervavo puteshestvya Rosskikh vokrug zemnavo shara . . .* ("Journal of the first voyage of the Russians around the globe . . . compiled by the chief commissioner of the Russian-American Company"), St. Petersburg, 1816.

Shelekhov, Grigorii I., *Rossiiskavo kuptsa imenintavo Rylskavo grazhdannina Grigorya Shelekhova pervoe stranstvovanye s 1783 po 1787* ("The first voyage of the eminent Rylsk citizen, the merchant Grigor Shelekhov, from 1783 to 1787"), St. Petersburgh, 1793.

—— Correspondence, in Tikhmenyev, *Istor.*

Shelekhova, Natalya, Correspondence, in Tikhmenyev, *Istor.*

Simpson, Sir George, *Narrative of a journey around the world*, London, 1847.

Solid Men of Boston, Mss., Massachusetts Historical Society.

Sturgis, Captain William, *Remarks on the Northwest Coast*, Publications of the Massachusetts Historical Society.

Swanton, John R., *Social conditions, beliefs, of the Thlingit Indians*, Bureau of American Ethnology, Vol. 26, 1908.

Tarakanov, Vassili, *Account of captivity at Santa Barbara Mission, California, and the Scheffer expedition to the Hawaiian islands*, Mss. trans. by Petrov, Bancroft Collection, Berkeley, from Morskoi Sbornik, vol. of 1852.

Tchitchinov, Zakhar, *Adventures of an employee of the Russian-American Co.* Mss., Bancroft Collection, Berkeley.

Tikhmenyev, Pyotr, *Istoricheskoye Obozrenye obrazovanya Rossiisko-*

Amerikanskoi Kompanii i deistvii eya do nastoishchnavo vremenii ("Historical Review of the formation of the Russian-American Company and its proceedings down to present times"), two volumes, St. Petersburg, 1863. The *Appendix* contains the main correspondence extant relating to Baranov's early administration.

Tikhmenyev, Pyotr, Same, *Appendix*. Mss. trans. by Dimitri Krenov, University of Washington Library, Seattle.

—— *Materialui dlya istorii russkikh zaselenii po beregam Vostotchnavo okeana* ("Materials for a history of the Russian settlements on the Eastern ocean"), four vols., Press of the Ministry of Marine, St. Petersburg, 1861.

Turner, R. J., *Russian expansion to America*. Papers of the Bibliographical Society of America, Vol. xxv, Chicago, 1931.

Unalaska and St. Paul, Archives, Mss. in Bancroft Collection, Berkeley.

Vancouver, Capt. George, *Voyage of Discovery . . .* , London, 1798.

Waliszewski, K., *Paul the First of Russia*, London, 1913.

Wickersham, James, *A Bibliography of Alaskan History*, 1724–1924. Cordova, Alaska, 1927.

Yarmolinski, Avrahm, *Rezanov*, in Dictionary of American Biography.

—— "Some Rambling Notes on the Russian Columbus," Bulletin New York Public Library, September, 1927.

—— "On Shelekhov," *Bulletin*, New York Public Library, March, 1932.

Yanovski, Simeon I., *Correspondence*, in National Archives, Washington, D.C., and in Kodiak Mission, *Istorya*.

Yevgueni, the Metropolitan, *Rezanov*, in Slovar Russkikh Svetskikh Pisateli, Moscow, 1845.

Zagoskin, L., *Pyesnya Alek. Baranova slozhena iv 1799 goda pri pervom osnavanii rieposti Novo-Arkhangelska iv Sitkhinskom zalivye* ("The Song of Aleksandr Baranov, chanted on the establishment of Fort New Archangel in 1799 on Sitkan shores"), Mss. trans., Fairbanks.

Zavalishin, Dimitri, *Dyelo o Kolonii Ross* ("The Affair of Ross Colony"), trans. from Russkii Vyestnikh, Vol. III, Bancroft Collection, 1866.

Zelenii, Ivan, secretary to the Board of Directors, Russian-American Co., *Correspondence*, in National Archives, Washington, D.C.

Index

Rushalov, hunter, 193.
Rylsk, 21.

St. Anne, Order of, conferred on Baranov, 189; on King Tomari, 274.
St. Elias, Mt., 133, 135, 290.
St. Helens, Fort, 290.
St. George, Fort, 57, 58.
St. George, ship, 78.
St. Ivan Boguslav, ship, 78, 148.
St. Michael, Fort, founded, 165; Baranov leaves, 170; destroyed, 192 et seq.
St. Michael Archangel, church of, founded, 279, 280; Irina Baranova married in, 288; 303.
St. Michael Archangel, ship, built, 22; leaves Kodiak, 62; represented on Shelekhov's tomb, 142.
St. Nicholas, Fort, 60, 77, 148, 149.
St. Paul village, founded, 63, 64; built, 85; first church at, 139; Baranov pays for school at, 190; 291. (*See also* Kodiak.)
St. Petersburg, 20, 22, 24, 29, 36, 124, 129, 169, 206, 216, 224, 229, 253, 258, 259, 266, 273, 277, 278, 286, 295, 302, 303, 305.
St. Vladimir, Cross of, conferred on Baranov, 189.
Samoilov, Konstantin, 23, 25, 37, 56, 61, 76, 78, 132, 203.
Sandwich Islands, 20, 72, 92, 168, 169, 181, 211, 216, 227, 230, 233; Baranov's first mission to, 232, 238; 243, 248, 254, 255, 256; Scheffer expedition sent to, 267, 268; events of Scheffer expedition, 269 et seq.; 293; Baranov wants to retire at, 294.
San Francisco, 18, 19, 159; Rezanov visits, 228, 229, 255.
San Luis Obispo, 255. 294.
San Quintin, 212.
Santa Barbara, 255, 274, 294.
Scheffer, Dr., comes to Sitka, 259; origins, 261, 262; sent to Kamehameha, 267, 268; Scheffer expedition, course of, 270 et seq.; end of expedition, 275; results, 277, 278; remaining Russians return to Sitka, 293.
Shakh-mut, Ilyamna chief, 149 et seq.
Shelekhov, Grigor Ivanich, history of, 21 et seq.; 34, 36; hires Baranov, 37; correspondence with Baranov, 55, 82, 83, 117, 120, 121, 128, 129, 131; sends priests and serfs to America, 25, 115 et seq.; letter from Father Iosaph to, 124

et seq.; dies, 141; funeral and monument, 142; daughter of, marries Rezanov, 188, 207, 223.
Shelekhov, Straits of, 11, 48, 65.
Shelekhov, *the Travels of Grigor . . .* book, 23.
Shelekhova, Natalya Alexyevna, wife of G. I., 21 et seq.; writes to Baranov, 141; unites Siberian merchants, 143; 189.
Shields, James, comes to America, 80 et seq.; helps build *Phoenix*, 87 et seq., 91 et seq.; launches *Phoenix*, 110, 111; teaches Baranov navigation, 88; teaches navigation to colonials, 138, 139; explores Bering, 128; at Nootka Sound, 138; mentioned by Father Iosaph, 126; recalled to Russia, 143, 146.
Shvedzov, hunting-master, 212.
Siberia, conquest of, 15, 16, 17; influence of free trade in, 20; Catherine the Great and, 21.
Sidorov, hunter, 239.
Sitka, Baranov first explores region, 135 et seq.; 154; Baranov advances on, 158 et seq.; extent of early Yankee trade at, 168, 169, 170; massacre at, 192 et seq.; statistics on massacre, 203; Baranov drives to retake, 208 et seq., 212 et seq.; New Archangel founded at, 217; Baranov's second building at, 222 et seq.; Rezanov arrives at, 223; sufferings of Russians at, 225, 226, 227; Kuskov builds New Archangel at, 230; Baranov's rule at, 233 et seq.; library at, 234; Koch appt'd governor at, 244; Bornovolokov appointed governor at, 247; church established at, 279, 280; Yanovski appt'd governor at, 285 et seq.; census of, 290; Baranov leaves, 298; importance of, as a port, in Russian days, 232, 233; importance of, as port, wanes, 304; closing days of Russian rule at, 303, 304; Russian flag at, hauled down for last time, 305, 306.
Ska-out-lelt, Sitkan chief, 164, 165, 166, 167; directs Sitka massacre, 194 et seq.; 199, 200, 203, 217, 296.
Smith, Capt., 263.
Sokolov, Father, first priest at Sitka, 279, 280, 287, 290.
South America, 228.
Spain, 15, 18, 19, 185, 305.
"Spirit of Russian Hunters," song by Baranov, 214, 215, 235.
Stanovoi Mts., 22, 35.

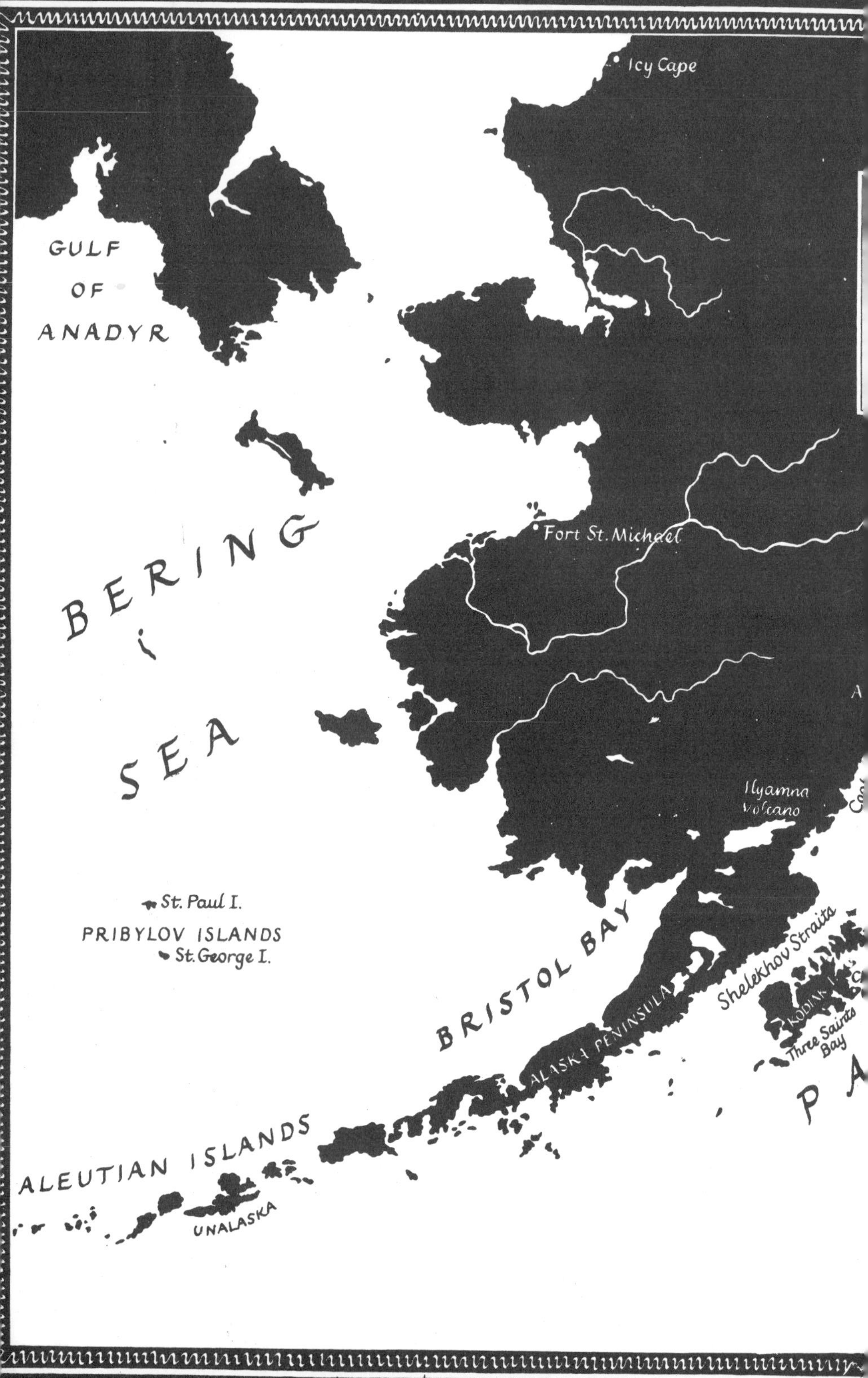
Icy Cape
GULF
OF
ANADYR
Fort St. Michael
BERING
SEA
Ilyamna
Volcano
St. Paul I.
PRIBYLOV ISLANDS
St. George I.
BRISTOL BAY
Shelekhov Straits
ALASKA PENINSULA
KODIAK I.
Three Saints
Bay
ALEUTIAN ISLANDS
UNALASKA
PA